Praise for *Generational IQ*

People of faith need solutions for the increasing complexities four generations create for their homes, friendships, workplaces, and churches. Haydn Shaw provides thoughtful answers about the different ways the generations can seek not only Christ but each other. Highly recommended.

JOHN TOWNSEND
New York Times bestselling author, leadership consultant, and psychologist

Generational IQ is one of the most thought-provoking, engaging, and genuinely useful books I have ever read on a topic that has never been more necessary than in this moment in time. With clear descriptions of each generation, Hadyn sheds light on why our generational standing affects the way we experience God and relate to others. While I would have thought I had a good understanding of this material to begin with, I realized I had used broad strokes to create caricatures of people in different generations and that many of them had missed the mark. Over and over again, I found myself nodding and whispering, "Ahhh . . . now that behavior makes sense." This is a profound book that I daresay should be necessary reading for all believers. It has truly changed the way I will approach my ministry, and I'm honored to share my praise for this spectacular book.

ANGIE SMITH
Author of *I Will Carry You*

This is a really important book. Our culture and, more important, our churches, need to continue to figure out not only how to live in a multigenerational climate, but how to thrive in it. Haydn's book will help us understand each other better so that we can work together better. *Generational IQ* will not only give you the information you need to know how to relate to multiple generations, but it will also give you the tools you need to do it in real life. I'm confident this book will be helpful to individuals and to churches as we seek to build a truly multigenerational approach to ministry, outreach, and following Jesus together.

KYLE IDLEMAN
Bestselling author of *Not a Fan*

It is said that for a pastor to minister successfully, he or she must correctly exegete both Scripture and the culture. Haydn Shaw's thoroughly researched and imminently practical new book, *Generational IQ*, places in pastors' hands an invaluable tool for interpreting the world in which we minister. No one else has offered what he explains in this encyclopedic survey of our society, particularly the critical implications that generational differences have upon ministry. The Church of God has benefited immeasurably from hearing Haydn speak at our largest gathering of pastors and church leaders, and we enthusiastically welcome this newest contribution to the work of church and Kingdom. In 2015 and beyond, any pastor who has this book close at hand will do a better job!

MARK L. WILLIAMS
Presiding bishop/general overseer, Church of God, Cleveland, Tennessee

I'm not smart enough to handle all the crazy stuff a church leader in the twenty-first century needs to know. I'm only smart enough to *find* smart people and ask them. Haydn is my *smart people*. He's been both a part of our congregation and a consultant with us through every stage a church can go through. In the past few years he's dedicated his life to helping the world understand the vast differences between the generations. The generational divide is quite possibly as deep as many ethnic and racial chasms have been in the past. I hardly have a conversation with another leader about "the church" without it coming up. This book is not only timely and important, but it's a great read. You'd expect me to feel obligated to give Haydn an endorsement, knowing *I've asked him to come* to a Saturday night service *and* critique *my sermon* every week. But I'm just honestly telling you—you need this *generational intelligence*. No matter how old you are.

TIM HARLOW
Author of *Life on Mission* and pastor of Parkview Christian Church

Haydn Shaw has combined outstanding research and practical application so we can understand how the various generations, spirituality, and the church all fit together. In his outstanding new book, *Generational IQ*, Shaw gives us a crystal clear picture of how different generation can work together for greater spiritual impact and more loving families.

DAVE FERGUSON
Lead pastor of Community Christian Church, lead visionary of NewThing, and author of *Finding Your Way Back to God*

Generational "rift" is felt everywhere in our homes and our churches, and it undergirds some of the most important conversations taking place in our culture today. *Generational IQ* is sorely needed. Haydn Shaw answers the big questions people of faith are asking. His book is as insightful as it is liberating. An important read.

DEBRA HIRSCH
Author of *Untamed* and *Redeeming Sex*

So much of life, faith, leadership, and ministry involves working with people, and generational intelligence offers countless insights to help us do this better. *Generational IQ* is a brilliant book based on significant research that can help us value and relate better with all generations.

JUD WILHITE
Senior pastor of Central Christian Church and author of *Pursued*

As a mom, there are so many things I worry about when it comes to my children. How can I help my children launch well? How will I pass on my faith, and how do I talk to them about their opinions that are so different than mine? Haydn Shaw covers these questions and more, putting to rest many of the fears and myths that we needlessly hang on to when it comes to our children. Filled with practical application, it moves us to an understanding of the Millennial generation that will not only inform our parenting but will help all of us to understand how they view God and the church.

SHERRY SURRATT
CEO and president of MOPS International

Haydn Shaw has blown off the roof with his new book about generational issues in churches. *Generational IQ* is witty, readable, and packed with observations and strategies that go way beyond a book for church leaders. It hits everyone—giving five generations a way to enrich their personal, work, and church lives. The content is so rich you could amplify each chapter into a book so valuable as to become viral. As a church consultant, Haydn Shaw brings reality to strategy planning that moves leaders and lay members into new areas of application of their gifts and skills. *Generational IQ* screams to readers, "Pick me up!" Get unstuck from the ineffective, dry, despairing rigidity of "the way you've always done it." Find the right questions—the ones that unlock the future. Transform your generation into facilitators for eternity. Packed with up-to-date and solid information, as well as brilliant options for releasing personal and organizational energy—Haydn Shaw's second book on generational issues management sets a new standard of excellence. He has created new terminology that will become the grist for conversations about dealing with generational issues for decades to come.

CARL F. GEORGE
Church growth consultant and author of *Prepare Your Church for the Future*

Yep, Millenials are everywhere! And yes, they *are* a force you need to understand for the future of your family, ministry, or business. But as Haydn Shaw shows in this refreshing book, they are also *not* the godless heathens intent on destroying American culture that they are often painted to be. In fact, Shaw gives an excellent overview of every generation and what you most need to know—because it is often different from what you think. This is a must-read for any parent or leader who works with anyone of a generation other than their own.

SHAUNTI FELDHAHN
Social researcher and bestselling author of *For Women Only* and *The Good News about Marriage*

Christians are called to be salt and light, to engage the culture around them, which in this day and age is no easy task. In *Generational IQ*, Haydn Shaw and Ginger Kolbaba provide Christian ministers and laypersons alike the intellectual framework necessary to tackle the communication gap between the generations. It is a timely and tailor-made treatment of generational awareness.

ED STETZER
Executive director of Lifeway Research

Christianity Isn't Dying,

Millennials Aren't the Problem,

And the Future Is Bright

Generational

IQ

HAYDN SHAW

with Ginger Kolbaba

Tyndale House Publishers, Inc.
Carol Stream, Illinois

Visit Tyndale online at www.tyndale.com.

TYNDALE and Tyndale's quill logo are registered trademarks of Tyndale House Publishers, Inc.

Generational IQ: Christianity Isn't Dying, Millennials Aren't the Problem, and the Future Is Bright

Copyright © 2015 by Haydn Shaw. All rights reserved.

Cover illustration of bird copyright © Soru Epotok/Dollar Photo Club. All rights reserved.

Author photograph taken by FranklinCovey, copyright © 2010. All rights reserved.

Designed by Ron Kaufmann

Edited by Jonathan Schindler

Published in association with Yates & Yates (www.yates2.com).

Unless otherwise indicated, all Scripture quotations are taken from the *Holy Bible*, New Living Translation, copyright © 1996, 2004, 2015 by Tyndale House Foundation. Used by permission of Tyndale House Publishers, Inc., Carol Stream, Illinois 60188. All rights reserved.

Scripture quotations marked NIV are taken from the Holy Bible, *New International Version,*® NIV.® Copyright © 1973, 1978, 1984, 2011 by Biblica, Inc.® Used by permission. All rights reserved worldwide.

Scripture quotations marked NRSV are taken from the New Revised Standard Version Bible, copyright © 1989, Division of Christian Education of the National Council of the Churches of Christ in the United States of America. Used by permission. All rights reserved.

Library of Congress Cataloging-in-Publication Data

Shaw, Haydn.
   Generational IQ : Christianity isn't dying, millennials aren't the problem, and the future is bright / Haydn Shaw, with Ginger Kolbaba.
      pages cm
   Includes bibliographical references.
   ISBN 978-1-4143-6472-8 (hc)
1. Christianity. 2. Intergenerational religious education. 3. Intergenerational relations—Religious aspects—Christianity. 4. Intergenerational communication—Religious aspects—Christianity. 5. Generations. 6. Age groups. I. Title.
   BR121.3.S53 2015
   277.3′083—dc23   2015019768

Printed in the United States of America

21	20	19	18	17	16	15
7	6	5	4	3	2	1

To Dr. Wayne and Janet Shaw, who taught
me to love Jesus more than air.
To Lyle Schaller and Carl George, who taught me to think
sociologically and practically about all of faith.
To Lola, who turned on the lights.

Contents

CHAPTER 1

Turning On the Lights

"HAYDN, I CAN'T see out of my right eye."

My wife, Laurie, and I were traveling home from my company's holiday party, and we were still an hour away.

"What do you mean you can't see?" I asked, fighting the temptation to take my eyes off the road and stare at her.

"It wasn't so noticeable at the party," she said, "but now that we're on the interstate, it seems like I'm peering through thick steam."

"So it didn't happen just now—it was bothering you at the party?" I confirmed, relieved that my forty-nine-year-old wife probably hadn't had a stroke. "Why don't you look it up on your phone and see what's going on?"

"Haydn," she said patiently, "I can't see."

I pulled over to the shoulder, put on the hazards, and spent the next seven or eight minutes scrambling over the Internet on my phone so we could decide whether we needed to race to the nearest emergency room. Cancer stared at me from every website.

If you've ever looked up medical symptoms on the Internet, you know how the possibilities are a mix of the horrifying and the ordinary. I read the list to Laurie:

> Stroke
> Cancer
> Brain tumor
> Eye tumor
> Macular degeneration (which had taken her mother's eyesight at sixty-two)
> Retinal detachment
> Ocular migraine
> Allergies

I thought this was an ominous list, but to my surprise, she said, "I wonder if it's allergies."

"To what?"

"To this sweater. I just bought it today for the party, and I've never worn angora before."

She decided to go home, remove the sweater, and take some Benadryl to see if that helped. Ten minutes after doing this, she couldn't see any better, so we went to the emergency room. Often there's a long wait, but since she suddenly couldn't see out of one eye, they were worried about stroke and took her straight to a CAT scan.

By the time she got back from the CAT scan, her vision was almost completely clear.

Within an hour, the emergency room doctors concluded from

a clear CAT scan and dissipated symptoms that it *was* allergies and sent us home.

I'm happy to report that Laurie has had no other problems, because that was her first and only experience wearing an angora blend. With the emergency room cost added in, we joke that the angora sweater was the most expensive she'll ever wear. But we were happy to pay for the doctors and the test because we had no way of knowing which of the possible Internet diagnoses was right. We didn't have the information, the training, or the know-how to interpret all the frightening reports we found to tell us about Laurie's problem.

A Frightening Diagnosis

Many of us are in a similar situation with our families, friends, and churches. We see the United States and Canada becoming less Christian, and many of us long for the good old days. We hear that in three generations Christianity will all but disappear unless something radically changes. We hear that 88 percent of young people have sex before they marry and that the statistics for Christian young people aren't much different.[1] We see hundreds of news reports that for the first time, people who claim no religious affiliation, the "Nones," make up as much as 23 percent of our population. Even more frightening, we hear that the Millennial generation is the biggest part of the "Nones"; they are leaving church and aren't coming back.[2]

Like my wife and me with her vision loss, we recognize that there are problems. We may even panic about the problems, and then when we see books or news stories about them or do our own investigations on the Internet, we panic even more. We ask ourselves and our friends questions like these (if we bring them up at all):

> Is Christianity really going to be dead in three generations?
> Why is my twentysomething still living in the basement?
> Is it even possible for young people to save sex for marriage when they don't marry until age twenty-eight?
> How do I pass on my faith to my children when they don't respond to the things I find most meaningful about it?
> What can I do now that my child is walking away from the faith?
> What do I say to people who claim they're spiritual but not religious?
> Why won't the younger generations come to our church?
> How does our church keep both the youngest and the oldest generations happy?
> How do I help my church figure out what to do with retirees like me who have real skills and want to do more than fold bulletins?

All of these problems share one thing in common: they are rooted in generational differences. Yet we often don't know enough about the problem to know how big of a deal it is or what to do about it. We don't know whether, as with my wife's allergic reaction, the solution is as simple as returning a sweater or whether we will struggle with it for the rest of our lives. We need intelligence to help us sort fact from terrifying fiction.

That's where *Generational IQ* comes in.

Generational Intelligence

I've been providing generational intelligence reports to individuals, businesses, the government, churches, and other organizations for twenty years, helping them make sense of the generations: Traditionalists (born before 1945), Baby Boomers (born 1946–1964), Generation Xers (born 1965–1980), and Millennials (born 1981–2001).[3] I've pored over countless studies and interviewed people from each generation, but I've learned the most from interacting with thousands of people in classes and speeches each year. That research allows me to advise my clients (and friends) which generational challenges are important and which ones are no big deal.

But it's not only when I speak at churches that the questions I listed above come up. When I speak in the marketplace, people of faith come to me after the presentations with their worries. They realize after being introduced to generational research that it can help us understand and answer all of them, yet many of these people lack the tools or experience to wisely diagnose what's happening in their relationships. We're making these issues harder than they need to be because we don't have the time to study all of the generational research and sort through the nuances of the data until we can draw balanced, thoughtful conclusions.

It's like the employee who has been at your workplace almost six months and still gets overwhelmed looking at his e-mail. He doesn't know whose e-mail matters and whose he can safely ignore. Or like medical researchers who must sort through millions of bits of data to find why some people can lose weight easily and others struggle for every half pound. Or like our country's intelligence community sorting through the "noise" of thousands of rumors to find the one terror cell that plans to blow up a marathon. Finding the relevant information in a sea of data requires more than just facts. We are drowning in facts; what we need is intelligence.

Close to Home

In my previous book, *Sticking Points*, I tackled generational tensions in the workplace. I wrote *Generational IQ* so I could bring people of faith the same help I've brought to businesses, because if we don't have generational intelligence, we overreact to the small things, ignore the big things, and do the wrong things, making our relationships worse. From what I've observed, people of faith overreact to generational differences even more than business-people do. And understandably so. The reason is that the people we worry about aren't just employees. They are our children, our friends, and our church members. Or we worry about our faith itself.

That's why we need generational intelligence, and we need it now. The questions I listed earlier (and others like them) keep Christians up at night because they hit us in the heart. The more we read about them in the news or online, the more frightened we get. It's like we're watching one of those scary movies where the girl heads into the dark basement, and we know the bad guy is there, and the ominous music reminds us that the bad guy is there, and we're yelling at the screen, "No! Don't go down there! Run away!" (I've always wondered why she never turns on a light.) It's as though we see our families and communities going down into that basement, and we feel just as helpless as we do watching the movie. We're left yelling, "No! Don't go down there! What's *wrong* with you?"

My aim in *Generational IQ* is to bring the best of genera-tional research close to home, to help you find a way to dispel generational tensions in the relationships that are closest to you. I also want to shed light on the outright mistakes, hearsay, and distortions—as well as the actual facts—in the dismal reports I mentioned above. I'm worried about some of these same things—the future could be bleak—but right now, despite what you've heard, Christianity isn't dying, Millennials aren't the problem in your family or your church, and the future really is bright if people of faith start learning generational intelligence.

The best research, combined with understanding the big mental shifts over the last eighty years, will help everyday Christians get startlingly smarter in dealing with the things that scare them about their faith, family, friends, and church. If we don't get smarter in dealing with generational issues, I'm afraid. I'm very afraid.

Generational tensions and problems aren't going away anytime soon. We may be tempted to ask, "Why can't we go back to the way things were?" Like the young woman going forward into the dark basement, we *can't* go back. But we can turn on the lights.

CHAPTER 2

Generational Intelligence

EVEN THOUGH I spend much of my time helping organizations understand the generations, I first learned about generational differences at church. I had heard plenty of sermons and church people complain about "that generation," including my father.

My Traditionalist father, as a professor and then dean of a seminary, was on the front lines of the generational gap in the 1960s and '70s. He was frustrated that "the younger generation"—my generation—was causing a lot of problems for colleges, churches, and society in general. He didn't like our music. ("Why does it have to be so loud? You can't understand the words!") He often said that rock and roll was "the corruption of the teenage mind." And he certainly didn't like our long hair. To save money, my father cut my brothers' and my hair until I began to pay for my own haircuts in eighth grade. His rule was simple:

"The more you fuss about how short I'm cutting it, the shorter I will cut it." I remember sitting on a hard stool, tears slowly coming down my face, while my coolness fell in clips onto the floor. He didn't buzz it like a kid in my seventh-grade class whose father was ex-military, but my hair was way too short to swing when I was playing air guitar to DeGarmo and Key.

My father didn't like that my generation talked freely about things like sex. He said we had no sense of delayed gratification. We didn't understand respect and were naive about how hard it is to keep churches going. As we will see later in the book, he wasn't wrong on some of those, and at eighty-three he has made his peace with guitars in worship and preachers in blue jeans as long as they get the job done. But at the time, the generations accused each other of some serious problems with their values.

I wasn't old enough to know much about it, but the church I grew up in had a split in the seventies after the young Boomers didn't see enough change. When I was able to drive, I remained with my parents' church, but I thought the other church had some strong points. Like any new generation, I had my own frustrations with church. I didn't like pews. I scared people when I asked questions, and I didn't want to talk only about doctrine. I wanted to learn how to have a relationship with God.

But most of all I was bored. I was bored with the organ music, the corny jokes, the Sunday school classes, and all the things that no one ever discussed. It was a good church, but it wasn't paying much attention to my generation. I shared my faith regularly but was reluctant to ask anyone my age to go to church with me.

The problem was that no one saw the need to flex. The older generation saw my generation's behavior as moral failure and essentially told us, "The way we've always done church should be good enough for you, too, so get with the program." The younger people came across as attacking the leadership, as demanding and disrespectful. I didn't know any of the sociological words for what was happening, but I could tell that much of it was over styles and preferences, not right and wrong. It started with people from different generations and ended up with a fight.

Sound familiar?

An Important Discovery

I didn't know anything about generational intelligence until I was not paying attention in a youth ministry class in Bible college, where I trained to be a minister. You know the moments—we only have a few of them in our lives—when we come across something, and it's like somebody flips a switch and the lights come on. Suddenly, you see everything you saw before, but it makes so much more sense.

While I wasn't paying attention in class, I stumbled across a chapter in my textbook called "Youth Culture Today: Backgrounds and Prospects." I read it and was stunned by what I learned. The author, Gerald C. Tiffin, explains why younger people today are less "responsible" and why they don't "settle down." He writes,

> In many [earlier] societies, early marriage, the ability to work physically, the assumption of economic independence, or the early death of parents served as an informal but functional rite of passage. The movement from childhood into adult status was less complicated, more clearly defined, and more easily achieved than in the twentieth century. . . .
>
> This well-defined and predictable life cycle prevented anxiety over "What will I be when I grow up?" . . . Work roles were clearly defined and easily achieved, and, in general, the culture offered a harmonious message and

instruction to the growing child. Youth viewed parents as appropriate models of their future, since youth expected to inherit a similar world, land, and life, relatively unchanged. Parents raised children anticipating that their children (and grandchildren) would live in a world basically the same as theirs, creating continuity between generations.

There was no need for excessive anxiety over life roles or expectations in a world that changed very slowly, and in which religious and political leaders viewed life in static and unchanging terms. Such a world neither fostered nor needed adolescents.[1]

Tiffin goes on to explain why all the things the Boomers were doing that so scared their parents at the height of the generation gap came from sociological reasons, not simply declining morals. They were acting differently because they faced different challenges from those their parents had.

Boom! The clouds parted, and I realized that there are legitimate reasons why the generations are different. I had just stumbled upon generational intelligence!

I had heard from so many that our generation was messed up that I believed it: the older generation was the "greatest," and my generation was soft, pampered, and ungrateful after having it so much easier than they had. But we didn't have everything come easily; many of the new challenges we faced were more confusing and complex (as we'll see in chapter 4). My generation needed older Christians who understood the new pressures and philosophies and could help us think them through. I could see that condemning a generation as they struggled through their issues wasn't helping. And I could see that Baby Boomer Christianity had weaknesses—some values had declined—but it also had strengths. Even more, Boomers could see the moral flaws of the older generation that they brushed aside. Could we sort through those? Tiffin's argument was that it wasn't just that this new generation didn't care about the things of God. Rather, they faced a different *world*.

We needed generational intelligence in the seventies during what was known as "the generation gap," but we need it even more today because the world really is different. People now live thirty years longer than they once did. In 1900 the average life span was forty-eight; today it's seventy-eight. But as people live longer—for which we're all grateful—it presents new challenges that previous eras didn't face. In previous eras, there were only three generations. The oldest generation had the money and made the decisions, and the younger generation of adults raised the children and did what the older generation asked them to until their parents died, and then their turn came to be in control. Changes in families and churches came slowly and naturally, with little disruption. Younger generations didn't push for what they wanted; they waited their turn because their parents would likely be gone soon enough.[2]

But today, for the first time in history, we have five generations in our families, churches, and communities. *Five.* That's a huge change, and it causes quite a shake-up because every generation is pushing to be heard and understood, to find their own way, to recover what they feel the previous generation fumbled away, and to work out their parents' unfinished business.

To handle this new world, we need generational intelligence. The reason we struggle with other generations is not that they are "the problem." The reason we struggle with other generations is that we don't understand them. We don't know *why* they think differently, so we stereotype, criticize, or make jokes. But when we start to understand another generation—rather than attempting to maneuver others into seeing things our way—we open ourselves to new possibilities of relating, helping, reaching, encouraging, and loving them.

It Goes without Saying

We are shaped by our generation in ways we don't realize. The historical events during a generation's childhood years shape their values, worldview, and definitions of success. Their shared experiences are what distinguish them as a generation in the first place.* When you were born colors and affects your perspective of *everything*. The era when you grew up fills your head with ideas and images that tell you what you can do with your emotions, how you should enter a conversation, what it means to be a male or a female, how you respond to others, and what you think about God and family and country. We don't think a lot about these ideas and images. We may not even realize they are there. Certainly we take them for granted—"it goes without saying"—and that's what makes them so powerful in controlling our lives. We don't think about them; we just do what they tell us, even if it's not good for us.

Most often we see the images and ideas of each generation through the pop culture of that generation's time. For instance, the first half of the Baby Boomers, the much more optimistic half, still gets tingly talking about the Beach Boys and how they felt when the rock group first released their tight harmonies and happy songs about young love at the beach, whereas the generation following mine will roll their eyes and say the group was

---

* I want to acknowledge that a generation's life stage also impacts how they think. The trickiest part of generational research is sorting out which characteristics a generation shares because they grew up with the same influences and which characteristics are the product of the life stage they are in (and are common to what other generations faced at that stage). Emerging adulthood is an example of a life stage. People in their twenties today share many characteristics with the Boomers' and Xers' twenties. In my opinion, half of the criticisms of Millennials come from a failure to understand the life stage of emerging adulthood, not the historical events that shaped their generation. That's why almost a third of this book focuses on this new life stage. For more detail on life stage versus generational differences, see my discussion in *Sticking Points* (Carol Stream, IL: Tyndale, 2013), 235.

over-the-top naive while they listen to Kurt Cobain and Alanis Morissette singing about angst (which all seems like wallowing in cynicism and pessimism to the Traditionalists and older Baby Boomers).

Older Boomers' unbridled optimism and high expectations are one of the reasons they are now 4 percent less happy than the other generations and have been lower throughout their life-time.[3] Life just hasn't worked out the way Tinkerbell promised each Sunday evening at the beginning of *The Wonderful World of Disney*. When Bart Simpson, in the longest-running cartoon in the United States, showed Generation X the foibles of families and the checkered backstory on corporations and government, it reinforced a more cynical view of the world that seemed to fit their era better. They've expected less, and as a result have been happier.

The movies, the music, the television shows, and even the schools we attend all pump images and ideas into our heads that shape our generation and are at the crux of our complaints about other generations. Another generation's behavior makes no sense to us because we don't understand the images and ideas that shape their minds.

We can get especially upset when another generation questions the ideas that go without saying in our generation. Of course we put the cell phone down when we're having a conversation with someone. Of course we let the oldest generation determine the traditions for Christmas or family reunions. Of course we plan our family reunions through e-mail because nobody has time to make twelve phone calls to get everyone on the same page. (If Aunt Agnes won't get e-mail, then she just won't get a say in the plans. She's being ridiculous. Really, it's just a power play on her part, and she's always made people bend around her.) Of course . . .

Most people don't realize that their own images and ideas are governing their lives, just as other images and ideas are governing the people they're criticizing.

For example, three male soldiers with post-traumatic stress disorder (PTSD), each from a different generation, would likely deal differently with the overwhelming emotions it creates, based on the era in which each was born.

With the ongoing conflict in the Middle East, soldiers are diagnosed with higher levels of PTSD when they return to the United States. Suicide in the military is on the rise. Recently when I spoke with General Martin Dempsey, chairman of the Joint Chiefs of Staff, he mentioned multiple times how much focus the military is placing on suicides among our military. Today, everyone in the armed forces from its top commander to chaplains and counselors is vigilant to identify soldiers who may be suffering and to get them help. Because of greater education, the public is more attuned to PTSD and its symptoms. Soldiers and their families are encouraged to speak freely about it, to face it bravely, and to work through it without trying to cover it up. The military is working hard to change what goes without saying: the image of what it means to be a "tough" soldier and the inherited ideas about how soldiers deal with their emotions when they reenter civilian life. These are all important strides in helping soldiers and their families deal with this unseen casualty of war.

But if we go back one generation, things were different. The Vietnam War was so politically volatile back in the States that soldiers returned home not to fanfare or counseling but to people spitting on them and to posters that stated they were "baby killers." Returning soldiers sometimes didn't admit they had been in the war—which many people refused to acknowledge was a war at all, but rather a "conflict." Many chaplains and counselors didn't know PTSD existed, so there was very little help unless someone had an obvious mental breakdown.

If we go back another twenty-odd years before Vietnam, World War II veterans certainly didn't discuss what happened to them on the battlefront. They returned home to fanfare and praise and then picked up life where they had left off before the war, never mentioning anything—and certainly never seeking help for post-traumatic stress. They shut the door on those memories so they could focus on their lives back home. It wasn't manly to talk about feelings or to complain about what they had experienced. Plus, the war was over and done with. Why drag it all up again? Many of these soldiers went to their graves never giving up their "secrets" about what they encountered in war. Their generation's idea was that talking about the past would do no good.

So a World War II veteran wouldn't be as open to seeking help for "shell shock," the old name for PTSD, because that generation didn't openly discuss emotional pain, whereas today's soldier has many options for opening discussion. And the images of what it means to be a soldier and the ideas of what's okay will be different in the next generation. There will be a new set of expectations that go without saying.

Let's bring it a little closer to home. Since there's been marriage, there's been divorce. But until the 1970s, 85 percent of those in first marriages were still together, and the older generation didn't discuss divorce. If a divorce happened in the Christian community, the divorced couple felt ashamed and was often ostracized. Throughout the 1970s, when Generation X was growing up, the divorce rate almost doubled (until 1980, when it began to decline).[4] Today divorce is much more commonplace in the church and is discussed much more openly than it was in the past. Churches have established ministries to help people and their children deal with and talk about their family's divorce. While even liberal churches and synagogues don't condone divorce, all religious organizations, no matter their view on divorce, have to deal with the larger society's changes in images and ideas about it. It's a different world.

For instance, I know one man my age whose grandmother hung up the phone on him when he called to tell her he was getting a divorce. But before she did that, she gave him an earful: "You made a vow in front of God and everyone. You don't walk away from a commitment just because you don't love each other anymore or whatever excuse you're giving. You think your grandfather and I have liked each other every day of our marriage? There were *years* when we didn't get along, but we didn't give up. We said until death do us part, and we meant it."

Both he and his grandmother held the view that the Bible teaches us not to divorce. As a Christian man, he hadn't anticipated that divorce would ever be part of his life. But his grandmother still held the older generation's view that divorce is something you never do except in horrific situations—even if you don't love the other person. He, on the other hand, had grown up in an era whose image of an emotionally destructive marriage was as equally stigmatized as divorce had been earlier.

Churches may wring their hands because so many marriages break up today. But if most people think that most marriages are unhappy because they believe the inaccurate but constantly repeated statistic that 50 percent of marriages end in divorce, and if in our larger society the image of marriage has changed from an economic necessity or a sacred trust to a matter of friendship and romance, then when friendship fails and romance fades, what's the motivation to stay together? Living in an unhappy marriage for twenty years "for the sake of the children" or "because we made vows" no longer made sense to the latter half of the

Traditionalists and the Baby Boomers. As a result, the divorce rate jumped, but not nearly as high as the 50 percent figure we have heard so often. (Shaunti Feldhahn has discovered through an exhaustive analysis of the data that over 70 percent of women are married to their first husband and 80 percent of people are happy in their marriage.[5])

Because many Christians absorbed those same ideas, their divorce rate increased as well, although it has never been as high as those who don't attend church.[6] Ministers and churches struggled to stem the tide, but it did little good to condemn divorce without addressing shifting images and ideas about marriage. Additionally, and ironically, those very sermons reinforced the idea that marriage makes most people unhappy, even as they lamented the 50 percent divorce rate.

The generation we were born into changes our relationships, because each era plants inside our minds images and ideas that we take for granted.

A New Lens

What does that mean for us? It means that we respond to the church, to the culture, and to our relationships based on the ideas of *our* generation—the things that go without saying—whether we realize it or not. Often we miss opportunities to connect with others because our assumptions are based on our own generation's experiences and culture.

I mentioned earlier that generational intelligence requires us to understand the ideas that shape the other generations. But there's another part to generational intelligence. Not only do we need to understand other generations' assumptions, we also need to understand our own. Each generation has unique spiritual strengths God wants to use. Each generation also has temptations that hold back their spiritual growth. That's why we can't grow in our own faith and relationships if we don't understand how the things that go without saying change our relationship with God.

This is the first time we have five generations alive at the same time, and we don't have the generational intelligence to handle it yet. While living with five generations naturally makes some things more difficult, it also provides one opportunity no other time period has had to grow our faith. With five generations living together and interacting with each other, we have an amazing opportunity to learn from each other so that our view of God gets bigger and our faith gets stronger. If we can set aside our complaints about the other generations for a moment, we can learn from their spiritual strengths (yes, they do have them). And then we can help them recognize their spiritual vulnerabilities, which set up their gravest temptations, as they can help us recognize our own.

As I've researched the generations, I've been surprised by something I hadn't expected: generations relate differently to God and often fight about those differences based on their unique generational characteristics. Those who care deeply about their own and others' spiritual lives search for the factor that will bring real spiritual growth, but they often overlook how the era they grew up in can propel them forward or hold them back spiritually. The truth is that when we come to Jesus, we bring our generation with us. Once we see the generational differences behind many of our conflicts in our homes and churches, it's impossible to miss them the next time. Suddenly, they seem obvious, and they no longer have to hold us back.

Recently I led a workshop on this topic at my church. I started the seminar by asking the group of forty why they came to a session on generational differences, and one guy said, "I'm open to the fact that I see things based on my generation, and I might need a new lens."

His acknowledgment was the first step to learning how to get along with the other generations. He's on the right track.

To help you develop a new lens as well, in the next four chapters we'll dive into how each generation breaks down—the basics of what they believe and how the time in which they were born affects who they have become. We'll also look at each generation's greatest strengths and temptations based on these generational characteristics. Not only are these four chapters crucial for laying the foundation of generational intelligence, they will provide you with insights into how to grow in your own spiritual life. Then throughout the rest of the book, we'll get more detailed about how to apply generational intelligence and these new spiritual insights to answer the frightening questions posed in chapter 1 about our families, our friends, and our churches.

We struggle to love people we don't appreciate or understand. When we understand other generations, we will quit judging them and start learning from them. Generational intelligence doesn't make the key teaching of Jesus to "love one another" easy, but it does make it easier.

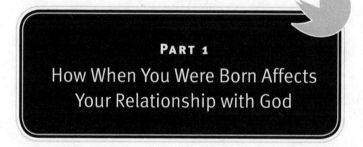

PART 1

How When You Were Born Affects
Your Relationship with God

CHAPTER 3

Traditionalists

Born before 1945

TODAY CHRISTIANS WORRY that Christianity is declining, people no longer believe in the Bible, sex outside marriage is expected, church attendance is falling, and "pop" psychology is replacing religion. And when they complain about how things have changed, they wistfully remember America or Canada before World War II, when Protestant Christianity dominated public opinion, when family values were intact, and when their country hadn't lost its morals. We picture our God-fearing grandparents and great-grandparents reading Scripture around the fireplace, heading to church in their one car, and courting in the parlor under the careful scrutiny of a chaperone.

When many people long for the return to a simpler time and family values and a Christian America, they picture the era the Traditionalists grew up in—1900 to 1945.

Surprisingly, America was not as Christian as people remember, our grandparents were not nearly as chaste as we think, and most startlingly, all the trends above that worry Christians today actually had their start in radical shifts that gained momentum in that era.

While that new way of thinking was gaining popularity, most people didn't realize it or even see those changes as particularly significant. The changes in thinking were there, under the surface, and didn't surge into the open until those ideas bore fruit in the generation gap that emerged between the Traditionalists and their Boomer children.

It's not that people weren't paying attention; it's that two different worlds existed simultaneously. As we who live in a world of constant communication forget, most people in the 1920s lived around farms and had very little experience with the city, where most of these changes were occurring. Until people had access to radio, their lives were largely oriented around their region rather than the country, so these ideas didn't reach much of the United States or Canada until later.

I live outside Chicago, a city famous for its museums. My favorite is the Art Institute of Chicago. In its Modern American Art gallery (and on our kitchen wall) you will find Grant Wood's famous *American Gothic*, painted in 1930. You know the one: a daughter with her stern-faced, pitchfork-holding father standing in front of an Iowa farmhouse. It's one of the most well-known paintings in US history and appears on T-shirts, postcards, and television commercials. While Grant Wood was expressing many layers of meaning—some of them tongue in cheek—even a person with little understanding of or appreciation for art can easily figure out what he was attempting to represent. His picture is popular because it communicates clearly to the average person: this is a portrait of the steadfast, hardworking American spirit.[1]

Go up one floor and you can see another painting from just one year later. Picasso's *The Red Armchair* (painted in 1931) shows a flat and cartoonish representation. The woman looks as if she has two faces, because Picasso was trying to show the front of her face and her profile at the same time. And it's hard to tell that she's even sitting in an armchair.[2]

While Wood was highlighting, if not spoofing, the clearly defined roles of tradition, Picasso and other modern artists were rejecting the conventional way of painting—because they were rejecting the traditional ways of understanding the world and the universe. After Einstein's theory of relativity, why couldn't a portrait have two faces? After Freud told us that our dreams showed us more of the truth about ourselves than did our waking hours, why shouldn't paintings be dreamlike rather than realistic, exploring internal perceptions and feelings rather than outward appearance?

Those two paintings illustrate the two worlds that were thriving as the Traditionalists grew up.

What Shaped the Traditionalists

Also called Builders, Elders, the Silent Generation, and the Greatest Generation, Traditionalists grew up in the 1920s through the early 1950s. Traditionalists have four stories that shaped their ideas and images so that their values "go without saying."

The Great Depression

You can't understand the Traditionalists unless you understand how the shift from the Roaring Twenties to the Great Depression (beginning in 1929) left an entire generation cautious, thrifty, and focused on saving. With little welfare and no Social Security, millions of people barely fed their families despite sacrifice and hard work. Anyone who has Depression-era parents or grand-parents has heard slogans like "Waste not, want not" and "Make do and mend."

When one of my grandmothers went to a nursing home at age eighty-nine, my aunt and uncle moved into the family farmhouse and threw out approximately 2.3 billion plastic Cool Whip containers from the cellar. My grandmother figured if there came a time when she didn't have enough food, she would certainly have containers for what little she did have.

Most of the Traditionalists who lived through the Great Depression have passed, but the shadow it cast shaped the mind-sets of those alive today, even though most aren't as frugal.

World War II

The Great Depression taught Traditionalists to sacrifice and show patience. That lesson served them well during World War II. The most popular war in US history, World War II united the country like no other war before or since. Families gathered around the radio for war news and prayed for their men to come home. The soldiers believed in the sacrifices they made. They jumped out of Higgins boats on the beaches of Normandy on D-day knowing that most of them would die but convinced that death in victory was better than life under a totalitarian regime. So the Traditionalists learned to sacrifice their individuality for the cause—to sit down, shut up, and do what they were told.

Traditionalists learned not to complain and often think younger people get upset about trivial things. Traditionalists who ate cold C-ration meals in foxholes have little patience for those who complain that the kale in their salad isn't fresh.

Because of World War II, Traditionalists witnessed the power of large government programs, larger-than-life leaders, and the accomplishments of a unified nation where everyone did his or her duty. They didn't question authority at home, because the threat overseas was far more terrifying. However, greater individualism grew out of the war because people saw the dangers of blind conformity in Europe and Japan. The Traditionalists raised their kids to value democracy and the importance of individual freedom.

Most of all, Traditionalists learned the power of sacrifice and patience. Ironically, the most famous British poster from the war, produced in case Germany invaded Britain, was never used. It later became so popular because it captures the wartime perspective of the Traditionalists: "Keep Calm and Carry On."

The experience of World War II also affected religious belief. Before World War II, most people in the United States and Canada assumed Christianity was true. The Bible said it, and that's what everyone else around them believed. But soldiers who previously had never left their hometowns returned having seen whole civilizations that believed different religions and defined truth in different ways. It became difficult for many of them to assume Christianity was the only true religion. On the other hand, after two world wars, the unbridled optimism of the previous century, which proclaimed that science and democracy were the keys to the inevitable progress of the human race, seemed delusional. Science had been a tool of devastation. Nations that had thrown off the shackles of religion had invented new ways to kill each other. And after the Nazis and the Fascists, democracy seemed much more fragile than inevitable.

The Move from Farm to City

After World War II, the migration from farm to city accelerated. Johnny came marching home from the war and married Rosie the Riveter. She told him she wasn't going back to the farm and the outhouse now that she lived in town and used indoor plumbing.

So she took him out to the suburbs to see the prefab houses with all the modern conveniences. These post–World War II subdivisions sprang up on the edges of every major city. At the beginning of the twentieth century, two-thirds of the US population lived on farms or in rural towns. By 1970, almost three-quarters lived in the cities and suburbs.

The city exposed people to new ideas and new opportunities. While rural settings have always had their problems, the closeness of rural communities made certain crimes more difficult to commit. (It's harder to rob people if they know who you are.) And while some atheists who believed that science could answer every question lived on farms, skeptical and even atheistic ideology was gaining ground in the universities during the years the Traditionalists were born. Because the universities were in the cities, these new ideas were becoming much more prevalent there.

According to these ideas, the Bible is full of legends that developed over time rather than descriptions of historical events. Skeptics and atheists at the universities believed the faster we dropped those outdated beliefs and put our trust in science and smart thinking, the faster society could continue to evolve.

Others in universities didn't reject God completely, even though they were also skeptical of the Bible. They thought that those stories, like stories in all religions, contained a kernel of truth that must be set free from the husks of man-made legends. They believed that people of all faiths needed to leave behind their outdated theologies so they could continue to evolve from individual religions like Christianity or Buddhism into a higher universal religion.

In addition to those ideas, Sigmund Freud and the growth in the influence of psychology swept the country. Freud was an atheist who popularized the fledgling field of modern psychology as an alternative to religion for explaining human behavior and health. Forget the soul and the father figure in heaven—psychology would tell us how to live.

While these ideas were not widespread in the older half of the Traditionalists' generation, the move from the farm to the city made them a growing influence on the younger Traditionalists and Baby Boomers.

Mass Marketing and Confidence in Experts

The generation before the Traditionalists was regionally based because they had little immediate contact with the "outside world."[3] But radio changed things for the Traditionalists. Some call Traditionalists the Radio Generation because it became their link to the broader world. And it did something else: it created the voice of "the expert." With the radio came not only news and entertainment but also mass marketing.

The golden age of radio (1920s–1940s) was also the golden age of mass marketing. Each radio show was sponsored by a single company. Week after week, the stars of that show plugged the sponsor's products before and after each episode. With whole families gathered around the radio in the evening, this mass marketing created powerhouse brands.

Traditionalists have always valued the guidance of experts. Previous generations either made their own essentials or purchased them at a dry goods store. City grocery stores carried multiple brands to choose from, so Traditionalists turned to trusted experts for guidance. "If Lux soap was good enough for 'four out of five' households, why shouldn't it be good enough for ours?" "If Little Orphan Annie needs all kids in the Radio Orphan Annie's Secret Society to 'Be sure to drink your Ovaltine,' then Ovaltine must be good for you." (Although Ralphie was pretty ticked off that Annie's secret message was just another "crummy commercial" in *A Christmas Story*, the movie that plays on a seemingly endless loop at Christmastime.)

The Traditionalist generation began regionally isolated in 1901 and ended with an unprecedented national unity that had won World War II. And who got them through those years? Experts—President Franklin D. Roosevelt during the Depression with his radio "fireside chats" and the scientists and engineers who created the weapons that ended the war. Many Boomers have told me that they accompany their parents on doctor visits because to this day their parents won't ask questions. Most Traditionalists grew up trusting the voice of experts—they didn't question their doctors or their lawyers. But as we saw earlier, for a growing group, that was beginning to change.

No wonder Traditionalists were shocked when their Baby Boomer children began questioning the experts they trusted. Archie and Edith Bunker, sitting at the piano and singing "Those Were the Days" on their weekly television sitcom, *All in the Family*, were a perfect picture of how the Traditionalists felt when their children disagreed with them on almost everything.

Traditionalists' Strengths

Each generation has spiritual strengths and temptations that were shaped by the ideas and images of the times in which they grew up. But describing the historical events that shaped them is easier than trying to summarize how these events determine their strengths and temptations, because short summaries can feel like stereotypes rather than generalizations. As I said in a column for *Huffington Post* on why experts disagree about the Millennials, it's impossible to make generalizations that apply equally to eighty-four million people.[4] Any sociological research requires making generalizations about groups of people, and marketing researchers do it successfully all the time. But summaries as brief as this require hitting the high points without exploring the exceptions and some of the nuances of the ideas and images for each generation.

So while I think it's invaluable to understand these high points for each generation, I want to warn you against applying them to any one person you know in that generation. Generalizations make sense when talking about thousands of people but not when talking about one person—the person you know. Applying a valid statistical generalization to one person is stereotyping. Instead, these summaries should invite you to get curious and give you a starting point to talk to the people you know from other generations. I will move more quickly through the strengths than the temptations of each generation because most of us can accept generalizations of our strengths more easily than we can of our weaknesses, even though other generations often see them clearly.

Oseola McCarty illustrates what is great about the Traditionalists. Oseola was a washerwoman from Hattiesburg, Mississippi. At the age of eight, to aid with the family finances, she began helping her mother wash and iron clothes. Then when her aunt became ill, Oseola dropped out of school in the sixth grade to wash and iron full-time. She never returned to school, but instead spent the rest of her life washing. Every week she took some of her money to tithe, pay bills, and buy food, and then put the rest into a savings account. Faithfully she saved.

When arthritis forced her to retire at the age of eighty-six, she decided it was time to pull out her $280,000 and spend it. But instead of using the money on a new car or a luxury trip—things that surely she deserved since she had worked so hard all those years—she donated a portion to her church, some to her family, and more than $150,000 to the University of Southern Mississippi because she wanted "to give some child the opportunity I didn't have. . . . I hope this money can help children, for years to come, make their dreams come true."[5]

Oseola McCarty illustrates some of the wonderful spiritual strengths I've observed both personally and in the literature about the Traditionalists: they cooperate, they serve with lower expectations than other generations, and they give generously.

They Cooperate

Life in extended families, on the farm, and in World War II developed in the Traditionalists a strong sense of cooperation. World War II created the greatest national unity in our nation's history. Organizing millions for battle (and even more at home to conserve critical supplies), eating tripe and pig's feet instead of hamburger, and buying wartime savings bonds required people to set aside their own interests and cooperate. That same "We Can Do It" attitude that adorned the famous World War II Rosie the Riveter poster stayed with a generation after the war as they saw cooperation create medical breakthroughs, interstate highways, and technological miracles. They flocked to clubs and started associations. Most of them had a church, even if they didn't attend regularly. Going it alone made no sense to them. In true Traditionalist form, Oseola McCarty gave her money because she wanted others to receive the support she didn't get.

My four-foot-eleven grandmother Emily assumed even the mob embraced this notion of cooperation when she went door-to-door collecting for the March of Dimes. The other women in her group wanted to skip the houses owned by mobsters, but my grandmother said, "They're not going to shoot me in broad daylight for asking for a donation. Who in this neighborhood has more money than they do? Plus, they're Catholic, so they feel guilty about their life of crime and always give generously."

Sure enough, she always raised the most money because she knew that mobster families were actually quite eager to cooperate with respectable pursuits.

They Serve with Lower Expectations

Traditionalists have lower expectations for organizations than the younger generations do. For instance, they are comfortable in smaller and less elaborate buildings.[6] Big wars, the Great Depression, and medical breakthroughs taught them that even though organizations are imperfect, they can still accomplish great things. So if the organization mattered to the community or their family, the Traditionalists did their duty and didn't complain. Oseola McCarty didn't do research on the academic standing or job placement record of the University of Southern Mississippi when she donated her savings; she gave to her local university precisely because it was her local university. It wasn't about the university anyway; it was about the greater good. Even, as we saw with my grandma, if you were in the mob.

They Give Financially

Traditionalists approach money differently than the other generations do. As Oseola McCarty illustrates, they are famous savers, and they are also givers. When this generation hears about a need, they're the first to pull out their checkbooks and write a check. Traditionalists give more money to the church and to missions than the other generations do.[7]

Because Traditionalists still embrace self-sacrifice, they're more willing to do without in order to support others. The church I attend had a big push to take care of orphans and sponsor impoverished children in Kenya. While I sponsor three children, neither I nor the other Xers I know gave up cable (or Hulu or Netflix) to do it. But a wonderful Traditionalist woman at my church who is on a fixed income decided that those children needed the money far more than she needed multiple channels. She sacrificed in order to sponsor.

Traditionalists are also more trusting in organizations. In fact, in some cases their willingness to give and their reluctance to ask questions has led them to financially support unworthy ministries, such as in the 1980s, when televangelists embezzled money, spent it on themselves, and served jail time for it.

This strength hasn't carried over to the next generations, however, and many ministries have had to do without, and in some cases make major cuts or even close their doors. I was on a conference call with leaders from fifty large churches and ministries who were concerned because they've already seen a 10 percent drop in giving as the Traditionalists die. Even with the greatest transfer of wealth in human history from the Traditionalists to their kids and grandkids, these ministries don't expect the younger generations to give it but instead to spend it on luxuries and to pay off debt.

Traditionalists' Temptations

While the Traditionalists' upbringing developed wonderful spiritual strengths, it also created some spiritual blind spots that other generations see more easily. Traditionalists struggle with purposeless retirement and their orientation toward the past over the future.

They Struggle with Purposeless Retirement

Several years ago I was teaching Stephen Covey's famous process for how to find your mission in life, and I had in my class a dedicated Lutheran man who had just retired with a couple million dollars from the insurance company he had built. I asked what his mission was now that he didn't have to continue the nine-to-five grind.

"Nothing," he told me. "I carried my load; now it's someone else's turn. I'm on my time now. I've earned it. I plan to sit by the pool and play with my grandkids. What's wrong with that?"

Well, a lot, actually. First, it doesn't work for most people; we live too long today. Second, the image of retirement that Traditionalists inherited from their upbringing is too small, even though it has become the expected ending to the successful American Dream. But God has a different and better dream for retirement: he has given Traditionalists money, health, and opportunities that he has given to no other generation in history, so they can have a big retirement, not this small, self-serving one.

You don't find retirement in the Bible, because people couldn't retire. Throughout history, most people have been farmers, and a farmer's work is never done. My great-grandfather Grover Cleveland Jackson Howard insisted on raking hay at eighty-eight because many farmers of his era were ashamed when they couldn't pull their weight anymore and had to rely on their families. He finally relented at ninety-three and moved in with my grandparents (who had indoor plumbing). He let my uncle rototill his garden rather than dig it by hand because "my knees hurt too much."

While we now take retirement for granted, the idea of it was a massive social change made possible by the move from the farm to the city following World War II, combined with the pension and Social Security system. Between 1900 and 1910, only 20 percent of men who reached age fifty-five retired before they died. Only 15 percent of males sixty-five and older are employed today.[8]

Suddenly a generation saw retirement as an opportunity to quit working and enjoy the fruit of their labor: a life of leisure. Because people at the turn of the 1900s didn't live as long, they often died a couple of years after they retired, making it a short "vacation" at the end of a life of hard work.

Now that Traditionalists are the longest-living generation in history, they've created a new life stage. Two-thirds of life expectancy gains have come in the last hundred years. Today, a man who reaches age 65 can expect another eighteen years of life, and a woman who reaches age 65 can expect almost twenty more years.[9] This new life stage goes by many names, but I prefer "second adulthood." Traditionalists are the first generation to face the challenges of constructing another life after retirement. They have the health, the money, and the freedom to live another twenty or thirty active years after they finish their first adulthood, their working years. Another twenty or thirty years means Traditionalists get almost another adult lifetime compared to earlier generations. In previous generations, adulthood started at twenty-one and ended at sixty-five, when old age kicked in. Today, people are still fully engaged at seventy-five and often at ninety.

So in this second adulthood, between the time people can financially retire and their health requires them to stop their activities, people get to construct their second adult identity, focused more on their own values and interests than on earning a living and doing their duty. Though the idea of a retirement filled with freedom, travel, and family sounds wonderful, second adulthood has so changed the game that Traditionalists struggle to figure it out.

Fifteen years ago, I was speaking in Orlando and decided to visit Universal Studios. I arrived about twenty minutes before the park opened, and as I stood by the turnstiles waiting to enter, I noticed an older, distinguished-looking employee in a blue jumpsuit uniform. I asked him what he did before he retired and moved to Florida. He mentioned that he had worked in research and development at Lockheed Martin.

"What did you do there?"

"I was a senior vice president," he demurely told me.

"You don't need to work," I shot back. "Why are you doing a minimum-wage job that starts at seven in the morning?"

"I love golf," he told me. "We moved here so I could golf every day. But I discovered after two years that if you do something every day, it's no longer a hobby; it's a job. When I began to dread getting up to go golfing, I knew something was wildly wrong with my retirement plans. My wife made it clear after a couple of weeks that I couldn't just sit around the house, so a friend told me about this job opening. At sixty-seven, I'm too old to sleep late anymore, and they provide the work clothes. I've always enjoyed meeting new people, so this job is perfect. Plus, if I feel like golfing, they'll let me go at 10 a.m., and I can still get in nine holes before it gets too hot."

Traditional retirement works only if you die a couple of years after you retire. The rest of us will have to figure out something meaningful to do, or we will suffer all the boredoms of the "idle rich" with too much leisure and not enough purpose.

Whole cottage industries are sprouting up to help younger Traditionalists and Boomers figure out who they want to be in their second adulthood. A friend from church who runs Christian counseling centers and does executive coaching through the Young Presidents' Organization asked me if I had any time to help him coach business owners who at forty-five or fifty could sell their businesses and retire but don't know what they want to do. He said he can't keep up with all the people trying to figure out their mission in their second adulthood.

That people are living another thirty years is one of God's greatest blessings. But it comes with a number of challenges, and Traditionalists have struggled, as any pioneers do, to forge this new path. Many have been stuck, like the gentleman at the beginning of this section who thought he would sit by the pool.

How did he respond? With the mentality, *I carried the load; now this time is mine. I worked hard. I volunteered at church. Now it's the next generation's job.*

But Jesus had something to say about that mentality. He told the parable of a man whose land produced a terrific crop:

> The ground of a certain rich man yielded an abundant harvest. He thought to himself, "What shall I do? I have no place to store my crops."
>
> Then he said, "This is what I'll do. I will tear down my barns and build bigger ones, and there I will store my surplus grain. And I'll say to myself, 'You have plenty of grain laid up for many years. Take life easy; eat, drink and be merry.'"
>
> But God said to him, "You fool! This very night your life will be demanded from you. Then who will get what you have prepared for yourself?"
>
> This is how it will be with whoever stores up things for themselves but is not rich toward God. (Luke 12:16-21, NIV)

God didn't design us for this small retirement. As a result, it's one of the great temptations for the Traditionalists. It's tempting for them to think that second adulthood is theirs because they did their duty in the first adulthood. While nothing is wrong with enjoying golf or vacationing in a warm climate in the winter, God didn't give Traditionalists—or any of us—more life, more money, and more health for our quality of life alone. God gave it to get his work done in the world. All gifts are God's—including our additional years—but how many people build their retirement around what God wants from them rather than their own interests and climate preferences?

What do I want to do in retirement? is not a Christian question. A better question is, What exciting adventures might God have for me, where I can get caught up in his great plan for the world and feel the power of his holy purpose blow through me, so that every day is rich with meaning and every trip or time of leisure provides refreshment and joy along the way? We've been telling young people for twenty years that their generation could be the difference makers, that their lives could be big and they are dreaming too small. It's time to tell their grandparents the same thing.

They Cling to the Past and Lecture

Waxing nostalgic is more a product of life stage than of a specific generation. I already see it in myself and my generation. But since Traditionalists and now early Boomers are the oldest, they face the temptation to remember the past as better than it was and to see the future as scarier than it is. This may be more pronounced with the Traditionalists because they grew up being taught that children should respect their elders and should "be seen and not heard." Now they are dealing with the Millennial generation that was taught to express their opinions and was invited into family decisions. Whether it will be more pronounced with the radio generation or not, nostalgia and worry can cause them to retreat from the new generations and harrumph to others their age about these kids today and about what they don't know yet and what the world is coming to. But even the Bible says, "Do not say, 'Why were the old days better than these?' For it is not wise to ask such questions" (Ecclesiastes 7:10, NIV). And it's especially not wise because it makes the younger generations pull back from the Traditionalists when they really would like to learn from them.

Sometimes Traditionalists withdraw because they feel as though nobody's listening to them. And while it's true that harrumphing turns people off, sometimes others don't listen because Traditionalists are communicating in the ways that worked for their generation but don't work today. Traditionalists were used to experts telling; they grew up on lectures at school, at work, and especially at home. But even the way younger generations explain Christianity has changed significantly: it used to be Evangelism Explosion, where dedicated folks learned a script and then delivered it to people who allowed them in their homes. Today, sharing our faith is much more about conversations and discussing questions than it is about presentations or scripts. It worked for their generation, just as they had sat quietly while their parents talked. But it's not how the younger generations communicate.

One way Traditionalists get stuck in the communication patterns from their era is that they lecture. The younger generations don't want lectures; we want coaches who will talk *with* us. Millennials most respect and want to emulate the Traditionalists.[10] One Millennial said, "I'd love to learn from them—if they weren't busy telling me I'm wrong all the time."

Traditionalists have a great contribution to make in mentoring and coaching. I think this Millennial's review of Bob Dylan's 2006 album *Modern Times* captures the key ingredient Traditionalists need in order to impact the younger generations: "The older Dylan gets, the more we trust his ever-folksier koans. *Modern Times* is the product of age, hindsight and intuition. . . . But rather than cranky old-manisms, the album twinkles with a knowing wink, a graceful boogie, with blue-collar poetry and a bar room waltz."[11] If Traditionalists can keep the twinkle and hold down the cranky, more Gen Xers and Millennials will value their insight and intuition. They may even agree, at times, when Traditionalists complain that the times are a-changing, and not all for the better.

CHAPTER 4

Baby Boomers

Born 1946–1964

"WHICH GENERATION IS the most rebellious?" a Baby Boomer asked me in the question-and-answer session at NASA's Goddard Space Flight Center. I surprised him when I said Millennials are the least rebellious and the Traditionalists were the most rebellious, although each generation rebels against the excesses of the previous generation. He expected me to say Millennials (because they are shaking up the workplace with values and skills different from the older generations) or the Baby Boomers.

Everyone knows about the generation gap. Take the Beatles. These rebels may have started out with mop-top hair and cute love songs about wanting to hold your hand, but they ended up long-haired and singing about LSD in an ashram where they learned Eastern religion. Rebel Boomers grew up with parents whose main goal was to provide a better life for their kids, but they told each other not to trust anyone over thirty. They were taught to be polite and well-groomed so they could succeed in modern society, but they grew their hair long and tie-dyed all the undershirts they used to wear to church under a shirt and tie. They were taught the old-time religion, but they left it for free love, communes, and drug use.

The Boomers appeared to reject all the accomplishments the previous generations had worked so hard for: successful businesses, the triumph of democracy, the emergence of the United States as a world superpower, confidence in Protestant Christianity, the epic fight against Communism.

Parents in the sixties never knew what hit them. Traditionalists who had moved from the farm to the city and suburbs had no idea that the new affluence and education they gave their children would introduce them to these new ideas.

If the generation gap is distinctive of the Boomers, why did I tell the scientist at Goddard that the Traditionalists were the bigger rebels? As we saw in the last chapter, they formulated the ideas that shook and shocked the world when the Boomers embraced them. Most Traditionalists embraced the philosophy of life that the *American Gothic* painting, rather than Picasso's *Red Armchair*, expressed. Still, the shifts in thinking during the first half of the century that formed what Daniel Yankelovich, the leading researcher on the Boomers, termed "the New Morality"[1] were firmly in place by the time the Boomers were teenagers. So that made them appear to be rebels when they were only embracing the ideas the Traditionalist intellectuals and artists formulated. The Boomers' generation gap, the Xers' cynicism (and punk rock), and the Millennials' self-esteem and approach to moral reasoning all grew out of the new ideas symbolized by that Picasso painting.

The Boomers were raised with high expectations because the

decades they grew up in, especially the older Boomers, seemed *magical*. Boomers grew up as the most optimistic generation in American history, and they had good reason:

> Kids knew their grandparents and sometimes great-grandparents due to increasing life spans.
> Penicillin and vaccines eradicated and controlled long-standing health threats.
> Television constantly marketed to, captivated, and entertained them.
> The postwar economy boomed, and the middle class prospered.
> Boomers believed that the world was theirs for the taking if they worked hard.

Baby Boomers grew up in the 1950s, '60s, and '70s. They got their name from the surge of births (the Baby Boom) after World War II. From the time they were babies, Boomers were told they were special. Their parents had great expectations for them because, compared to the Traditionalists' childhoods, they were living in a great time. That's why the generation gap shocked parents so much when their children rejected their values.

What Shaped the Baby Boomers

Boomers have four prominent ideas and images that shaped their lives, behaviors, and mind-set: the Baby Boom, affluence, television, and the shift from sacrifice to self.

The Baby Boom

The first prominent Boomer story is the biggest—literally. Never before in history were so many babies born so quickly. Johnny came marching home from the war, missing his girl and wanting to settle down and start a family. And start a family he did. But society wasn't ready for what happened next: the boom of babies. (One example that illustrates this boom is that baby-food sales jumped from 2.7 million cases in 1941 to 15 million in 1947.[2])

Overcrowded hospitals, grade schools, sports teams, college campuses, and job markets taught the Boomers that you have to compete to get what you want. Everyone made the park district Little League team in third grade, but only the best got to play, and only the very best got a trophy. The Boomers learned that if you didn't put in the hours, somebody else would.

Boomers are used to being heard. The sheer size of their generation made them the center of attention. So they reshaped markets as well as business and political priorities at every stage of their lives. And they reshaped childhood: smaller families meant they were the focus of their parents' attention and dreams.

Boomers have reshaped each stage of their adult lives as well. They redefined parenting styles and roles in marriage, reworked everything from the coffee shop to the church (and even put a coffee shop *in* their church). They have stayed active (and Botoxed), hoping to hold on to youth longer. And this huge generation is now reshaping retirement: they plan for retirement, but they don't plan to retire. According to one survey, Boomers think old age begins at 79.5—the age of current life expectancy![3]

Affluence

"For the first time, a civilization has reached a point where most people are no longer preoccupied with providing food and shelter," *Life Magazine* announced in their 1959 year-end issue.[4] Boomers grew up in one of the most economically optimistic times in history.

Because World War II wasn't fought on American shores, our factories and transportation systems were in place, whereas much of Europe's and Asia's infrastructure had been destroyed. The economy boomed because the United States stopped producing bullets and started producing more than a third of all the world's manufactured goods. Almost overnight the political slogan "A chicken in every pot and a car in every garage" was coming true. By the 1950s many people even had a dishwasher and a television. The country thought this new generation would not need to strive for the American Dream as their parents had—they were born into it.

Affluence created "great expectations," to use the title of Landon Jones's landmark history of the Boomers.[5] For example, the Boomers didn't save money the way their Depression-era parents had. The economy was booming, and they were confident the money would be there when they needed it.

Television

Television allowed the entire country to see the same thing at the same time. And when the "thing" was Kennedy's funeral or the first moon landing—powerfully emotional events—the nation shared common experiences as never before. Unlike radio, where individual people form different pictures in their heads as they hear a story, television assures a stronger common experience, since everyone sees the same image. That's why MTV launched their channel in 1981 with photos of the Apollo 11 moon landing, because everyone had seen it live or replayed dozens of times. Since there were only three major network television channels during the Boomers' formative years, the entire nation saw the same stories the same way at the same time.

A Millennial participant in a recent workshop couldn't believe that when his older classmates were growing up, there were only four channels, television programming turned off at 1 a.m., and a pattern appeared on the screen until 5 a.m. Horrified, he asked them what they did once the TV shut off. Today a thousand people can watch a thousand different things on TV or the Internet. It's difficult for Xers and Millennials to grasp how having such limited television channels powerfully connected the Boomers and scripted their common language. *Gilligan's Island* may have been corny, but Boomers can still sing the theme song because it was one of the few shows on.

Shift from Sacrifice to Self

The generation gap signaled a massive shift in values far more important than the music, tie-dye, or protests that usually get the focus. Daniel Yankelovich described Boomers' new values as self-expression, self-exploration, and personal satisfaction.[6] Boomers saw the new freedom from want and war and fear as a new opportunity—not to fulfill their parents' expectations but to figure out what *they* wanted. The hierarchy, conformity, and suburban sameness of the post–World War II decades became stifling, and Boomers accelerated a shift to individual freedom of expression and self-fulfillment.

The affluence described above explains many of the Boomers' distinct values. No longer worried about survival, Boomers changed their value system and focus from sacrifice to self. Affluence also meant that parents no longer needed to have lots of children to support the farm, so they could channel their expectations and their attention into their 3.5 children. As a result, Boomers were the first generation to be raised in an era that emphasized that people are special. In 1940, only 20 percent of men and 11 percent of women agreed with the statement "I am an important person." In 1990, 62 percent of men and 66 percent of women agreed.[7] Instead of hearing, "Who do you think you are?" as the Traditionalists had, the Boomers were told they were extraordinary. It's no surprise that Boomers are idealistic and confident.

It takes cash to become the "Me" generation, and Boomers were the first generation to have the money, time, and freedom to explore self and search for meaning. If the Boomers had a slogan, it was "Do your own thing." This central commandment of the new morality was chanted in songs and printed on psychedelic posters.

The media (and thus much of the population) focused on the more symptomatic stories of the Boomers' youth—sex, drugs, rock and roll, and the Vietnam protests. But those realities did not cause the generation gap. No more than 2 percent of Boomers joined civil rights or antiwar protests or the counterculture.[8] Television's focus on the counterculture magnified its size in the minds of Traditionalists. Woodstock (1969) was a symptom, not a cause, of the generation gap. Affluence allowed a much more profound shift to self over sacrifice, optimism over caution, and the new morality over traditional religion.[9]

Baby Boomers' Strengths and Temptations

The Baby Boom, affluence, television, and the shift from sacrifice to self, in addition to greater education and the emergence of the discipline of psychology, all contributed to two major shifts in thinking: the shift to hyperindividualism and the corresponding shift from theology to psychology as the authority for daily living. In the case of the Boomers, these two shifts created their generation's greatest spiritual strengths—which are also their greatest spiritual temptations.

Hyperindividualism

Baby Boomers' parents and grandparents told them stories of the hunger of the Great Depression, the dread of polio, and the hope for a better world after defeating the tyrants in World War II. The moral of their stories was how much the Boomers should appreciate their nice suburban homes, war-free childhood, medical miracles, and that the Communists had not yet conquered America and placed all the children in work camps.

Most Boomers were grateful to be born in this magical time, but they took their parents' stories far beyond what their parents meant. They coped with the Traditionalists' expectations that they would do great things by becoming the "Me Generation." After seeing hundreds of photos of goose-stepping Nazi soldiers and Japanese kamikazes, those living in the post–World War II era focused on the individual. This spread into how the Boomers approached the spiritual life.

One benefit of this focus on the individual was that Boomers brought God closer. The greatest single discovery of my life came out of my only time of prolonged depression, for which I sought counseling, when I thought I would never be good enough to please God. While my generation was taught we were loved by God and saved by grace, we were taught that after we were saved, Christianity was simply believing the right things and doing the right things. But I had questions and doubts about my beliefs, and more often than not, I failed at doing the right things even though I was trying hard. One day during my sophomore year in high school, I thought, *If I work this hard and I'm* still *not getting it right, maybe I can't do this. I don't know what else to do.* That thought began my clinical depression.

But then I read a book by John White,[10] who wrote about his spiritual struggles. He said that the further from success and God he felt, the harder he tried to be holy enough to please God. He spoke of his despair until he realized that Christianity is a *relationship* with God: God first reached out to us to bring us close to him, and then we obeyed because we loved him and were grateful to him. Though the difference is subtle, it lifted my depression. I forever gave up trying to please a distant God and began to look at obedience as a way of getting closer to the one who was already close to me.

This move from religion to relationship with God transformed my life and many other Boomers' lives. This Boomer focus on the individual rather than the Traditionalists' focus on the group brought God closer. Christian Boomers also put a greater emphasis on experiencing God rather than simply learning doctrine. Their songs reflected this. Instead of four full stanzas of "A Mighty Fortress Is Our God," they sang, "That's how it is with God's love, once you've experienced it: You want to sing, it's fresh like spring, you want to pass it on."[11]

Boomers were drawn to the idea that Jesus called his disciples "friends" (John 15:15). Instead of going outside to learn right doctrine from experts or authorities, as their parents and grandparents had done, Boomers applied the larger societal shift from sacrifice to self to their faith and went inside themselves to experience God. They helped shift the emphasis from doctrine and commandments to the God who loves us deeply and profoundly and wants to be involved in even the minor details of our lives.

This is a huge strength—the realization that God has been brought near through Christ. But the generation raised with "great expectations" and told they were special also had a tendency to want to make worship "all about me." If society valued self-expression, self-exploration, and personal satisfaction, there was little to keep Boomers from becoming self-centered. Boomers were not just individualistic; they became *hyper*individualistic. This hyperindividualism has led to two temptations that Boomers (and the rest of us) face: a focus on self and church hopping.

FOCUS ON SELF

We see the focus on self in the way Boomers studied the Bible. In Sunday school, Traditionalists covered the entire Bible every six years by using the Uniform Series International Bible Lessons for Christian Teaching (begun in 1872).[12] Traditionalists emphasized learning the Bible and doctrine rather than application. But the focus changed as Boomers grew up. Sunday school and small groups began asking questions like "What does this verse mean to you?" "How does this help you feel closer to Jesus?" "What will you use from this passage in your life this week?" None of these questions is inherently bad—I've grown spiritually by asking them myself—but taken collectively, they illustrate a significant shift to a greater focus on self. The Me Generation had come to church.

I saw that firsthand when I planted a church. I had hundreds of conversations with Boomers who said they were trying to find a faith that "works for me," even if that meant skipping parts of the Bible. The Traditionalists may not have obeyed all of the teachings in the Bible, but the Boomers were the first generation to widely believe you could pick and choose.

Are parts of the Bible boring or difficult to understand? Sure. But God put them there for a reason, and sometimes we have to chew, as on a steak, rather than slurp, as on a shake. The writer of Hebrews went straight at spiritual milk shake lovers:

> We have much to say about this, but it is hard to make it clear to you because you no longer try to understand. In fact, though by this time you ought to be teachers, you need someone to teach you the elementary truths of God's word all over again. You need milk, not solid food! Anyone who lives on milk, being still an infant, is not acquainted with the teaching about righteousness. (Hebrews 5:11-13, NIV)

The writer of Hebrews is frustrated because he can't teach the people what he knows they need, because they're not even trying to understand the harder parts of the faith. It's hyper-individualistic for us to pick and choose to read only the parts of the Bible that we easily understand or that encourage us in the moment. Don't misunderstand me: the majority of Bible readers seek answers, help, and comfort for their own lives.[13] That's as it should be if we don't skip the "hard parts" and miss out on passages that are necessary for understanding God beyond "the elementary truths." Jesus knew the Old Testament deeply and found it a source of comfort and practical guidance when being tempted, for example.[14] He didn't skip the hard parts.

CHURCH HOPPING

The Traditionalists were loyal to the churches they grew up in— or at least to one in their denomination if they relocated. Boomers began to evaluate their churches from a more self-focused perspective: Am *I* growing spiritually? Am *I* happy? Are the minister's sermons relevant to *my* life? Their hyperindividualism shaped their ideas and images of church. Just as with Scripture, they believed they could pick and choose their church. So they left the church they grew up in for whichever church best suited their needs. Because of a greater awareness of other intellectual options and a reaction against denominational infighting, Boomers were far more likely to switch denominations or marry outside their denomination.[15]

Over the last twenty years, as Boomers chose nondenominational churches based on the quality of their programs, their music, and their preaching, denominational labels began to appear in tiny letters underneath the church name or disappeared completely from church signs. This greater focus on quality over denominational affiliation also gave rise to nondenominational parachurch organizations, such as Promise Keepers and Women of Faith. Why should you go to your denominational conference, which offers only a small slice of what Christianity has to offer, when you can join fifty thousand other people and hear the best communicators of your generation?

I love that my generation isn't as caught up in theological debates between denominations. Two of my children went to my alma mater, a college in our denomination, and two didn't. But it doesn't matter as much as when I attended, because both campuses have students who don't agree theologically with all the details that their school teaches. (We'll see how critical this openness is to keeping our kids in the Christian faith in chapter 9.) When I overhear my kids talk or I stand by them at church and watch how they worship, I'm beyond grateful to both schools. I have my interpretations of theological questions, but if you believe in the resurrected Jesus yet disagree with me doctrinally, I'm still in this with you. We Christians have our hands full dealing with the new morality and new philosophies; we don't have the luxury to spend much of our energy fighting each other today.

I'm also a fan of the greater focus on quality. High tech when I was growing up was a new flannel board in the fourth grade boys' Sunday school class. Attention to quality has transformed the religious landscape.[16] I know it's a sweeping generalization, and those can be dangerous, but I know of few churches that have grown beyond two hundred over the last thirty years if they continued to emphasize allowing everyone to lead or participate regardless of their talent. The Boomers left the small churches of their childhoods for ones that have better programs and more polished worship. They knew Miss Stella was the only one willing to do it, but they just couldn't take another Sunday of hearing her play the piano like she was wearing mittens.

There is nothing wrong with appreciating quality in our churches, but I think church hopping is one of the worst things that ever happened to our spiritual lives. You can't date and dump churches *and* grow deeper spiritually. If your church is practicing spiritual abuse or heresy, or if it has so much anger and bitterness and you aren't spiritually strong enough to deal with it, by all means, get out of there. But most churches aren't horrific; they're full of humans, and that makes them imperfect, frustrating, and sometimes boring.

Just like marriage. I didn't grow much spiritually when Laurie and I began dating, because everything was new, shiny, and exciting. She was amazing—what wasn't to love? It was only after dating three years and getting married that I had to grow up in order to love the real Laurie, whose complaints about my not putting things away were getting old. Thirty years later, I love my wife more than ever (she still complains I don't put things away), though I don't have the same feelings for her that I did at first. That was infatuation, which was really all about how she made me feel. This is the real thirty-year deal. I am crazy about this woman, but it is not the same feeling. It's a much better one.

Church hoppers are hooked on a feeling more than on God. When they find a church they like, it's all new, shiny, and exciting. The sermons are different and the people are wonderful—unlike those needy or irritating people from the last church. Then a year passes, and they discover that these people are needy or weird just like the people in the last four churches. Three years later, the worship songs don't move them anymore. They wonder why their minister can't preach more like this guy they've been listening to on the radio. And they begin to wonder if God perhaps wants them to go someplace where they can be fed spiritually, because they're certainly not feeling it here. Individualism brought God close; hyperindividualism applied a consumer's attitude toward churches, and it has stunted Boomers' spiritual growth.

John of the Cross (who lived in the 1500s) compared Christians who need those warm and exciting feelings to infants who want to be held and regard their parents with self-centered love for what Mom and Dad can do for them. In response to this temptation, John talked about the "dark night of the soul," when God withdraws his warm and supportive feelings from us so that we can begin to love *him* more than the feelings of being close to him. John of the Cross described how God takes us out of his arms, places us on our feet, and asks us to walk beside him.[17]

When we take individualism too far and become hyper-individualistic, we can't get beyond our attachment to an emotional experience of Christ. We leave a church in search of a new "Jesus buzz" before we grow up through the dark night of the soul, or learn to love ordinary people, or deal with our boredom.

So I hope we learn to go to church not so much for what it gives us but because this is Christ's body; this is where the Holy Spirit is at work. If we are constantly searching for a better place, we'll miss what he put us on the earth for, we'll live small and shallow lives, and we'll get older and grouchier. We'll be like those Boomers who are now going on eco-vacations because they're looking to do some "good" in the world, when we could have just shown up right where we live and made a difference for eternity.

Psychology

I'm a fan of psychology. When I was depressed, I prayed and went to a godly, trained psychologist. When my wife and I were stuck in our marriage, we prayed and went to another godly, trained psychologist. We have told our married son that if he and his wife get stuck in their marriage and don't have the money, we will pray and pay for them to go to a godly, trained psychologist. Thank God Boomers are nine times more likely to seek psychological help than their parents.[18] Thank God mental illness is coming out into the open. Thank God neurology is teaching us so much about the bodies God created and sin corrupted.

Modern psychology has brought us so much obvious good and is so much a part of our lives today that its benefits go without saying.

While I'm a fan of psychology as a servant of theology, I think my generation's often unconscious faith in psychology instead of theology is also one of their greatest temptations. In society, psychology has replaced theology as the explanation for why we are the way we are and the source of guidance for living.

Modern psychology was in its infancy when the youngest Traditionalists were born, but it reached maturity with the Boomers. Boomers may not know Scripture, but they do know psychology. Everyone has an opinion on when a friend needs therapy. Parents debate in great detail the strengths and weaknesses of different child-rearing approaches on park benches while the kids play.

Celebrities talk in psychological categories in interviews and tweets. A psychological evaluation form from the late 1800s I found in an inherited family Bible placed self-esteem in the least important category. It prioritized moral character. People from that era would be shocked that when *Time* magazine asked Jennifer Lopez if there was anything she knows now that she wishes she would have known at sixteen, she replied, "You've got to love yourself first."[19] We are so steeped in psychology that we nod at her answer because today it goes without saying. But that was not the case even fifty years ago.

Psychological terms such as *defense mechanism*, *ego*, and *low self-esteem* pepper everyday speech. Little surprise: psychology dominates everything we read. Reporters quote psychologists as the reigning authorities, and new studies make the front page (or the front screen) of the news. Now that society no longer calls actions sinful, bloggers ransack psychology trying to explain human evils like child abuse, date rape, or governmental corruption.

The Boomer generation searching for self-fulfillment turned not to God but to Oprah. Instead of church, every Sunday morning you can now catch Oprah talking with a self-help or feel-good guru on her show *Super Soul Sunday*. It illustrates how the Boomers redefined the core theological word *soul* into a psychological replacement for religion in a time slot that replaces church. It's about humans looking into themselves to find the answers to why their souls aren't "super."

I realize Protestant Christianity no longer dominates the mind of society on this continent or in Europe, so you can't have a mainstream show that talks about just one view of God, as the Traditionalists could. But psychology, while a helpful hand-maiden to faith, is a fourth-rate substitute for it. Without God's wisdom and power, it has nothing to rely on but itself, which means when it runs into difficult challenges, it has nothing to recommend but more psychology and more analysis.

Take the problem of overeating. It is listed among the seven deadly sins as "gluttony," because Christian theology says the deepest cause of overeating is, like those other six foundational sins, our desire to do what we want when we want. I didn't gain thirty pounds over the last three years by eating healthy. I can give you valid neurological and psychological explanations for why I gained weight. I got whiplash that messed up my metabolism, which was already slowing as I turned fifty. I don't sleep enough (which creates cravings and reduces resistance), and I've worked too much researching two books while doing more than a full-time job trying to put four kids through college in seven years.

I've got great reasons why I have been eating too much for my age and weight. But the fact remains, I'm also a glutton. On the rare occasions I can get to LC's Bar-B-Q in Kansas City, I have been known to eat a full slab of ribs and a pound of smoked pork. When I'm eating like that, I'm not thinking about feeding my body because I want to be healthy. I'm a barbecue snob, and LC's makes my favorite ribs and pork in the world. I don't get there more than once a year, so I sometimes eat all I can hold. *Hey,* I think unconsciously, *it's my body, and I get to do what I want with it, even if it's not what God designed it for. I am king of my mouth; I bow to no one.* But that, my friends, has been the classic definition of gluttony for centuries.

Right out of college, I did a lot of work with addictions and dependencies, so I saw the power of psychological concepts and tools to help people who couldn't control their drinking or their eating. I get that until people deal with those underlying emotional causes, avoiding gluttony will be much more difficult. Psychology may explain the factors that make it harder for me to avoid gluttony, but theology calls the overeating a sin. I need them both, but I need to hear the word of the Lord first.

Since only Christian psychologists can refer to God and Scripture, most psychologists can't speak of sin. So psychology calls our inability to control our eating and drinking a "dependence" or an "addiction." And it can become that. But it's psychologically uncouth to call overeating a sin, because that makes people feel guilty, which puts them into a negative emotional cycle, which then causes them to eat more. They may discover they are eating because they are angry at the pain caused by a mentally ill mother or an emotionally distant father. What does psychology do with that? There's no God who forgives our sins so that we can forgive others. There's no eternal emotional security that comes because we know that "the LORD is my shepherd; I have all that I need" (Psalm 23:1).

Without the power of God, there's just more analysis and then more psychological tools like "mindfulness" to master.

(Mindfulness, the current fad in pop psychology, helps people focus on the present rather than pain from the past or anxieties over the future.) Then when we fail at mindfulness and the old fears overcome us, we have to dig deeper into the reasons we are self-sabotaging. Since they can't turn to the promises of God to comfort us, secular therapists have only more psychological techniques to help us try to get our souls back to "super." And we go back around that circle again.

That circle makes psychology more demanding than religion. If I'm unhappy, that means I haven't bought the right bestseller or figured out the right secret or found the right therapist, and I've got to keep reading, trying, and searching. If I've done all that and I'm still not happy, I've just got to make it till next Sunday, because there will be another psychologist on *Super Soul Sunday* with a whole new plan.[20]

No wonder the psalmist pleads with God to "open my eyes to see the wonderful truths in your instructions. . . . Don't hide your commands from me! I am always overwhelmed with a desire for your regulations" (Psalm 119:18-20). He recognizes that he needs wisdom beyond what humans offer.

Christian Boomers helped us by asking how to apply Scripture and theology to our lives. They are willing to use therapeutic tools to better handle their emotions and lives. But because psychology has so shaped our thinking today, we have gone too far in the worship of the therapeutic.

Jesus cares deeply about how we feel, which is why he came to show us how to put our faith in God and to "have life, and have it to the full" (John 10:10, NIV). Therapeutic teaching is often the starting point for reaching people, but it's never the destination. The Good News Jesus came to bring is that we are all irreparably broken sinners who have messed up our lives. As long as we're in charge, we will always suffer from insatiable desires.

(LC's ribs really are stunningly good.) We're hopeless cases, and we need Jesus to save us from ourselves and give us his new life. Christ's message is much more powerful and hopeful than the psychological and therapeutic:

> On the last day, the climax of the festival, Jesus stood and shouted to the crowds, "Anyone who is thirsty may come to me! Anyone who believes in me may come and drink! For the Scriptures declare, 'Rivers of living water will flow from his heart.'"(When he said "living water," he was speaking of the Spirit, who would be given to everyone believing in him.) (John 7:37-39)

When we are no longer ruled by insatiable desires, living water flows from within us. Psychology can give us insight into some of the things that block that living water, but it can never make it flow. The good news is we're all hopeless cases, and we will find rest for our not-so-super souls only when we surrender to Jesus, because his Holy Spirit will flow from within us, a never-ending source of supernatural life and joy.

Chapter 5

Generation X

Born 1965–1980

GENERATION X IS the most misunderstood and invisible of the generations.[1] The name itself illustrates the problem. Generation Xers don't like the label. Who can blame them? When it first became obvious that this new generation didn't think like Traditionalists or Baby Boomers, no one knew what to call them because they were still unknown. Douglas Coupland called them "X," the unknown in algebra, and to their (and his) horror, the name stuck. His 1991 novel *Generation X: Tales for an Accelerated Culture* described disengaged, pessimistic, and well-educated twentysomethings who could neither find a job in their field nor find their way to the good life the Boomers had. You can still find blogs where Xers wonder when they're going to get a better name than the one the older two generations pushed on them.

Gen Xers grew up in a world that was running out of the

pixie dust that Tinker Bell spread over the Boomers' child-hoods every Sunday evening on *The Wonderful World of Disney*. Divorce, latchkey kids, multiple recessions, global competition, missing children on milk cartons—Gen Xers faced a world full of bad news.

Xers learned that life threw surprises at them that were often beyond their control, so they became realists, hedging their bets. They found new families in their friends, constantly rewired their lives, and cautiously enjoyed things today rather than betting on an idealized future that might never happen. Instead of relocating seven times in ten years as the Boomers had, they stayed put so they could be close to their friends. Instead of jumping into home ownership, they traveled. Instead of conspicuous consumption, they chose the simpler "grunge" look or wore khakis to work.

But what Gen X saw as realistically coping with life's never-ending challenges, the older generations saw as cynicism—and whining. Even the name "Generation X" is partially a slam. Gen Xers feel misunderstood because they never saw themselves as whiny slackers but as open-eyed realists. And they've always wondered if the Traditionalists and Boomers know the difference. In 1994, journalist Piper Lowell explained,

> It's not that we're whiny. We're cynical and isolated. I, for one, had a hard time trusting anything: Love is forever (my parents divorced when I was four). Uncle Sam is your friend (if you're American, and sometimes not even then). Technology will solve the world's problems (just turn off the TV, dear, and take your Prozac). And Richard Nixon is not a crook.[2]

While the Boomers tried to fix society so it was fair, Xers learned that life isn't fair. Xers' experiences of life's unfairness have shaped their mind-set, giving them a different collection of ideas and images that "go without saying."

What Shaped Generation X

Being Squished

The Traditionalists focused on their Boomer children, but the Boomers didn't do the same with their Xer children. Instead of having two or three children, they had one or two—and often none. More than a million Americans a year had themselves surgically sterilized during the 1970s.[3] Simply put, children were no longer viewed as the best way to find happiness. One survey found that children had dropped behind automobiles on the list of what made people happy.[4] Numerically, Generation X is 25 percent smaller than the Boomers who preceded them and the Millennials who followed them. So the Xers are squished by virtue of being smaller than the generations on either side, and they are smaller because they grew up in a time less interested in children. Is it any wonder they are more individualistic and pragmatic? Ironically, many of them had more children than their parents did—children they made the center of their lives. So in a very real way, the Xers squished themselves by creating a Millennial generation larger than their own.

Divorce

A surge in divorce during the seventies (after no-fault divorce was introduced) as well as the surge in working Boomer mothers meant that Generation X grew up in the midst of unprecedented changes in family structure.

The first half of Generation X watched divorce become more commonplace during their childhood. That meant the percentage of Xers who grew up without both married parents

(29 percent) doubled from that of the Boomers (15 percent) and Traditionalists (13 percent).[5]

Divorce impacted the ideas and images of Xers more than the other generations, even though more Millennials have grown up in single-parent families. Because we have now become used to higher divorce rates, children no longer feel that their families aren't normal if their parents divorce. Society has created support systems like child care and after-school programs. We are far too scared of child predators today to allow "latchkey children," but many Xers had to walk home from school and let themselves into the house before Mom came home from work.

Unlike the Millennials, when the Xers were growing up, television didn't have shows about divorced families. So they watched *Father Knows Best* or *Leave It to Beaver* while their single mothers left for a second job in the evenings to make ends meet.

Because divorce left many Xers feeling alone and without a stable family life, more than other generations, they turned to friends to find a family. In between the slapstick, the long-running television show *Friends* told many of the stories that made sense of Xers' lives. The show didn't focus on family, because the characters' parents were distant and dysfunctional. Since their family relationships were unsupportive, the friends turned to each other, just as many Xers had done.

Downward Mobility

Generation X missed the growth of the economy but arrived just in time for the growth in prices. The huge Boomer generation pushed housing prices up. As a result, only a third of twenty-five- to thirty-year-olds (and half of thirty- to thirty-five-year-olds) owned a home in 1990 despite a decade of economic growth.[6] Ironically, fewer homeowners meant more renters, and that raised rent prices by 28 percent.[7]

In addition to being squished for jobs and housing by the larger Boomer generation, Gen Xers saw college expenses quadruple while grants and aid were slashed. Caught in the aftermath of the 1990 recession, more than 40 percent of the class of 1990 had either no job or one that did not require a college degree.[8] Xers began their adult lives with unprecedented personal debt. They missed the heavy college subsidies and the boom years of the economy but arrived just in time to use credit cards to cover the higher costs.

Parody
Parody creates a poor imitation of something serious in order to make light of it and expose its perceived flaws. Access to information creates parody, as does skepticism—and the Xers have both. They got a modest American Dream, divorced parents, a downsized deal at work, and a computer to check facts.

Xers are computer/Internet natives. (If you carried a typewriter into your college dorm instead of a PC, you are a digital immigrant, not a native.) This gave them access to what was going on behind the scenes in a world that was taking itself pretty seriously. Xers were the first generation to gain access to information beyond the news. They were the first to question and verify the backstory behind the news on their computers, so they knew that news is always shaded by someone's perspective. Gen X learned you can't believe everything you're told, so they wanted those in authority to "get real"—to quit spinning things, quit trying to force a happy ending, and quit producing the sentimental, simplistic sitcoms of the Boomer era.

Xer skepticism is most clearly seen in its parodies, epitomized in the long-running cartoon shows *The Simpsons* and *South Park*. Whereas Boomers would have tried to use the microphone to push for change, Xers want humor. Ben Karlin, who produced

Jon Stewart's *The Daily Show* and Stephen Colbert's *The Colbert Report*, told *Rolling Stone*, "The biggest mistake people make is thinking that Jon and Stephen sit down before every show and say, 'OK, how are we going to change the world?' . . . They both really just want to get a laugh."[9] The age of parody expresses the underlying skepticism of a generation. Despite remaining squished between two massive generations and juggling family and jobs in an up-and-down economy, Xers still retain their sense of humor, and their edge.

Generation X's Strengths

Technology is often mentioned as one of Generation X's most obvious differences from the earlier two generations. While ties to technology are indeed one of their strengths, this often invisible generation has far more important things than technology to teach the other generations.

They Reclaim the Priority of Community

Baby Boomers were such a large generation raised with such high expectations that they were always competing—for school desks, grades, college entrance, and jobs. Xers, on the other hand, were a much smaller cohort group that saw each other as comrades, not competitors, in a society focused on the much larger groups of Boomers and Millennials.[10] Because so many more Xers experienced divorce in their families or through friends, finding nontraditional sources of "family" or community became a high value. Ironically, the first generation to be criticized for always being on their phones used those phones to construct families and communities.

While some Xers come to church small groups,[11] many want a more stable form of community than groups that divide or reproduce every two years.[12] When two great Xer friends, who spent five years helping me start a church, announced they were moving to Golden, Colorado, no one was surprised, because they loved the mountains and outdoor sports. But we were surprised when they bought a house with two other couples. They explained that saving a little money was nice, but the main reason for the arrangement was to live in community all week long rather than only on Sunday mornings and at small group on Tuesday nights. After ten years, when the couples had kids, they bought separate houses, but almost twenty years later, they still live as next-door neighbors. Most Xers don't choose to move into the same house, but my friends illustrate how their generation moved the focus from the individual back to the community.

They Reclaim the Spiritual in All of Life

For the past five hundred years, life has become increasingly divided between sacred and secular. The division between the two worlds is evident for most of the generations. We believe that when we say our prayers, we are doing something sacred. When we shop, however, it is secular. When we get married, that is sacred. When we go to work, secular. This way of thinking would have shocked most Christians throughout most of the church's history because they saw themselves playing an important role in God's created order no matter what they were doing. Today it would seem that only ministers get to combine the sacred and secular because they work in "full-time Christian service."

Whether or not we acknowledge it, the truth is that all of life, no matter what we are doing, is sacred if lived within the Kingdom of God. When we see our restaurant or engineering job as furthering God's Kingdom, the focus shifts outside the church walls as we live in Christ each day. This is one reason Gen Xers volunteer in their churches less than Boomers or Traditionalists.[13] Xers have grown up in a world where the philosophical questions of the Baby Boomers have been replaced with the practical question, Does it work for you? Xers are more concerned that Christianity "works," that it makes a difference, than that it can answer all the intellectual questions raised about it. Therefore, many Xers believe that the command of Christ to bring justice to those who are poor or disadvantaged and to serve the community is also the best way to create opportunities to interest people in the gospel. Xers know their friends at work won't be impressed by a big concert of the hottest Christian bands or by a famous apologist debating an atheist but by a big project to remodel classrooms in elementary schools in underresourced neighborhoods. They don't volunteer as much at church, because they see playing with their kids, enjoying their marriage, and volunteering in the community as equally sacred.

They Reclaim the Value of Life and Family over Work

Rebecca Ryan, who founded Next Generation Consulting, discovered in five thousand interviews between 1998 and 2002 that Xers value control over their time more than anything else organizations offer. To emphasize how important this is to Xers, she called her book *Live First, Work Second*. She suggests that companies show how little they understand Xers when they refer to "work-life balance" instead of "life-work balance."[14]

Even so, many are not finding work-life balance. The Center for Work-Life Policy found recently that three out of four Xers consider themselves ambitious,[15] 31 percent of Xers earning more than $75,000 a year have an "extreme job" (which demands more than sixty-hour work weeks, short deadlines, and 24-7 access), and 28 percent work an average of ten hours more per week than they did three years before.[16]

This generation, originally called "slackers" by the older two generations because they wouldn't come in early and stay late if there wasn't critical work to do, is not using work-life balance as a way to get out of hard work. A greater focus on family is one reason many Xers want more balance. Gen X women have had more kids and work less than Boomer women,[17] while Xer fathers are pushing for greater time with children and more flexible policies from organizations.[18] Surprisingly, Xers' commitment to family is a major reason that 40 percent of Xer women and 33 percent of Xer men reach forty years of age without having children. Many said they would not be able to juggle demanding careers and still be the kind of parents their children would deserve. With Generation X, we can no longer assume most people will eventually "settle down" and have kids. Growing up under divorce's shadow, Xers treasure children and long-term love relationships (married or not) and the stability they provide.

While the older generations may roll their eyes at the "child-centered parenting" that has become popular over the last decade and the $600 strollers and the over-the-top birthday party extravaganzas, Gen Xers bring a focus to their families that many younger Traditionalists and Boomers lost in their search for self-fulfillment. Their focus on family and friends is an invaluable spiritual strength.

Generation X's Temptations

To Traditionalists, Xers epitomized everything that was accelerating the world's decline. But that was a misperception. Xers weren't slackers; they were rewriting the world with the new philosophy, new technology, and new expectations they had inherited. Xers have lived through a massive shift in thinking, which has quietly and subtly rewired our world in much broader ways than most of us have noticed. That shift is a mixed bag, providing spiritual strength and also temptation. We must understand this shift because it has dramatically changed the way all of us think, and because we also can't comprehend the Xers' spiritual environment unless we do.

They Build Their Own Truth

Xers were the first generation to be taught that something can be true for you but not for me—that truth is constructed by a group of people, not revealed by God or discovered by science. That's the opposite of what Traditionalists and Boomers learned. As a result, Generation X may be on the hinge of a shift in thinking five hundred years in the making. We will never understand Xers or Millennials if we don't understand this shift from "we must find the right answers" to "true for you but not for me."[19] So a bit of history helps us grasp how we got to this generation's particular temptation.

For more than a thousand years in the West, from the most educated people to illiterate peasants, everyone believed that something was true because the Bible said it. But about five hundred years ago, that changed. People increasingly came to believe that something was true when human reason and scientific discovery had proved or would prove it.[20] Although many still believe this view, people began to doubt that science or rational thinking could discover all the answers. Here are some significant reasons why faith in reason and science began crumbling:

> Smart people, using their best reasoning, weren't any closer to agreeing on the answers to basic philosophical questions, even after five hundred years. It became evident that instead of coming together into shared agreement (as Enlightenment philosophers in the 1700s had predicted), really smart people interpreted things really differently.
> Science and technology, instead of finally proving truth, did a number on our world in two world wars.

> World War II introduced Eastern religions and
philosophies to millions of soldiers who fought in Asia.
These beliefs redefine the very meaning of truth and place
their confidence in inner enlightenment, not scientific
proof or logical arguments. If other cultures have a
completely different approach to truth, then maybe
societies determine what is true and there are no objective
answers.

Possibly the biggest reason the average person is less confident
there's a right answer to every question is that we've all become
much more aware of how biases influence our conclusions. We
see it in what we expect from news sources. Any newscaster today
who ended his or her broadcast with Walter Cronkite's famous
tagline, "And that's the way it is," would be ridiculed into the
unemployment line.

Instead, some of the most popular news shows of the past
decade, such as *The Daily Show* and especially *The Colbert Report*,
have actually parodied the idea that newscasters are objective.

After five hundred years of people having faith in human intelligence and the scientific method, the "true for you but not for
me" mentality went mainstream. The Xers entered grade school
and learned that we use the scientific method and rational thinking to discover truth (such as that two plus two equals four) and
left the university having been taught that truth is whatever the
majority of people agree it is rather than something actual or
objective (in other mathematical systems, two plus two doesn't
equal four). Frank Schaeffer, son of Francis Schaeffer—the most
well-known defender of Christianity in the seventies—left his
father's faith and embraced this new philosophy: "There are no
objective facts, just personal histories and the coincidences of time
and place seen through the lenses of short lives. Deal with it."[21]

No one group can tell another group what to think or do, because . . . what's true for you isn't necessarily true for me. If objective truth *is* out there somewhere, humans can't discover it because they can't get beyond their own assumptions and biases.

A more realistic view of the limits of human reason and science is good news for Christianity. For five hundred years smart people have been telling Christians that no one can believe that faith stuff anymore because it can't be scientifically proved or discovered by reason and logic alone. In contrast, today's Xers and Millennials are more open to the spiritual because they worry less whether it's true for everyone than whether it works for themselves. They don't care as much if the Bible is accurate—many don't think it is. They care if it *works*.

This focus on what works creates additional good news for Christianity. Jesus is popular among Xers and Millennials outside the church, even if they don't like Christians or churches. They like how he loved and hung out with people who were judged and rejected by the religious leaders of his day. Many quote his teaching to "judge not" in blogs or on Twitter (even though their application isn't what Jesus had in mind). They like that he was antiestablishment and didn't sell out to "the man." They like that he came to bring a spiritual Kingdom, not a political one. I, too, admire Jesus for those reasons. That's why this new philosophy of "true for you but not for me" is a mixed bag. Xers and Millennials understand a lot about what Jesus taught, and sometimes try to emulate him, but many don't accept the way Jesus thought.

In one episode of *The Simpsons,* Bart asks his father what religion they are. Homer replies, "You know, the one with all the well-meaning rules that don't work in real life. Uh, Christianity." Homer speaks for millions of people, some of them regular church attenders, who don't understand that what Jesus taught doesn't work unless you believe what Jesus thought. For example, how do you emulate Jesus' constant caring for and loving people at great personal sacrifice? (Today he would be labeled codependent and sent off to a support group.) In 1995, rock legend Van Morrison wondered in his song "No Religion" if anyone could be meek enough to always turn the other cheek. The book of Hebrews explains part of Jesus' motivation: "Because of the joy awaiting him, he endured the cross" (Hebrews 12:2). In order to see joy on the other side of the cross, Jesus had to believe certain things *about* God and not just believe *in* God.

What Jesus taught about love and sacrifice only makes sense because of what Jesus thought about God. You might admire Jesus, but you won't follow him if you think he was wrong about God. It wouldn't make sense. It would demand too much, and it wouldn't work in the real world. It would be crazy to try to live the dangerously different way Jesus did if we didn't believe in the God Jesus believed would take care of him. In the 1990s thousands of people—even those who didn't consider themselves Christians—wore WWJD? (What Would Jesus Do?) bracelets in a well-intentioned fad. But it won't work to focus on what Jesus did without first putting on another bracelet: WDJKAG? (Okay, "What Did Jesus Know About God?" is kind of long for a bracelet.)

You may know what Jesus taught about being good, but he says you don't get him if you reject what he thought about God:

> If anyone hears my words but does not keep them, I do not judge that person. For I did not come to judge the world, but to save the world. There is a judge for the one who rejects me and does not accept my words; the very words I have spoken will condemn them at the last day. For I did not speak on my own, but the Father who sent me commanded me to say all that I have spoken. I know

that his command leads to eternal life. So whatever I
say is just what the Father has told me to say. (John
12:47-50, NIV)

Jesus thought that he had essential knowledge about God that
we can't get anywhere else. He believed God commanded him
to say what he did. Jesus thought that the information he was
relaying from God leads to a better life for us—eternal life—if
we keep his teachings. But that condemns the view that what is
true for you may not be true for me, because what's true for you
may be chock-full of misinformation about God. Jesus said *he*
didn't come to condemn us; the very things he taught us about
God will condemn us if we reject them because we preferred to
believe something else would work better for us. He came to save
us by teaching us to understand God and spirituality accurately
and then to save us from our love of sin that keeps us in the darkness (see John 3:19).

It's good that after five hundred years of antifaith thinking,
people are more open to spiritual things. It's encouraging that
people still admire Jesus. But Gen Xers are the first generation to
face "true for you but not for me" for most of their lives. This philosophical shift is such a new challenge that many Christians don't
understand it, let alone know how to communicate the claims of
Jesus without sounding arrogant or undemocratic to their friends,
their children, or the people their church is trying to reach. So we
will come back to it throughout the rest of the book.

They Are Cynical

Gen Xers see themselves as realists. The Traditionalists and Baby
Boomers were overly optimistic. While the Traditionalists grew
up with a depression and world wars, they had faith in their
families and the government and were optimistic that problems

could be solved. Boomers were raised with enormous expectations. Both generations had too much confidence in human goodness and ingenuity. The Xers grew up while that optimism unraveled with corporate downsizing, offshore manufacturing, increased divorce, much more explicit and critical news reporting after Watergate, razor blades in Halloween candy, and photos of missing children plastered on milk cartons. The Xers inherited the consequences of previous generations' excesses: Social Security slowly went broke, pollution increased, the American Dream stalled, AIDS surfaced, and petroleum supplies dwindled. Understandably, Generation X is cautious and skeptical. While the Boomers tried to fix society so it was fair, Xers learned that life isn't fair, and so they made fun of it. They had a powerful effect. As a society, we've been forced to "get real." How many people do you know who are now less confident in institutions than they were fifteen years ago? If Gen X is about lowered expectations, tongue-in-cheek comedy, and embracing technology, then I guess we are all Xers now.

Generation Xers overcorrected by getting cynical. This generation of realists can get jaded when Christians sin, church leaders disappoint, or families fail them. And that makes them vulnerable to cynicism.

Their realism helps them face life and roll with setbacks. Skepticism cuts through hype, reveals hidden agendas, stops the spin. But unchecked, skepticism turns into cynicism.

It's one thing to build your own community; it's more cynical to build your own world. I don't blame Xers for looking for lasting and meaningful relationships, especially if they didn't have them in their families. It's a spiritual strength that they realize relationships need to be a priority if they're going to last and be healthy. But it's a real temptation for Xers to build their own worlds with people of their own choosing. It's safer, and you don't get burned or disappointed that way. But doing so can keep Xers from truly engaging with others who are different from them. Xers may move jobs until they find a work culture they like. They may hang out online with other people of their generation or who likely share their views. Xers may say they value diversity, and they may serve people who are different from them in their communities, but they probably do so with people very much like themselves.

This tendency toward sameness is one reason we need the church. The church forces most of us to get out of our insulated worlds and learn to love people whom we wouldn't choose to be with in our carefully constructed worlds.

Boomers may church hop to find the next Jesus buzz and avoid the dark night of the soul. But Xers often take that one step further and never really engage with their churches enough to have those positive feelings in the first place. They can't be disappointed, because they can't lose what they've never had.

I admire my wife, Laurie, who, like me, is on the cusp of two generations—part Boomer and part Xer. We attended a church for almost a decade that never quite felt like home to her. We lived a half hour away, she had only a few friends there, and some of the older congregants felt it was time for the younger generation to take on the bulk of the work. Laurie prayed for God to lead us to another church more like the one she grew up in. But each time I got invited to relocate with FranklinCovey and she got her hopes up, she clearly sensed it was not the time, and God wanted her to learn to serve where we were even if she felt lonely and others didn't help. I turned down the offers to move, and we stayed. We provided special support to the senior minister and his wife, Laurie ran vacation Bible school with another dedicated woman, and we led a multigenerational adult Sunday school class with two other couples. I wish there were a happy ending where through our service the church became more of what we wanted it to be. It never did.

But we made a difference in our own corner, and then when the church my friend Tim led built a new location ten minutes from our house, we joined that church so our kids could attend youth group with the kids from their high school. We never anticipated that this church would be all we wanted, yet within six months, Laurie had twenty close friends. She ran the back end of the drama ministry. People were excited, they brought their friends, and the church doubled in size in two years. With all that growth, they needed my management training and organizational development experience. I helped the staff reorganize each of their ministries so the church would continue to grow. Laurie and I never saw it coming; we just thought it would be a better church for our kids. But as volunteers and then later, when I worked as a part-time staff member for a while, she and I made more impact on more people's lives in the first five years there than we did during all our previous years of ministry and church service combined.

The moral of our story is not that if you serve faithfully for almost a decade in a church that does not do much for you (as my wife did), God will reward you with the church of your dreams, and you won't even have to relocate to Denver to get it. That might happen. But realistically, it probably won't. The moral of our story is that God was just as pleased with our service and our faithfulness in both churches, even though one showed much bigger results from our labor and felt much more like what we wanted.

Looking back, I can say confidently that we would not have been ready for the second church if we had not learned to serve patiently in the first one. Especially me. God had to raise my maturity so I could lower my expectations of other people and of the church. I hate to admit it, but as a young minister, my leadership was still too much about what I thought was best. I had to learn to let other people do it their way, even if it didn't work as well as my ideas would have. I needed that first church because without it, I would have built my world around people like me and missed out on God's opportunity to mature.

Cynicism is dangerous because it leads us to build our own worlds, not just our own communities. It's dangerous because it assumes that since people's motives cannot be trusted, we shouldn't open our hearts to people. Jesus was skeptical about people and their motives (see John 2:24-25), but that skepticism never turned into cynicism. Jesus knew God was in control, even as he headed toward Jerusalem to die—abandoned and alone—at the hands of religious men. He opened himself up to the people who hurt him, and found joy in it anyway.

Knowing we'll be hurt but trusting anyway, knowing others will fail us but loving anyway, and knowing institutions will disappoint but God will not are all necessary parts of being useful for God's Kingdom. The apostle Paul reminds us that "hope does not disappoint us, because God's love has been poured into our hearts through the Holy Spirit that has been given to us" (Romans 5:5, NRSV). That's what Paul found despite his many disappointments when people and churches let him down.

Xers will do the same if they push beyond cynicism.

CHAPTER 6

Millennials

Born 1981–2001

LONG BEFORE SMARTPHONES and selfies, the Millennials were already the most photographed generation. Polaroids, the instant photos I grew up with that developed while you flapped them, were expensive, so families saved them for only the most special occasions.[1] But digital photography and video made photographs and movies significantly cheaper, so all three of the older generations took pictures of everything the Millennials did. They were the first generation to be widely videotaped being born. Their first birthday parties were well attended and well documented. And you would have thought that the girls at my daughter's first-grade dance recital had won some Olympic event by the number of camera flashes when the program was finished.

Millennials are still the generation that gets the most attention. When I tell people I tweet about the latest research or articles on the generations, what I should say is that I tweet about the Millennials because there are ten times more articles on them than on the other generations combined. (Sorry, Xers—even as you move into your peak earning years, you still get the least attention. I know what you're thinking: *What's new?*) To say Millennials get the most attention would be like saying the NBA gets more television coverage than curling (you know, the broom and ice sport). Because Millennials are the newest generation out of college and the first in four generations to live at home into their twenties, families as well as organizations want to figure out what they're all about. So I will give them extra attention in this chapter and the next as we look at what has shaped the Millennials and especially their spiritual strengths and temptations.

What Shaped the Millennials

Heavy Parental Involvement

You'll remember that Generation X is the smallest of the generations because their Boomer parents didn't have as many children. But around 1985, a change was underway. "Baby on Board" signs showed up in minivan windows as younger Boomers and then older Gen Xers began to have children—a lot of children. The second Baby Boom, or Echo Boom, had begun—and it was bigger than the first.[2]

The Millennials were a "wanted" generation. There were half as many children per family in the second Baby Boom compared to the first, but far more women gave birth. And by 1990, 80 percent of all fathers were in the delivery rooms attending their children's births, up from 27 percent halfway through Gen Xers' birth years.[3] The hands-on dad had arrived! (With a camera.)

Millennials and their parents have a mutual affection and admiration. Almost half of Millennials pick their parents as role models and heroes over celebrities or political leaders.[4] In 1974, 40 percent of Boomers told Gallup that they would be better off without their parents. In contrast, more than 90 percent of Millennials told Gallup that they have a good relationship with their parents.[5] Boomers saw their parents as part of the establishment, while Millennials see their parents as resources to help them get established.

Millennials *want* their parents involved in their lives. A study by Thom Rainer found that 77 percent of Millennials seek their parents' advice regularly.[6] Millennials believe their parents can offer guidance for navigating the university and the workplace, while many Boomers knew their parents couldn't. Boomers were often the first in their families to go to college. Their Traditionalist parents could show them how to farm or build a house but knew little about college or the corporate world.

Fear of Low Self-Esteem

Millennials are confident. Their parents and teachers convinced them they are special, and the Millennials believe it. In one survey, 96 percent of Millennials agreed or somewhat agreed with the statement, "I can do something great." Not one respondent disagreed strongly.[7]

Whitney Houston had a song, "Greatest Love of All," that captured this sense of esteem. And who *was* the greatest love of all? Herself. That is part of the reason everybody got a trophy in organized activities. Boomer and Xer parents wanted to make sure their kids could feel good about themselves because they were at least coming out and playing. Millennials were raised not keeping score in organized youth sporting leagues until they were at least nine years old—for fear the losing team would feel bad. So everybody got a trophy, not just those who had achieved something, because *everybody* was good enough.

Part of building their children's self-esteem involved parents dialoguing with their kids rather than commanding them. In 2009, *Qualitative Sociology* looked at three hundred advice columns and editorials from *Parents* magazine spanning 1929 to 2006. According to this survey, while Millennial children had less freedom to be outdoors without parental supervision, they had more freedom to disagree with their parents and wear whatever clothes they wanted.[8] Parents encouraged the Millennials to express their feelings.

Gen Xers put a protective shield around their children's self-esteem. From participation trophies on the soccer field to bouquets of roses after preschool dance recitals, Millennials have been made to feel special.

The Consumer Age

Millennials were raised as consumers. Their parents could offer them choices previous generations never had. Who hasn't seen an SUV leave one fast-food restaurant and go across the street to another, presumably just to stop the whining from the backseat?

Millennials have always had so many options that they need search engines to sort through them all. That has taught them to ask for what they want and to look someplace else if someone can't give it to them.

Technology Everywhere

Millennials are the first generation to grow up digital, surrounded by technology. Millennials spend more than fifty-three hours a week with media because they use more than one kind at the same time.[9] Boomers learned computers at work, and Xers learned them at home or school. Millennials never had to learn computers—they were built into their earliest toys. For

Millennials, a smartphone is a bodily appendage. McCann Worldgroup discovered that half of Millennials would give up their sense of smell to keep their computer or mobile phone.[10]

Emerging Adulthood

This new life stage is so important that I make it the focus of chapter 8. Today, we don't believe a person is an adult until around age twenty-six. Remarkably, twentysomethings agree with that assessment. They think it takes that long to figure out what they want to do so they can settle into a career, commit to a long-term love relationship, and have enough saved up to get their own place.[11]

The New Generation

In this book, I've talked about five generations at home and at church. The fifth generation (children of the second half of Gen Xers and the first half of Millennials) doesn't yet have an established name or even a start date. Although many researchers call them Generation Z, I think that name is a bad idea. If there's one thing we've learned about labeling generations, it's that generations don't like negative names or names that compare them to an earlier generation. Generation Z (the obvious end of the alphabet) does both. So until a consensus on the name emerges, I'll continue to call them the New Generation or Always On.

Assuming the Millennial generation is roughly the same span as the Boomers and Xers, the fifth generation starts somewhere between 2002 and 2004, which means the oldest members are in their teens.

I'm not focusing on them throughout this book because the research is still coming in and because the book would be huge— not because they aren't important. These children are already consumers and influence massive amounts of government and parental (and grandparental) spending. They are "always on"—always linked to technology. In fact, 25 percent claim to be actively connected (checking e-mail, text messages, etc.) within five minutes of waking up, while nearly 73 percent are connected within an hour or less. Every member of this generation spends at least one hour with technology each day, while almost half (46 percent) spend at least ten hours a day connected.[12]

The younger half of this new generation is born with a tablet in their hands. How many times have you watched a one-year-old swipe the television screen, puzzled that nothing is happening? Forty percent of newborns have a social-media profile that their parents have set up for them.[13] They are constantly interacting and entertained.

They are growing up in a world where class is rapidly replacing race. While flare-ups of racial tensions remind us that racial inequality has not been solved, the Occupy Wall Street protests and the last two US presidential election cycles have highlighted the growing divide and emotional wedge between economic classes. Marrying outside a person's religion was a major taboo for the Traditionalists. Marrying outside of race was the taboo for the Boomers. But I predict marrying outside of economic class will be the larger barrier for the "Always On" generation.

Fewer of their parents go to church or read the Bible, so fewer of them know Bible stories.[14] For decades, churches have assumed a common core of Bible knowledge. But the new generation is the first of what is most likely a growing trend not just of biblical illiteracy but also of biblical unawareness.

Millennials' Strengths

It's important to focus on the strengths of the Millennials, because they receive so much criticism, it's easy to miss what they can teach us. Because they're the newest generation of adults and we aren't sure what to make of them yet, Millennials take a beating. I've heard hundreds of criticisms about Millennials:

> They won't get off their phones.
> They aren't loyal.
> They don't show respect.
> They're naive about what it takes to make organizations work.
> They're impatient and drop out if you don't implement their ideas.
> They're materialistic.
> They have no work ethic; they want everything handed to them.
> They think they're entitled.
> They've grown up in a sex-saturated world.
> They're walking away from Christianity.

Some of those statements are true; some of them are not. I debunk many of them in my book *Sticking Points*, and we'll cover some in later chapters. But they distract other generations, who then miss the great opportunities to learn from Millennials. The times the Millennials grew up in shaped them to be spiritually strong in many areas. I've selected three that I think are most important both for Millennials to understand about themselves and for the other generations to understand about them.

They Want Meaning
Millennials are more focused on finding meaningful work than the Gen Xers before them. Xers needed a job to survive; Millennials want to be involved, expressing themselves and making a noticeable impact. They want what they do to matter. Growing up under the shadow of school shootings and the

terrorist attacks on September 11, 2001, they know that no matter how many organic kale salads they eat, life is unpredictable and can end at any moment. As a result, they want to make a difference *now.*

In her book *Got Religion?*, *New York Post* columnist Naomi Schaefer Riley suggests that Millennials drop out of church because the church isn't much different from the larger society in not entrusting them with serious responsibility until they get into their thirties. She also points out that while flashy may seem necessary to get people through the door, what Millennials really want is a meaningful place where they can settle in.[15]

They Want Authentic

Millennials grew up with cheating television evangelists, Britney Spears and Miley Cyrus shedding their Baptist faith, CEOs going to jail, and the constant TMI (Too Much Information) that celebrities share on Twitter. By the age of seventeen, they have seen and heard it all. They have grown up constantly sorting through what is authentic and what is hype. As a result, Millennials trust people less than any other generation, less than half as much as the Boomers.[16] They don't expect perfection, but they do expect people and even the brands they buy to be authentic.[17]

This desire for authenticity flows into religion as well. Millennials—and Generation Xers, for that matter—assume people are flawed. Whereas Traditionalists are often much more private and formal, Millennials, even more than Xers, are open with their lives and emotions and look for emotional openness as they search for authenticity. (See the books popular with Millennials, such as *Blue Like Jazz.*)

They Want Teams

Millennials grew up in teams. They went to preschool on a blue team or a green team. My Millennial kids took exams in high school as teams using the Internet. (When I was growing up, that was called cheating.) They learned peer mediation in grade school. And loyalty to friends is one of Millennials' highest values.[18] So it should be no surprise that they expect to work together. Even more, thanks to group text messaging and Facebook, they have more close friends in their "tribe."

Millennials are the most diverse generation, so they easily cross boundaries of ethnicity and gender because they are far more color-blind than the previous generations.[19] (Think of the recently popular TV show *Glee* as this generation's inclusivity battle cry.) They wish society and the church would quit fighting over differences and work together.[20] Even more, they cross generational boundaries more easily. They have grown up with their grandparents and sometimes great-grandparents and are closer to their parents. They have learned to get along, to roll their eyes and ignore the insensitive things their older relatives say. They may put in their earbuds and listen to music or head off into another room, but they are less likely to fight.

Millennials' Temptations

Millennials' spiritual strengths of meaning, authenticity, and teamwork don't require long explanations. They prepare Millennials to make significant contributions to their churches and communities and to the understanding of our faith, but they also come out of shifts in ideas and images that can be devastating precisely because they're seen as virtues. We will need to untangle the good from the bad—not only for their sake, but for the sake of all the generations. Millennials have inherited and intensified the new ways of thinking that tempted the other three generations, demonstrating that the sins of the fathers are truly visited on the children to the third and the fourth generations when it comes to how we think. Consequently, I will spend more time on their temptations compared to their strengths, not because they're bigger than the other generations', but because they are the culmination of what has tempted the other generations.

They Miss the Contradictions in Their Morality

Sociologist Christian Smith and his team studied the younger Millennials from the time they were in junior high through their entry into emerging adulthood. One of the most important things they learned concerned moral reasoning:

> Emerging adult [Millennial] thinking about morality
> (as with most of the rest of adult Americans) is not
> particularly consistent, coherent, or articulate. . . .
> Not many of them have previously given much or
> any thought to many of the kinds of questions about
> morality that we asked. Thus, much of what they have to
> say about morality is peppered with uncertain phrases,
> such as "I don't know," "like," and "I guess."[21]

Millennials have a morality, and their moral beliefs are important to them, but it's not classic morality in the sense that some things are right and some things are wrong because of universal principles, natural law, or God's will. It shouldn't surprise us that after the philosophy of "true for you but not for me" took over during Generation X's childhood, individuals determine what is right or wrong for themselves as long as they don't hurt anyone else.

Millennials are the most educated generation in history, so the contradictions and inconsistencies in their moral reasoning aren't due to a lack of knowledge. They picked up their ideas and images from the larger society and from their parents. Their cartoons, their storybooks, their movies, and even their classroom rules all centered around the idea that no matter how different you are from other people, you should be yourself because you're the only you there is. Just pick up Dr. Seuss's *Happy Birthday to You!*: "There is no one alive who is you-er than you."[22] Anyone who tells you that you're weird or wrong is a "hater." You should be yourself and feel good about yourself. It's their Boomer parents' hyperindividualism on steroids.

The highest goal in life, the noblest morality, is no longer to live a life of honor to some ideal standards. It's to be yourself, to feel good about your choices, and to do what works for you—and to not judge.

That was precisely Demi Lovato's sentiment when she explained her friendship with fellow Disney Channel star Miley Cyrus ended because they "don't have anything in common." Demi didn't want to be a hater, even as she distanced herself from Miley's controversial choices:

> Miley has been one of my best friends growing up and so I'm happy for her. She's doing what she wants to do and this is her time to break out and figure out, you know, what she wants to do in her career and her image and everything. . . . I'm happy seeing her happy because I love her so much. And, you know, she doesn't care what people think, nor should she.[23]

The new unpardonable sin is for one person to judge another person's moral behavior. So Demi Lovato said, essentially, "What's good for her isn't good for me, but that doesn't give me permission to criticize her. It's her right to make her own decisions, as long as she doesn't hurt anybody else."

That's the moral reasoning Miley Cyrus uses in her song "We Can't Stop" to defend all-night parties and provocative dancing:

"Remember only God can judge ya, forget the haters, 'cause somebody loves ya." No one has a right to tell you that you're wrong. In Miley Cyrus's case, the "haters'" truth may be her parents' truth or the Baptist denomination's truth, but it's not *her* truth. Each person has to decide for him- or herself what God will and will not judge. You are your own theologian.

"Haters" don't understand that. Like Demi Lovato, most Millennials don't make the same extreme choices as Miley Cyrus, but Christian Smith discovered that most young Millennials use the same moral reasoning she does: everyone sees things with their own perspective, so no one can claim to have some absolute moral standards that apply to everyone in every culture in all situations. That means that each person has to do what seems right to him or her, even if others strongly disagree, as long as that person is willing to live with the consequences and doesn't hurt anyone else.

Startlingly, 34 percent of the Millennials interviewed said they didn't know what makes something right or wrong, although most could explain some basis for their moral reasoning:

> Forty percent focused on what other people would think about them.
> Fifty-three percent mentioned that something was wrong if it hurt someone else, though that didn't apply to organizations nearly as much as it did individuals (so, for example, illegally downloading movies is fine, but stealing a friend's DVD isn't).
> Twelve percent said while there's no such thing as objective or absolute moral truth, societies do need values and have to agree on a set of laws or social norms that most people stick to so people can be happy without being hurt or taken advantage of.

> Forty percent said they base their values on the Bible or religious teachings.
> Seventeen percent pointed to Karma.
> Twenty-four percent recognized "religion probably operated as a general ethical influence in the background of their lives," even though they didn't follow a particular religion. But for most, the individual still had to decide if Bible-based morality made sense to him or her.[24]

You may have noticed that these percentages add up to more than 100 percent. That's because many people claimed more than one, if not many, of these as the basis for their moral reasoning, even though they often contradict. Millennials today face a more complex moral world with access to so many different beliefs. But the tools they've been taught to use are a reaction to science or religion as the final authority instead of a coherent approach to moral reasoning. They are contradictory and self-refuting, and therefore, unsustainable.

In contrast to this unstable morality, Jesus claimed he came to bring us the truth about God. He said that if people build their lives upon it, they will find rock-solid stability that can withstand even the strongest storms (Matthew 7:24-27). This confidence is a key part of the Good News: God has not hidden his commands from us. Throughout the past century, Christians could assume people shared similar approaches to morals, so we could argue for certain moral standards by saying, "This is what God commands." But today, that approach repels people before they ever have a chance to understand the beauty of this God whose perfection and holiness captivated and transformed so many from the beginning of the Bible until its end.

How do we bring this Good News to Millennials who neither see the contradictions in their morality nor want to think much about it? How do we interest Millennials in becoming disciples of Jesus when his rich and multifaceted teachings, long considered to be the greatest moral teachings in history, have been reduced to "love everyone and judge not"? This question is so big and so important that we will spend the rest of the book (and especially the next chapter) trying to answer it.

They Miss the Power and Importance of the Church

Most Millennials aren't antichurch; most of them think it's a good thing. They—including many Millennials who attend church regularly—just don't think it's that important. Christian Smith described religion as "in the background" for most Millennials. They may have gone when they were young and are glad they learned right and wrong, but now that they've learned it, there is less need for church.[25]

They are distracted, busy figuring out the transition to full adulthood, sorting through all the choices they must make to create their identity, and having fun before they settle down. Church is something they might do more once they settle down. Even if they attend a Bible study, it isn't where they find their sense of belonging—not as they do from hanging out with friends or family.[26]

Ed Stetzer surveyed unchurched Millennials and found that if they wanted spiritual guidance, only one in six would look for it at church.[27] More troubling, he discovered that nine out of ten unchurched Millennials believe they can have a good relationship with God or learn what it means to be a Christian without the church.[28]

On the positive side, unchurched Millennials are less fed up "with religion than older unchurched." More than 70 percent of the older unchurched are turned off by religion, compared to only 60 percent of Millennials.[29] Nine out of ten have at least one close friend who is a Christian, and 89 percent said they would listen to someone tell them about their Christian beliefs. Forty-six percent said they would join a small group to learn about the Bible and Christianity.[30]

There are a number of reasons why Millennials are less interested in the church. First, as we've seen, their parents are less interested as well. Millennials aren't rebels: they perceive their religious commitment and beliefs as *about as strong as their parents'.*[31] Parents who are committed and engaged with their church have one of the biggest influences on how engaged their children will be.[32]

Second, Millennials see more hypocrisy. While every generation accuses the previous generation of hypocrisy, the church is under particularly intense scrutiny today because technology can show the hypocrisy within one church to the entire world. Since we hear far more of the negative stories than the positive, the church looks worse than it is. Jesus told us that what would be whispered in the corners would be shouted from the rooftops (see Luke 12:3). Smartphones allow anyone to climb up with a megaphone. Additionally, the younger two generations don't stay and fight hypocrisy in institutions as much as Boomers did. They just leave or disengage. As with the other generations, some Millennials have been hurt by people in the church. Others feel that the church is not even trying to live up to what is described in Scripture.

Third, during the lifetimes of both Generation X and the Millennials, theology has shifted emphasis from the church to the Kingdom of God. Even though it is mentioned eighty-seven times in the New Testament[33] and was a central theme of Jesus' preaching, I never heard a sermon or lesson dedicated to the Kingdom of God until 1983, when a professor spent two days on it. For the Traditionalists and Boomers, the focus was on the church, usually growing or bringing people to "our" church but not to the larger Kingdom of God.

This effort to restore the biblical balance of Kingdom of God and church is huge. It's too easy to focus on what our individual church needs rather than to see where our church fits in God's plan. It's too easy to equate our church (or our denomination) with the Kingdom, when it's only a small part of it. But I think the scales have tipped too far. When we see how our own church has fallen short, it's tempting to disengage from real people in a local church and to put our focus on the universal church, the larger Kingdom of God.

I think that's what Donald Miller, author of Millennial favorite *Blue Like Jazz*, is doing as he wrestles with seeing the nasty side of churches. Here's how he described it in a blog post:

> My understanding of the church has radically changed. Since *Blue Like Jazz* came out, I've sat in many a green room and talked with many Christian leaders and I've discovered there's a lot of competition and power struggle taking place in the church and it reminds me of the world. I've taken part in those struggles. I've contributed to them and I've made some of them happen.
>
> But seeing that, feeling it, and wrongly participating in it has caused me to wonder if God's view of "the church" is very different than ours. I now believe the church from man's perspective is an earthly organization, and the church from God's perspective extends into man's organization of the church but is not defined by it.[34]

I agree when Miller says that God sees not just our individual churches but the universal church made up of everyone who knows him. But I think Miller minimizes the local church as he emphasizes the universal one. While the church has taken many shapes through the centuries, it has always been a group of people in some community like Ephesus or Sardis or Rio de Janeiro or Lockport, Illinois. While the Kingdom—the church universal— lives out God's grand story, unrestrained by our human failings or limitations, the only way you and I can experience the universal church is in an "earthly" church. While the church universal is like a mighty army always marching onward, the one I attend is full of humans, and they are flawed, fickle, and frustrating. Just like me and their other leaders.

Because I think Miller has made a much bigger distinction between the Kingdom of God and the group of people who gather on Parkway Boulevard, he struggles to love the local church as Jesus does, because he doesn't see it as the Bride of Christ.[35] Miller's distinction between the spiritual Kingdom and the earthly church has some practical implications he describes as he ends his thoughts:

> What's interesting about this change in my understanding
> of the church is I'm no longer interested in helping to
> build the earthly church, while I'm very interested in
> helping build the church God sees. And it's hard to know
> the difference. But I want to move where God is moving,
> not where people are "moving for God" if that makes
> sense.[36]

I agree it's hard to know the difference. It's too easy to believe that everything my congregation is doing is exactly what God wants. Even more, I think we are all interested in helping the church that God sees. But I suggest that God sees each local congregation or house church as a physical expression of the

Kingdom, not as something earthly or different. Your local church is not the whole Kingdom of God, but you are missing the Kingdom of God if you aren't in church, even if you have a long list of what needs to improve or are bored out of your head. Skim the second half of the New Testament for ten minutes and you will see that Paul, James, and Peter had quite a list of what they thought was wrong with the churches. But these apostles lost their lives starting and serving local congregations because they believed the local church was the Bride of Christ, whom Christ will eventually purify (Ephesians 5:25-27). Frustrating? Yes, but worth it.

Millennials, you don't have to like the local church, but you do have to love it just as Christ loves it. There are two reasons why I think you need to see the power and importance of the church. First, you need it in order to grow in your spiritual life. Similar to the Boomers and Generation Xers, you also need the boredom, the dark night of the soul, the disappointments, and the opportunities to serve without reward, as well as the joys, the fellowship, and the faithfulness that come from the hard work of loving real people from all the generations (although, I admit, you will want to scream or run at times).

Second, no matter how great your contribution to the Kingdom of God outside of a local church, no matter how great the work parachurch organizations do in the world, a thousand years from now, if Jesus doesn't come back before then, local congregations are what will survive. I'm sure they will be structured differently, and who knows what the music will sound like, but they will be putting hands and feet on the Kingdom of God. The local church is Jesus Christ's plan A for bringing his Kingdom to the world. He doesn't have a plan B. He's got one Bride, she's not going anywhere, and learning to love her as he does is a necessary process in Christian maturity. The church needs you. They need your insights, your spiritual strengths, and your understanding of how to communicate in the new world of interconnectivity, even if many don't realize it yet. You may have to "pay your dues" with the older generations in churches who think you are young and naive. That may drive you crazy or bore you to death. But that's okay, because you need them, too. And you'll drive them crazy as well.

Their Christianity Has Been Hacked

Just as computers can get hacked and bad software installed, an alternate version of Christianity, which I call "Be Good, Feel Good, Live Your Life (God Is Watching)," has replaced the Christianity of the Bible and the historic theology of the church. The majority of people, but especially Millennials, think it's Christianity, although a minority understands the difference. I've covered pieces of it throughout these last two chapters, but it's so important, I'll explain it in detail in the next chapter, because tragically, so many people have rejected this hacked version, thinking it is Christianity. If you get nothing else from this book, you must get this—it's that dangerous.

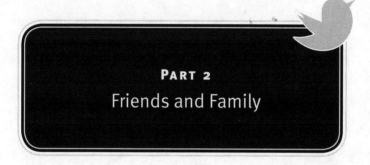

PART 2

Friends and Family

CHAPTER 7

What Do I Say to Friends Who Claim, "I'm Spiritual but Not Religious"?

I WAS HAVING dinner with two colleagues at a company meeting recently, and one of them told me, "You know, I really enjoyed the conversation we had three years ago about different religions."

"Oh yeah?" I said. "I did too."

We chitchatted for a few minutes, and then she asked me, "If you weren't a Christian, what religion would you be?"

Her question threw me for a moment. I shrugged. "I don't know. I've never thought about that before."

"Really?" She seemed genuinely surprised.

I said, "Well, I know for sure which ones I wouldn't be. I wouldn't be one of the Eastern religions."

The colleague on my right jumped in. "Those are the most attractive to me! Why wouldn't you want to follow one of them?"

"I would miss love," I replied.

"What do you mean? How would love disappear if you were a Buddhist?"

"Well, if everything is one, then anything that is distinct from something else, like a person, is an illusion. If everything eventually just folds back into oneness, then all those we love are part of the illusion we have to get beyond in order to lose our individuality and self-consciousness in nirvana. So I would stick with one of the religions that believes God is separate from his creation. It makes love possible."

"That's so surprising," my colleague told me. "Christians aren't loving—they're judgmental. Christians act like they're right and everybody else is wrong."

"I agree there are a lot of obnoxious Christians who seem to get a thrill out of condemning people," I replied. "But I think all religions are judgmental. They can't help it. Eastern religions say that all religions are different ways of getting to the same truth, so they seem less judgmental on the surface. But that's because they believe all the parts that matter most to the faithful of each religion are insignificant and will disappear when their adherents become enlightened. Eastern religions believe all religions lead to the same thing: their point of view. Buddhism, like every other religion, claims it has learned the ultimate answer to ultimate reality. They are all judgmental because they think other religions don't have it."

Why Is Being "Spiritual" More Attractive?

Our conversation was cut short at that point because the program started, but you've probably heard a similar conversation in which someone has said, "I'm spiritual but not religious." In fact, that may be the most common phrase we hear from people who are not actively engaged in church. A recent survey discovered that almost two-thirds of females and a little less than half of all males thought that most of their friends were spiritual. And 43 percent of unchurched Millennials said they were spiritual but not religious.[1]

Many want to take the best from each religion and build a spirituality that works for them. From famous celebrities to the people on your street, they don't want "religion"; they want to be "spiritual." Katy Perry, who grew up as a pastor's kid and started her career in contemporary Christian music, said in an interview that she liked to essentially cut and paste together her own religion—taking the nice, feel-good parts of the Bible and combining them with other religions and philosophies.[2] She, like so many others, is building her own spiritual playlist by downloading only the songs she likes.

Others are turned off by or don't want to be associated with Christianity, especially more conservative Christianity. Not long ago the Grammy-winning band Mumford and Sons' frontman, Marcus Mumford, told *Rolling Stone* that he wouldn't call himself a Christian even though his parents are both pastors: "I think the word just conjures up all these religious images that I don't really like. I have my personal views about the person of Jesus and who he was," he explained to the magazine. "I've kind of separated myself from the culture of Christianity." In another interview with *Big Issue*, he claimed that the band is "more about 'faith' than about 'religion.'"[3]

As we saw in the last chapter, the biggest sin—especially for Millennials—is to tell other people their choices are morally wrong. My colleague speaks for many: Christianity is seen as judgmental. It is judgmental because the founder of Christianity taught that certain things are wrong. We can't soften his teaching. But some Christians make it worse by thinking the best way to stand up for God is to push his commandments at everyone, even if others don't agree with their theological beliefs or even believe in God. The era is over when everyone shared the same basic assumptions about the Bible and morality, when Billy Graham could fill an arena, hold a Bible above his head saying, "The Bible says," and everyone would nod—even if they weren't following Jesus' teachings, because they knew they should be.

Instead we live in a pluralistic era when Christians are just one voice among many, not the moral majority they still sometimes envision. But many Christians don't know any other way to communicate God's instructions than to blurt them out with no explanation, as if everyone already agrees. Worse, the media obsesses on those Christians who seem to enjoy condemning others. It's no wonder my colleague thinks Christians are judgmental.

It's sometimes hard for Christians to appreciate how much this new moral standard of not judging is the norm. I heard a radio show recently that revealed how common it has become. The DJs were playing a game of "what's worse," where they offered callers two options. Finally, the choice was, "What's worse: being a cannibal or being a racist?" It's hard to be more judgmental than a racist. Unanimously, the DJs—as well as the call-in guests—said it was worse to be a racist. I wondered if they actually knew what being a cannibal was.

To them it was better to *eat people* than to judge them.

Spirituality has become more attractive than organized religion by the slow accumulation of mental shifts. The Boomers' shift to hyperindividualism, combined with society's replacement of theology with psychology, made it reasonable to decide which parts of religion made sense without relying on religious authorities or institutions. Mix in "true for you but not for me" from the Xer era and Millennials' embrace of the new morality. Add in the growing fear that religious fundamentalism in any faith can lead to war, and organized religion seems like the problem, not the answer. Woven together, it's easy to see why it's now popular to believe the seventeenth-century idea that all religions are basically the same underneath their rituals and doctrines. Researchers Ed Stetzer, Ritchie Stanley, and Jason Hays discovered that 57 percent of Millennials believe there is only the God of the Bible. However, 58 percent believe that the God of the Bible is the same god of the other religions—he's just worshiped differently.[4] The ideas of Picasso's era have gained momentum through the last century and have produced the perfect environment for people to feel more comfortable saying they are spiritual but not religious.

This chapter serves as a transition between the previous four chapters on the spiritual strengths and temptations of each generation and the rest of the book, which answers the questions Christians ask most related to generational intelligence. We have to raise our children and lead our churches in a world of spirituality and multiple religions and viewpoints. In this chapter, I'll offer practical ideas for what to say to people who claim they are spiritual but not religious. These ideas are foundational—I will refer to them throughout the rest of the book.

This chapter is also foundational because it covers the most important thing you need to know about not just the Millennials' faith but everyone's faith. Many people are spiritual but not religious because they have either unconsciously absorbed or mistakenly rejected a version of Christianity that's been hacked—it's not the real thing.

Hacked Christianity

In the last chapter I claimed that the Be Good, Feel Good, Live Your Life (God Is Watching) philosophy[5] is like malware that hackers have installed inside your computer. Many Christians have pointed out the various parts of it throughout the years, but it wasn't until sociologist Christian Smith and his team talked to teenagers that it became obvious how badly Christianity had been hacked.

Smith and his team interviewed more than three thousand Millennial teenagers, ages thirteen to eighteen, to discover what they thought about religion, faith, and the church. Then several years later, they reinterviewed many of them between the ages of eighteen and twenty-four and discovered that their main beliefs had not changed substantially.[6] The team categorized their interview results into five core beliefs that have almost nothing in common with Christianity:

1. A god exists who created and ordered the world and watches over human life on earth.
2. God wants people to be good, nice, and fair to each other, as taught in the Bible and by most world religions.
3. The central goal of life is to be happy and to feel good about oneself.
4. God does not need to be particularly involved in a person's life except when God is needed to resolve a problem.
5. Good people go to heaven when they die.[7]

During the interviews, few referenced even basic theological terms—such as *sin*, *grace*, and *holiness*—that appear throughout the New Testament. Even most teens who had grown up in Sunday school and youth groups didn't recognize those terms. It didn't matter whether the Millennials were Catholics or Protestants, from conservative or liberal denominations. Be Good, Feel Good, Live Your Life (God Is Watching) was their dominant worldview. With few exceptions, the teens spoke a language of happiness, niceness, and earned heavenly reward. They know the words of this new spiritual creed but not the language of the classical Christian creeds. But—and this scares me—*they think they are the same thing.* And what scares me most—they said they learned it from their parents.[8]

For fifty years, Christians have been worried about the increasing secularization of society. But while our attention was focused there, our own faith got hacked. Christian Smith summarized his overall conclusion:

> It is not so much that U.S. Christianity is being secularized. Rather more subtly, Christianity is either degenerating into a pathetic version of itself or, more significantly, Christianity is actively being colonized and displaced by a quite different religious faith.[9]

No wonder Millennials disengage from the church. Why do they need it? No wonder more people say they are spiritual but not religious. What they think of as Christianity is lame. I wouldn't believe it either. This alternate religion strips the power of Christianity to show us how to find our life (see Matthew 10:39) and instead reassures us that our current one just needs a little tweaking. It creates a "religion of me" that never experiences the joy of believing in the God Jesus believed in: a God of startling love who relieves us of the overwhelming burden of trying to make life work on our own.

Be Good, Feel Good, Live Your Life (God Is Watching)

Because this may be the biggest spiritual danger facing you, your family, and your church, I want you to understand all three parts of Be Good, Feel Good, Live Your Life (God Is Watching) and why Christianity is so much better.

Be Good

Good means being "nice, kind, pleasant, respectful, responsible, at work on self-improvement, taking care of one's health, and doing one's best to be successful."[10] Millennials see the main benefit of religion as teaching people what it means to be good, and encouraging them to avoid being mean or self-destructive.

Every hacker gets through some hole in your computer security. What spiritual hole allowed Christian teaching to be hacked into with the idea that we should just be nice and not judge other people? The spiritual vulnerability that most opened a hole for "be good" is the "true for you but not for me" attitude and the new moral reasoning. Of course, after three decades of religiously motivated terrorism, we could predict that the beliefs of any religion that are exclusive would be uncomfortable. Today, people are convinced that the only way for people to get along is if no one has strong conviction that their beliefs are true. So being nice to other people (as long as they are not big jerks) and pursuing your dreams without hurting anybody else has become what "good" people do. Those are the kinds of people who deserve to get to heaven.

I, too, prefer nice people over jerks. Especially in traffic. I am often stuck in Chicago rush-hour traffic, and those jerks who drive on the shoulder trying to get past all the other "good" citizens waiting to get on the ramp deserve the withering stares I give them. But Jesus didn't come to make us nice; he knew nice doesn't work in the real world. He came to transform us so we could live here in a way that anticipates how we will live in heaven (see Matthew 6:10).

Feel Good

The major goal of religion is to make you *be* good, and the major benefit God provides is to make you *feel* good. Millennials told

Smith that God wants you to feel good about yourself, and he is there to comfort you—like a cross between a loving uncle who is almost never angry no matter what you do and a therapist who helps you feel better about yourself.

The Boomers, like Homer Simpson, had lost faith that Jesus' "well-meaning rules" still "work in real life." So they latched on to psychology and its therapeutic techniques. This overconfidence in psychology and the therapeutic is the spiritual vulnerability that allowed Christianity to be hacked until it became about us rather than God. Boomers' trust in psychology grew to dangerous proportions until it redefined religion itself. This shift throws the created order into chaos: we regard ourselves with the kind of honor only God is worthy of, and so we love ourselves with the devotion only God deserves.

We keep messing up our lives, proving to ourselves that we are not worth loving supremely. So we are constantly looking for reassurance that we are worthy of love and adoration, even turning God into a source of reassurance, rather than worshiping him as the only absolute perfection worth loving. In the "feel good" mentality, God serves us rather than us serving God. Ironically, it's the worship of God that makes us feel good as we find our reassurance in the perfect reliability of God. It's when we try to get him to reassure us that our lives are fine that our insecurity takes over. The real God does want us to feel good, confident, joyful, and fully alive. But he knows that the most we can do on our own is try some therapeutic life hack that will ultimately leave us unsatisfied and searching for the next one.

Live Your Life (God Is Watching)

Christian Smith and his team discovered that Millennials see God as distant, observant, and only involved when they have a problem they can't handle themselves. In my opinion, this is the most debilitating of the three components of Be Good, Feel Good, Live Your Life (God Is Watching). For when God is watching us "from a distance" (thank you, Bette Midler), we are on our own. We see God as a teacher on the playground who steps in only when things get out of control.

Gone is the God who "never slumbers or sleeps" (Psalm 121:4), always working throughout history and in our individual lives to make right all that we have messed up. Gone is the God who pursues us, calling us by name to come and know him. Gone is the Holy Spirit, the baptism into the body of Christ, and the "God and Father of all, who is over all, in all, and living through all" (Ephesians 4:4-6). In this "live your life (God is watching)" mentality, we handle our lives on our own and hope for the best.

Our Be Good, Feel Good, Life Your Life Response

Just the thought of living without constant connection with God makes me shudder. Being "spiritual but not religious" gave Katy Perry a distant god who, unlike the one she grew up with, doesn't make demands, but now it's all up to her to assemble her own spirituality. Being into faith but not Christianity has kept Marcus Mumford from being lumped in with judgmental Christians, but it also means he's got to figure out on his own what he needs to do to become the person God created him to be. And if all you've known is a graceless Christianity or Be Good, Feel Good, Live Your Life (God Is Watching), I don't blame you for looking someplace else. But please don't mistake this philosophy for the God Jesus believed in.

Being "spiritual but not religious" sounds good, but the real problem is that it tries to prop up and fix our busted selves, and it can't.

First, Be Good, Feel Good, Live Your Life (God Is Watching)

is full of contradictions. One of the biggest contradictions is, how do we figure out what "nice" is in situations where someone gets hurt? For instance, adultery plays havoc with nice. If I think your wife looks nice, and I think I could treat her nicer than you do (although I'm not judging you for not being as nice to her), wouldn't it be nicer for her if I took her away from you? Your kids probably wouldn't think it was nice of me to break up their family, but I'm not judging them. They're nice kids, really, even though they would hate me. That's a nice mess of contradictions.

But the contradictions are not the biggest reason Be Good, Feel Good, Live Your Life (God Is Watching) won't work. It doesn't do anything to free us from being controlled by unfulfilled desires. For instance, I want to be nice, and nice people share—that's what I try to teach our kids. But now everyone in my neighborhood is getting a pool, and I really need a pool too. But that means the pool money can no longer go toward the soup kitchen I helped support. I know people are out of work and food is tight, but on the other hand, it wouldn't be nice if everybody else got a pool and my kids were left out. When we are controlled by insatiable desires for more stuff or more approval (what 1 John 2:16 [NIV] calls "the lust of the flesh" and "the pride of life"), then we see the good we should do and want to do but can't do. Our unfulfilled desires are too strong. They own us.

Being good or nice cracks under the pressure of the real world. If God is distant and only jumps in to save in times of crisis, we're left on our own to work things out, even though we don't have the power to ensure that bad things don't happen to us or the people we love. So sometimes we have to do things that are not nice—but aren't horrible, either—in order to get our lives to work. Like blaming another department at work rather than admitting we messed up. Sure, we lie from time to time and manipulate other people and pretend we care when we really don't. But if someone confronts us on that, we get angry because we're not really "bad." We've just got to do what we've got to do in this situation.

If we are controlled by unfulfilled desires and are trying to run our lives when we know we can't control everything, we feel forced to cheat on our own standards and then deceive ourselves into thinking we aren't that bad. Be Good is simply too much pressure unless we continually drop the standards.

Jesus came to show us that we can trust God to take care of making things work out right, so we don't have to. The good news is that God will look us in the eye and push through our self-deception by telling us this:

> No, you are not okay. What you are obsessed with isn't worth loving. You are messed up, and that's why you spend so much energy manipulating and maneuvering and worrying. You can't make your life work and will never be able to be good on your own, even according to your own low standards. I can't let you into heaven because even your highest standards are too low. Heaven is perfect, and you will ruin it.
>
> I know you struggle to understand this because you only love people who are nice, but I love you even though you are often a self-centered jerk. Actually, I've loved you since before I made the world. I knew then that you would mess up your life. Nonetheless, I love you so much that I made you anyway, knowing the price I would have to pay to cleanse you from your sins and begin the process of transforming you into someone who enjoys doing what is good, a person who will love the way I run heaven.

The real God is stunning. Being spiritual but not religious only makes sense if you've never met the real God, the one Jesus believed in. Learning the difference is the most important thing you or your children can do.

What Should I Say When Someone Tells Me, "I'm Spiritual but Not Religious"?

Now that we've looked at *why* people say they're spiritual but not religious and we've dug into the hacked Christianity that many reject because they think it's Christianity, we're ready to talk about what we say—or more accurately, what we don't say.

Back when most people said they were Christians and trusted the Bible, Christians could do most of the talking because people shared the same assumptions. Today our talking makes us come across as coercive and judgmental, when that's not what most of us mean. Many of us haven't realized things have changed, or we don't know what else to do. Since we can't assume anything today, we need to agree with others where we can, listen more, ask questions, and—most of all—talk less.

Agree with Them

In the conversation at the beginning of the chapter, my colleagues were asking the questions, so I did more talking than I usually do. But when someone says they're spiritual but not religious, I agree with them. If Be Good, Feel Good, Live Your Life (God Is Watching), or misunderstandings over how the Bible relates to science, or just plain mean Christians is their definition of religion, I agree with them because I don't like that religion either. I've found it helpful to ask, "The word *religion* means a lot of different things to different people. What does it mean to you, and what turned you off?" And then I listen.

Listen More; Talk Less

There's no canned approach or magic words for sharing your faith with someone who is spiritual but not religious. People reject Christianity for many reasons, as we've seen, so you have to listen to their story even to know where to begin. As you hear why they have been turned off by religion, you can determine whether they are open to a conversation about what true religion really means. If they're emotionally closed because they or someone they love has been burned in the name of organized religion, then apologize for how other Christians treated them and agree with them that the religion they've experienced isn't worth believing in.

You don't have to have all the answers. That's the biggest fear that keeps people from opening their mouths. If you haven't had much training on how to respond to doubts and disagreements, don't fake it. Just listen.

Sometimes people reject Christianity because of intellectual doubts. If you are capable of engaging in a conversation with individuals who are spiritual because they intellectually don't believe Christianity, it usually doesn't accomplish much debating them. When a person has made up his or her mind, you can only plant seeds. Direct arguing just proves that you're another one of those brainwashed types who is too scared to listen to somebody else's view. When I'm dealing with people who have rejected Christianity for intellectual reasons, I like to listen, acknowledge when I think they've made good points or asked thoughtful questions, and then pose some questions of my own. That way we'll both have something to think about. If you can't have those conversations, no worries. Love the person and take them to someone who can dialogue with them.

As an aside, let me say two words about intellectual conversations: *they're back*. All the generations have intellectual questions about their faith. You couldn't live in the Traditionalists' era, with its growing confidence in science and human reasoning, without having to respond to intellectual objections to Christian claims. The theological battles after World War II that split denominations into conservative and liberal were far fiercer than anything the following three generations have faced. And many Boomers had those same questions and learned just to shut up, because nothing freaked out the saints like someone saying, "How do you know Jesus was both God and man simultaneously?"

Because Xers grew up on that hinge of personal truth without absolute truth, they focused more on asking if Christianity works than on wondering about the intellectual conversations of the previous two generations. But intellectual questions are back.

One of the biggest challenges we have in responding is that Millennials are asking questions again. Generation *Why?* wants to know, "How do we know that?" Three of the six reasons Barna Group gives in their book *Churchless* for why Millennial Christians are leaving their churches are intellectual: Christianity is too shallow, churches seem antagonistic to science, and the exclusivity of Christianity is a turnoff.[11]

You don't have to be an expert in those topics, but you do need to understand that these questions are the big ones, and you need a go-to person when you don't know what to say. All four of my Millennial kids have wanted to talk through these three questions and many more. Whether inside the church or outside, we have to be willing to listen to those questions.[12]

Ask Questions; Talk Less

If someone disagrees with your basic assumptions, simply repeating more loudly what you think doesn't make you more persuasive; it makes you more obnoxious. So talk less and ask questions.

By the way, there's a big difference between leading questions and authentic questions. Every child knows that "Would you like to eat your peas?" is a leading question, not an authentic one. I've seen people move from lecturing to questioning without really shifting. It doesn't take long for people to realize you don't care what they think; you're simply using questions to make your points. It feels manipulative, even if that's not what's intended. If someone is spiritual but not religious, it's not your job to "sell" them on traditional Christianity. Jesus is a big boy; he can defend himself. But we can clarify what they misunderstand about Christianity and plant seeds that the Holy Spirit can use.

Questions lead to meaningful conversations if we are curious to hear others' answers. Here are some questions I've been curious to learn the answers to. Over half of them could come across as manipulative because I'm asking about things in others' views that don't make sense to me. But that's why I'm curious. I don't mind if they ask *me* hard questions, so I want to see if they have wrestled with hard questions about *their* beliefs. If not, I'm willing to help them wrestle with them. I offer these to help you think of your own:

> - It's huge that you care about feeling close to God and taking care of your soul. How do you do that?
> - Why do you think that all religions are the same underneath?
> - What version of Christianity makes no sense to you?
> - Why do you think Jesus was so religious and also epitomized all the best things people mean when they say "spiritual"?
> - How does your spirituality make demands on you to push you to become less of your unspiritual self?
> - There are certainly parts of any organized theology that are more challenging to accept and believe, so I

understand the attraction of picking and choosing. But if the goal of spirituality is to be more like God, how do you know you're picking the right parts?

"One Thing I Do Know"

Jesus healed a blind man one Sabbath—a big no-no to "work" on the Sabbath. When the authorities interrogated the formerly blind man with theological questions he didn't know the answers to, the man replied, "Whether [Jesus] is a sinner or not, I don't know. One thing I do know. I was blind but now I see!" (John 9:25, NIV). You don't have to know all the answers either. Just talk about what Jesus has done for you. In a world of personal but not absolute truth, we all get to tell our stories. Listen first, but also tell yours. Then if the other person is open, take him or her to someone who has the training to help.

While you don't need to be an expert on intellectual questions, you do need to learn enough about theology that you can explain the difference between Christianity and Be Good, Feel Good, Live Your Life (God Is Watching). It won't hurt to learn more about other religions as well. It comes up a lot more today. It's helped me have deeper conversations and ask better questions.

I've always found that my amazement with Jesus and my understanding of my own Christian faith deepens when I study other religions. Why? Because the God who revealed himself in words, nature, and our own hearts is a God of beauty, love, mercy, and justice. When I study Allah, I don't see the same God. And Buddhism doesn't have a god at all.

You put Jesus in the lineup with any other god, and his beauty outshines them all. Philippians 2:10 says that when we stand before God and see him face-to-face, "every knee [will] bow"— not because God has to grab us by the head and force us down to grovel, but because we will see him fully, without distortion, and it will blow our minds. Throughout the centuries, that moment of seeing God has been called the "beatific vision." When it happens, our knees will give way, and we will say, "This is the answer to every question."

To the intellectually sophisticated people in the Greek city of Corinth, Paul wrote, "All of God's promises have been fulfilled in Christ with a resounding 'Yes!'" (2 Corinthians 1:20). When God wanted to answer our big questions, he didn't send down a philosophy textbook. He certainly didn't send Be Good, Feel Good, Live Your Life (God Is Watching). He sent Jesus, his very self, love in action, to make his ultimate answers to the ultimate questions come alive in the real world. If only Homer Simpson were real, I would tell him that.

We've got a story to tell people who are spiritual but not religious. We just have to get better at telling it to people who come from different assumptions.

CHAPTER 8

When Will My Twentysomething Move out of the Basement?

"I LOVE MY son and daughter," Dana started apologetically, "but they *need* to move out of my house."

"How old are they?" I asked.

"Twenty-five and twenty-six. They both graduated from college and then came back home to their old ways—with the same expectations that I'm going to take care of them as I did in high school but not infringe on their lives. They want me to treat them like adults, but they would rather hang out with their friends than go hard at building their careers. They don't help around the house, and they don't offer to pay for anything." She bit her lip, ashamed as if she'd just confessed a sin.

"It's okay. I get it," I told her. "You're feeling something that a lot of parents are experiencing."

Every place I travel, I hear the same complaints from parents, lamenting their frustration with their children who are young adults and who fit the "young" description, but not quite the "adult" part:

> "He needs to stop changing jobs and girlfriends and settle down."
> "She's back in the house, living like a child but wanting to be treated like an adult."
> "Every weekend he plays video games until four in the morning."
> "She wants to join the Peace Corps while she's still young instead of finding a real job."

My answer to them always starts the same way: "Welcome to the most important life stage you've never heard of."

Emerging Adulthood

The good news is that most of what Dana and other parents worry about usually works itself out. Most Millennials are not lazy; they're just not sure they've found what they want to do, what organization they want to do it with, where they want to live, and who they want to live with.

A couple of years ago I joined a table of Millennials in a class I was leading. They were all well respected and productive, but they articulated the freedom of twentysomethings when they told a colleague, "You're not married, you've saved enough money your first three years working, and you're only twenty-five. This is the time to hike through Europe and Asia for a year. You'll never get this chance again because you'll settle down and have a house and a family. Enjoy the freedom and opportunities while you have them."

Millennials have redefined the transition to adulthood and the traditional benchmarks of maturity. They're extending their education, postponing career choices and marriage, and waiting to settle down. In fact, these milestones have been gradually changing for the last fifty years. In 1960, more than two-thirds of young adults had attained all five key adult milestones—leaving home, finishing school, becoming financially independent, getting married, and having children—by the time they'd reached thirty years of age. By 2000, though, less than half of women and less than a third of men had reached those same milestones by thirty.[1]

Today, almost one in three return home to live with Mom and Dad,[2] earning them the moniker "boomerang generation." (Though to be fair, one in five Millennials lives in poverty compared to one in seven in 1980.)[3] Unfortunately, many parents see the instability and indecisiveness that comes with this time as somehow deliberate. While some people call it "delayed adolescence," it's really more than that: it's a new life stage between adolescence and young adulthood that social scientists have labeled "emerging adulthood." The key distinctives of this new life stage are freedom, choices, change, and trying new things (ideas, jobs, and relationships). It's about discovering an identity within a much longer time frame. More parents are willing and able to provide financial help and/or a place to move back to. My friend Bob said, "I don't think our kids know how easy they have it. We will support them and let them come back home while they figure out what they want, whereas the day after we Boomers graduated from college, our parents told us we'd better have a job because we were not getting back in the house."

Millennials are not in the same hurry Traditionalists and Boomers were in. Because they've heard that their generation may live into their nineties, instead of thinking that life's too short to do a job that's not their passion, they think life's too long to grind it out for a paycheck.

Consider these statistics:

> One-third of twentysomethings move to a new residence every year.
> Forty percent will move back home with their parents at least once.
> Twentysomethings will go through an average of seven jobs during that decade of life—more job changes than in any other life decade.[4]

Jeffrey Jensen Arnett, who coined the term "emerging adulthood," compares it to what happened a century ago when social and economic changes helped to create what we now take for granted as adolescence.[5] In *Emerging Adulthood*, Arnett summarizes what makes this life stage so exciting and confusing:

> In emerging adulthood, no dreams have been permanently dashed, no doors have been firmly closed, every possibility for happiness is still alive. This is the glory of emerging adulthood, that it is the age of possibilities, the age of unvanquished hopes. . . . Most emerging adults . . . [have] lives characterized by exploration and instability, and [focus] on self-development as they seek to translate their possibilities into real life.[6]

They Aren't Adults Yet

You may be surprised to learn that this life stage actually has its roots with the Boomers. Thanks to a flourishing economy and government subsidizing universities, Boomers were able to go to college en masse—the first generation to do so. And those four extra years extended their freedoms by delaying when they entered the workforce. You may think the Millennials have it easier than the Boomers did, but back then Traditionalists complained the same way, insisting that Boomers were messing around rather than getting serious and getting a job as soon as high school was over, like they did.

Then when the Xers got to adulthood, because of the economy, they often had an even longer delay than the Boomers in finding the kind of job that would allow them to settle down.

But emerging adulthood has extended beyond the college years. For more than a decade, we haven't believed a person is an adult until around age twenty-six to twenty-eight.[7] Remarkably, twentysomethings agree with that assessment. They think it takes that long to figure out what kind of work they're passionate about, commit to a long-term love relationship (which we'll discuss more in chapter 10), and save enough money to get their own place.[8]

One thing all generations agree on is that today we become fully adult around twenty-six. Most twentysomethings see themselves as on their way to becoming adults. They like that they are not as much under their parents' control, but they don't believe they are able to stand on their own yet.

More than that, when you ask people who are thirty and younger what is an appropriate age to marry, they say, "Twenty-four or twenty-five." When you ask their parents, they say, "Twenty-seven or twenty-eight."

So when we ask what's wrong with young people these days, the answer is one we all agree on: they aren't adults yet.

Reasons for Emerging Adulthood

Sociologist Christian Smith learned that most emerging adults are enjoying their freedom and are not in a hurry to move through the five key adult milestones I mentioned earlier: leaving home, finishing school, becoming financially independent, getting married, and having children. I know people who think they wait simply because they want to party. But there are actually larger reasons than that. Here are some reasons why Millennials have delayed the five key adult milestones.

They Pursue More Education

Almost two-thirds of Millennials will at least try college (though half of them won't finish), and almost a quarter of those who graduate will go on to earn a master's degree.[9] The information age requires more education to get ahead, which further postpones finishing school, a key adult milestone. Between 2007 and 2012, US funding per student fell 27 percent, but costs rose by 20 percent.[10] Seventy percent graduate with student loans compared to less than half in 1993. That has created an average of $33,000 of debt per person, which when doubled in a marriage is more than the down payment on most houses.[11] College debt is one of many reasons emerging adults are postponing getting married—another milestone.

They Are Trusted Later

In 1901, a fifteen-year-old boy who could throw hay or pick apples as well as any of the men would be invited to sit with them at lunch. They would expect him to listen a lot more than he talked, but the rite of passage from boyhood to adulthood was clear, predictable, agreed upon, and supported by everyone in the community. Exactly how old do employees have to be, and what rites of passage do they have to demonstrate before a company today will trust them with key accounts or critical projects? Even after four to eight years of additional schooling, emerging adults typically apprentice themselves for the next five or six years before they're promoted to positions of responsibility and allowed to join the "adults" at lunch. (Look around the cafeteria in almost any organization, and you will see more segregation by age than any other demographic factor.) That's double the time to transition from child to adult than it was a hundred years ago.

This is one of the reasons given for why video games so appeal to twentysomething men. If the modern world is beating them down, at least they can be heroes in the digital world. Judging by portrayals of young men in the popular media, people don't expect much of them anyway.[12] Could your twenty-four-year-old son be doing something better with his time than playing video games twenty hours a week? Probably, but I doubt his second-shift supervisor job at Starbucks or even his third-year engineering job depends on him to do something someone else couldn't do.

Well-Paying Jobs Take Longer

Since emerging adults are trusted later, it's likely they are paid less and can't afford to become financially independent the same way their parents did. Nor do many of them see much reason to struggle as they would if they left home. In my generation, you would never move back in with your parents, especially if you were a guy. You would move into an apartment with seven other people in a room the size of a closet. You would live in a van down by the river before you would *ever* move back into your bedroom. No woman would date you. Horror films tell us what we're afraid of, right? Alfred Hitchcock made a movie in 1961 about what society thought of men who lived at home too long: *Psycho*.

The Great Recession and the jobless recovery since 2007 have pushed back the five key adult milestones even further, but emerging adulthood is not going away if the job market heats up. All five key adult milestones were being postponed even when the economy was booming and companies were eager to hire Millennials. That said, this jobless recovery has made finding a job harder for Millennials, even for those with college degrees.

I know a woman whose daughter just graduated with a degree in graphic design. She came home to live while she sent out her résumé and looked for work in her chosen field. Nothing but rejection notices sent the Millennial—and her parents—into a deep sadness and disappointment. When someone suggested to my friend that her daughter could work at her company doing some administrative tasks, my friend refused the invitation because it wasn't in her daughter's field. "Thanks, but no thanks," she said. "Her father and I didn't spend all that money on a degree so that she could get a job in some other field."

Finally, the family realized that to get a job in her field, the daughter would need to take on some internships to get experience. Today, she has an unpaid internship in her field—and she works part-time at Target.

For many college graduates, starting a career and getting their own place to live isn't an option as it was for the Traditionalists and Boomers. So they either rack up more debt (and delay paying their already-accrued school loan debt) by going back to school; accept a low-paying (or nonpaying) internship in their field; or put that expensive degree on the shelf and take what Douglas Coupland famously called "a McJob": a "low pay, low prestige, low benefits, low future" job in the service sector.[13] With the housing market so unstable and rent sky high, moving back with their parents makes financial sense.

When our son Josh was in the seventh grade, Laurie came to me one day and said, "Josh and I were talking about how much he would pay in rent when he moves back in." *He was in the seventh grade.*

"Our children are *not* moving back in with us," I told her. "Once they're out of the house, they are out."

"Don't you like Josh?"

I was still stuck in the past, projecting my own experiences on my son. I was remembering the conversation I had thirty seconds before my wedding. My father performed the ceremony. Dad and I were standing next to each other, waiting to walk to the front of the sanctuary, when he leaned over and whispered, "You know, after this, you can never move back in with me."

"I'm doing this because I don't *want* to," I whispered back.

My dad smiled at me, squeezed my hand, and said, "That's good. I'm glad we're on the same page." And with that, I walked in and got married at twenty-two, both of us happy for our little talk.

So Laurie had to shake me out of my generational time warp by saying, "With housing prices rising like they have, how long do you think it will take before your kids work their way up to a job that pays enough to afford even a small home anywhere close to us? And they *will* live close to us, because I will see my grandkids."

Now that the taboo for both parents and their twenty-somethings is lessening, many families admit they like living together during emerging adulthood, even if they get on each other's nerves from time to time.

They Are Still Trying to Decide What They Want to Do

Only a third of Millennials say they are confident they have found their career.[14] We, their parents, told them to find something they're passionate about because they'll be doing it for a long time, and they actually listened to us. Plus, they know they may be working for another fifty or sixty years. The Social Security Administration says that eighty-eight is the *average* life span of Millennials, and half will live longer than that.[15] So think that through.

Today, we live another thirteen years if we retire at sixty-five. So if many Millennials live into their early nineties and the government doesn't pay out benefits until thirteen years before they die, our kids can't retire until they are eighty. (Sorry if I bummed you out, Gen Xers. It's your generation that looks shocked and depressed when I explain this in my speeches or workshops.) Well, if people are going to work into their seventies or eighties, it's understandable they might wonder, *Why do I have to choose a career right now? If I did that same career from twenty-two to seventy-five, wouldn't I be really bored?* The thought of being in the same career for half a century seems like playing the same video game year after year until you go crazy.

How Do We Respond?

Think back to when you stood at the precipice of adulthood and how scary it was. For Boomers and Gen Xers, we looked into adulthood alone—our parents or many of the other adults in our lives hadn't been to college, had died, or didn't think it was their place to help us navigate that transition. Plus, emerging adulthood was brand new, and older adults hadn't experienced it before.

Boomer and Xer parents have the opportunity to be more involved, so we've walked alongside our kids, helping them navigate adolescence, first jobs, school, friends, and everything in between. Some Boomers took it too far and earned the title "helicopter parents,"[16] but most of us were much more involved than previous generations had been. So our kids know that we're going to be there for them during this life stage as well.

But how do we help them through this new life stage without becoming codependent? Dana was stuck here when she complained that her twentysomething children still expected her to take care of them and wouldn't help around the house or pay for anything. Later in our conversation, I asked why she allowed her children to act like high schoolers while expecting her to give them the freedom of adults. She admitted that she was stuck in a time warp, treating them as she did in their high school years because she didn't know what she should expect of them, since she had already been out on her own at twenty-five. She didn't know if she was being too lenient or if the world had changed and this was just how it is now. I suggested to her the three things that can also help you get along better with the emerging adults in your life.

Be a Person They Can Think Out Loud With

It's easy to beat up on Millennials. Obviously, asking, "What's wrong with you?" shuts down dialogue and communication. What this generation really needs are adults whom they can talk stuff over with, who won't yell or lecture, and who will help them think through the transitions.

Millennials in this life stage feel "in between": they know they aren't adolescents anymore, but they aren't sure what kind of adults they want to be. The freedom and choices feel liberating, but assembling an identity in this different world is overwhelming at times. They value older generations who can listen as they wrestle through this stage.

My twenty-five-year-old contact at a factory I was working with outside Toronto reminded me of that last year. It was my third day there, and she was feeling more comfortable talking openly with me. As we walked the ten minutes from the lobby to the training room, she told me that even though she had a degree in human resources, she could only find this job as a temporary administrative assistant for the human resources department. She hoped the company would hire her full-time because she was still too financially dependent on her parents.

Then she paused and said, "But I'm not sure if I should take an administrative assistant job in human resources or keep looking for a human resources job." She asked my advice and continued, "I know I sound confused, but it is confusing. The older generations think that all this freedom is so great. But it's scary, and really stressful, because if you make a wrong decision on some of these things, it can mess you up throughout the rest of your life. I've been dating this guy for the last six months, and he's great. But could I marry him, could I really live with him until I'm ninety-two? My family tells me not to marry a 'fixer-upper,' but how do I know if he will grow out of some things by the time he is thirty or will stay a fixer-upper?"

As we set up the training room, we continued to discuss my ideas on how to tell which frogs could become princes and which ones would still be frogs. It reminded me how eager many emerging adults are for conversations with people from older generations who will listen more than talk and let them think out loud.

I'm the first to admit that it was easier letting her think out loud because she isn't my daughter. Parents find it harder to know when their children want advice or just a listening ear. When we're with our adult friends, we listen a lot more than we give advice, because they would think we're pushy if we kept telling them what we would do. Plus, they're paying for their own dinner, so their bad decision isn't our problem. That's part of the complexity of navigating our transitioning relationship with our kids. Should we listen to our twenty-four-year-olds as we would our adult friends, or should we give them more advice, as we did when they were adolescents? Like Dana, we know how to relate to them as adolescents, but how do we relate to them at each new year of their emerging adulthood?

We will probably be three or four years behind what they need from us if we don't stop and have a Define the Relationship (or

DTR) talk. DTR is what Millennials call the conversation with that special someone they've been "hanging out" with for the last six months, to find out if they are dating or just good friends, and then three years later to find out if they are dating or are headed toward marriage. Just like a couple who dates for seven years, we will need DTR talks at different points throughout our children's twenties. It gives them an opportunity to redefine how much parent and how much friend they want from us. It gives us an opportunity to redefine the boundaries. While we often talk to them like they are five years younger than they are (which drives them crazy), they often act as if we're going to take care of them the way we did five years ago (which makes us resentful).

So if things are going well in your relationship, you can define the relationship in a casual conversation by asking these questions:

> Are there times I treat you like a seventeen-year-old and give you too much advice when really you just need me to listen more so you can think out loud?
> How do I tell when you really want my advice or when I should listen more?
> What do you want me to do with the big issues? I would definitely say something to my best friends if I was 80 percent sure they were about to make a mistake that would have lifelong consequences, so how do you want me to handle that with you?

If it has been tense, you have been driving them crazy, and the resentment is building inside you, you may need to schedule a DTR. You will want to ask those three questions to redefine how they think you're stepping over their growing adult boundaries, but you also want to redefine when they are stepping over yours. But first you need to decide what those boundaries are.

Set Boundaries, Especially with Your Money

When a person is growing more frustrated and resentful about their kids' emerging adult behavior, as Dana was, it's usually a symptom that they haven't determined their boundaries. So I asked Dana, "At this stage in your relationship, how much are you willing to do for your children? And how much do you want them to do for themselves?" It didn't take her long to figure it out; her resentment pointed the way. She wanted them to pay rent, buy groceries, and pay their cell phone bills. She realized they were going to delay getting serious about their careers until they needed more money. She wanted to rotate who cleaned the house each week, though she admitted she would have to get over that they wouldn't do it the way she would. But most of all, she wanted her children to interact with her like she was an important person in their lives rather than the front desk attendant at a hotel. If they were going to live as a family, she wanted to feel they *were* a family, even if it was a different kind of family than when her kids were teenagers.

Dana's situation illustrates that we can't define the relationship with our emerging adult children until we sort through our resentments and let them help us define our boundaries. It's not fair to complain about our kids if we haven't decided how we want to update the relationship and then talked to them about it.

Let your emerging adults know you love them and that you want to treat them as adults, and if they live at home, that you want to live in an atmosphere of mutual affection and respect. In order to best do that, you need to set clear boundaries. These are not the curfew boundaries of your kids' teenage years. These are boundaries about how you will and will not intervene and help them and how you expect to be treated if they really do want a more grown-up relationship.

But especially clarify your boundaries about what you're willing to do with your *money*. Money talks in this life stage, and it often tells them the opposite of what you've been saying. If, like Dana, you're complaining that your kids prioritize going out with friends over their careers but then don't make them pay rent, your mouth is saying one thing and your money is saying another. If you tell them they've got to stand on their own feet more but then buy them the latest smartphone the day it comes out, your mouth says one thing, but your money whispers—far more effectively—*Mom isn't emotionally ready for you to become more independent.*

According to some estimates, parents spend an average of $38,340 per "adult" child between the ages of eighteen and thirty-four.[17] It may be that you are not only their parent but also their sugar daddy. So if you want your children to move into adulthood, maybe it's time to tighten the purse strings. Money talks, so we need to talk about money in our DTRs.

Dana admitted that it was going to be hard for her to stick to her boundaries. She was so used to relating to her children as teenagers that she knew it would be easy for her to go back to doing their laundry two weeks after the DTR. She also admitted that she was worried she would push her children away from her if she was too firm. It's a common worry, but nothing pushes our children away like our resentment, nagging, and endless advice.

Relax
When I have people pull me aside and say, "Should I worry that my twenty-seven-year-old son still plays video games?" I respond with, "If he's still doing it at thirty-six, then yes, you probably should. But your kid is going to be fine."

Inevitably the comeback is "But he spends four hours playing *Call of Duty* with people he doesn't know. He's an adult. Why does he still play video games?"

He plays because he likes them.

One woman asked me about this and then said, "But is that natural?"

I responded, "Does your husband watch television for four hours on a Saturday?"

"Yes, but I don't think that's the same thing."

"No, you're right. Watching TV is far less interactive. Your husband is experiencing significantly more brain atrophy watching TV than your son is playing video games."

Isn't it funny how we judge another generation by what feels right to us?

We need to relax.

A Millennial woman I know and work with expressed the other side of this concern: "How can I make my parents understand and accept my choices?" After she graduated from college, she joined AmeriCorps to serve and do something mission related before she settled into a career. But her father wanted her to get a job right away. He warned her; he complained he'd wasted his money sending her to college; he left job ads on her pillow (so subtle). This young woman is bright and hardworking. She just wanted to take some time, serve, pursue other opportunities, and discover herself in the midst of all the changes. I told her what I tell other Millennials: your parents will eventually get over it when you turn out okay. And don't ask them to fund it.

To her father I would have said, "Relax. Lecturing doesn't do any good. Just because she isn't working on your timetable doesn't mean she isn't moving into adulthood." We get much further by relaxing and loving than we do by lecturing.

I'm glad I knew about emerging adulthood when my son

Barton was twenty-three and worried about a job. He moved in with us after college and a one-year internship, and he freaked out when he couldn't find a job right away, worrying that it would postpone his wedding plans or that it would push him into a career he hated just to pay the bills. I told him to relax and that he and my daughter-in-law could live with us for a year if they needed. I knew the job market for new grads was way down.

He ended up living with us for a couple of months, taking a paid internship for six months, landing in a job that he loves, marrying Emily, and making his way in the world as a financially strapped but happy adult. And that's the good news for us all. (I think he's close to paying his own cell phone bill.)

We don't have to freak out when our kids come home. We can relax knowing that things usually work out. It won't be on our timetable, because our era is over—but they'll figure it out, and so will we.

CHAPTER 9

How Do I Reach My Twentysomething Who Is Drifting from God?

THE WOMAN HAD come to the workshop desperate. Her eyes filled with tears as she asked the group, "What can I do to get my son to come back to the faith? I've done everything I can think of, and nothing has worked." She rattled off at least a dozen things she and her husband had tried, and then she complained about her church's youth minister, who "should be able to think of something because he's a professional. If only he would spend more time one-on-one with my son, I'm sure my son would turn the corner."

I did not give her the comfort she expected when I told her she had missed the most important thing she could do to help him: first, she needed to understand that at some point in their lives, one in three Americans leaves Christianity[1] and accept that her son might be one of them. I added, "That also means he will probably come back—but you need to stop crowding and nagging him."

She cried harder. "I couldn't sleep at night if I thought I wouldn't be with him in heaven."

I think most religious parents can relate to that, as can grandparents, aunts, cousins, and friends. They may be able to keep their wits with everyone else stepping away from Christianity, but when it comes to their kids, they get crazy. If this is your situation, then this may be the most terrifying chapter in the book for you. It may feel as if *you* are the person in chapter 1's scary movie, and you're heading down the basement stairs in the pitch black, thrashing around, trying to find some way to get through to the other side.

But if one out of three people leaves Christianity—some for a time and some for good—it means most families of faith will face this. So there may be no more important topic where we need generational intelligence to turn on the lights than this one. Emerging adulthood makes it harder. Losing faith can happen at any age, but it's especially complicated when our children or grandchildren drift from their faith in this new life stage because we often react as we did when they were in high school, even though the relationship is more complicated than we realize.

The Same but Different

In the last chapter we looked at how emerging adulthood is a time when twentysomethings are trying new ideas and figuring out who they are and where they fit in life. Emerging adulthood also has all the challenges that previous generations went through—it's just that the Millennials' challenges last longer. Drugs, sex, and rock and roll didn't die with the Boomers; they became an industry.[2]

Historically, as we enter adulthood, we try out what we

believe, which means we have to distinguish between our beliefs and our parents' beliefs. Do we believe something because we know it to be true for us, or have we blindly accepted our faith because that's the way we were raised? That has been the same for all the generations. What is different, however, is how each generation has managed this transition.

So, for instance, Traditionalists tended to stay in the faith they grew up in because they valued duty and loyalty. They went to church whether they liked it or not, because respectable people went to church. But when Boomers came to their own "age of accountability," they rebelled against that mentality and threw off their parents' religion, opting instead for an individual-focused search for spirituality.

After the Boomers married and had kids (still mostly in their early twenties), many of them came back to the church and to a more active faith. But now that Millennials have pushed off marriage and children for ten to fifteen years (or more) after high school, the time between leaving church and returning with toddlers is much longer, if they return at all. Plus, the Boomers grew up in a world that was still sure of many Christian assumptions, so it was easier for many of them to return to God and the church. The Gen Xers, however, grew up with anti-institutional suspicion and the individual-truth atmosphere that made returning to the faith less certain. Millennials quit going to church just as the other generations did when they were young, but they live in a world of greater religious diversity and skepticism of Christianity and the church.

Millennials spend a majority of time with their "tribes," so peer pressure is a factor. They are surrounded at school and at work by their friends, who may believe the greatest sin is to say that someone else is sinning and the greatest arrogance is to make the claim that your belief is capital-T True. So while that may not have been the environment that *you* grew up in or spent most of your life in, it is definitely the world that today's twenty-somethings are in and will continue to live in. They are learning how to deal with that world, which is one of the primary challenges of their spiritual lives.

How Bad Is It?

I was speaking recently with my doctor, who had just retired from twenty years of teaching at a medical school. She quit because of her growing frustration. When I mentioned that I was working on a book about the spiritual life of the generations, she responded, "Does this younger generation have any? I didn't see it when I was teaching."

"Yes, they do," I told her, "but it doesn't look the same as with the other generations."

She asked if Millennials had made more idols. That surprised me since we'd never discussed religion before and I'd never heard her use a theological term.

"No, it's about the same," I said. "All generations make their own idols; that's one of the things that makes them different."

Next she wanted to know what any patient wants to know from their doctor: How bad is it? It seems as if everywhere we turn, we hear about some new study showing that Millennials are leaving the faith in droves, and we wonder if our kids will be next. That's why it's important to understand what's really going on. We'll focus on these issues in greater detail in chapter 11, but here's a quick summary of some top findings regarding Millennials and faith. (Be warned: some of these will surprise you.) We need to understand them so we don't overreact to the small things, ignore the big things, and do the wrong things when it comes to transferring our faith to our emerging adult children:

> Emerging adults, ages eighteen to twenty-eight, are still less religious than teenagers and older adults.[3]
> There has been little change in the last forty years regarding how often younger adults pray, whether they believe in God or in the accuracy of the Bible, and how important they think religion is.[4]
> Most emerging adults believe in the existence of God, though that drops the most in the years right after high school.[5] That drop in faith, which has existed during emerging adulthood for forty years, may explain why Millennials are also more likely than any other generation to doubt Jesus' sinlessness and bodily resurrection.[6]
> Thirteen percent more conservative Protestant emerging adults thought that their faith was "very or extremely important" in shaping daily life back when they were in high school than they do now.[7]
> Seventy percent—yes, *70 percent*—of eighteen- to twenty-two-year-olds quit attending church for at least a year (although it's lower for evangelical young people). Eighty percent of them did not plan to do so when they were in high school. Ed Stetzer, the author of the survey, summarizes it this way: "Our teenagers aren't primarily leaving because they have significant disagreements with their theological upbringing or out of some sense of rebellion. For the most part, they simply lose track of the church and stop seeing it as important to their life."[8]
> Two-thirds of them came back to church.[9]
> They are still deeply committed to Be Good, Feel Good, Live Your Life (God Is Watching), although they have a more sophisticated understanding of different faith options.
> Millennials compartmentalize their religious beliefs and

their lifestyle choices—which is why many Millennials are fine with being Christian and having sex outside of marriage. (We'll talk more about that in the next chapter.)

How bad is it? Not nearly as bad as we often hear or fear, but emerging adulthood is still a challenge. So when we see our kids drifting from the faith we embrace, it's understandably difficult to figure out what to do—when everything in us wants to grab them and go straight back to where we last felt safe: in that parent–young child relationship. Unfortunately, that won't work.

Forcing Faith on Our Kids

My wife was born in Hammond, Indiana, the setting for the movie *A Christmas Story*. In one scene that always makes me laugh, the younger brother, Randy, won't eat his meatloaf and mashed potatoes, so the father threatens to use a tool called the "plumber's helper" to spread Randy's jaws apart and shove the food down his throat. He's not the first father to get frustrated with a picky eater. Although we may be able to force-feed meatloaf and mashed potatoes, we can't force-feed our faith when our children (or friends) lose interest in God. But what's our first inclination? To try to fix them—to find some technique that can pry their brains open while we shove our faith in.

Why doesn't fixing work? The people we're trying to fix don't think they're broken. Instead, they think we're the crazy ones who get wacky over religion. An even bigger reason fixing doesn't work is they don't want to be told what to do or think. They want to make their own decisions. Even your dog gets nervous when he hears the word *fixed*.

For almost four decades, Vern Bengtson and his team from the University of Southern California have been studying 3,500 people from all five generations in 350 families to see why some families pass on their faith to their children and others don't. Most people assume that with all the technology and the thought shifts like Be Good, Feel Good, Live Your Life (God Is Watching), it has become significantly more difficult for families to transmit their faith to their children. But the good news is the opposite: more than half of the young adult children have stayed in the same religious tradition, the same as it was in the 1970s. Evangelicals, Jews, and Mormons hand on their faith more often than mainline Protestants or Catholics.[10] Seventy-four percent of couples who are still married, both attend church, and are both evangelicals also had kids who were evangelical.[11]

The families that are emotionally distant and rigid in their beliefs actually drive their children from their faith. The research is clear: parents who are deeply committed to and model their faith will not compensate for an emotionally distant dad.[12] In addition, those parents who are so worried about losing their children that their response is to hold them tight—who don't let them ask questions about other religions, don't let them explore other denominations, and don't allow them to express doubts—discover that their children are more likely to leave and not come back.[13]

We shouldn't be surprised. We witnessed it ourselves when we left home or went to college. How many kids who were raised by very strict parents and who had never been allowed any freedom self-destructed? They discovered beer kegs and for three years never stepped away from the tap. They partied hard. Their parents had never allowed them to make even the smallest decisions, and when they were finally on their own, they had no idea what to do with all the freedom and went crazy because there was no one there to control them.

Some people will rebel no matter what approach parents use, but this is one case where, in allowing our fears to overcome us, we end up pushing our children further away, which in turn makes our scariest nightmares come true. That's why I interrupted the mother at the beginning of this chapter who was rattling off all the things she had done to get her son interested in religion again. I needed her to know that she had missed the most important thing she could do to help him. She was trying to force *her* faith onto him rather than helping him develop his own faith.

So What Do We Do?

Since we know that forcing our emerging adult and young adult children into faith doesn't work, what *can* we do?

Know the Shifts

I know I sound as repetitive as one song set on repeat, but the secret to generational intelligence for people of faith is understanding the shifts in thinking that created the spiritual temptations in each generation. You can understand all you want about generational characteristics, but if you don't understand that Boomers absorbed the shift to hyperindividualism, Xers had to deal with "true for you but not for me," and Millennials have grown up under the full force of Be Good, Feel Good, Live Your Life (God Is Watching), you will have the wrong conversation.

Drew Dyck tells of a friend whose dad rushed him a copy of C. S. Lewis's *Mere Christianity* when he found out that his son had left his faith. C. S. Lewis was the rock-star defender of the Christian faith for the Traditionalists, and this was his most popular book, so the father had high hopes it would help his son see things differently. But C. S. Lewis wrote before the shift to "true for you but not for me," and Dyck's friend, an Xer, did not have the same confidence in logic as his father. Dyck wrote that his friend told him, "All that rationality comes from the Western philosophical tradition. . . . I don't think that's the only way to find truth."[14] Thousands of Christians still read *Mere Christianity*, and all my kids have loved it, but Lewis doesn't answer many of the questions the new generations are asking.

There's no way around it: you have to learn the spiritual temptations that impact the generations. You need to read chapters 3–6 until you understand them enough to see them in your conversations. You don't have to be an expert, but you need to recognize the temptations. I know—some of you are probably thinking, *But those chapters were kind of philosophical. I'm not into that.* If you didn't understand what was medically wrong with your child, you would read anything you could find until you understood what was going on. You'd never expect to do surgery, but you would want to know enough to be able to help. You have to know the shifts, especially Be Good, Feel Good, Live Your Life (God Is Watching) (see chapter 7) and how to explain why it is not Christianity. It really *is* the most important shift in thinking that's impacting the people you care about most.

Model Your Faith

Of course you model what you hope your children will believe, because if there's anything that matters to this generation, it's authenticity. They don't expect you to be perfect—and they wouldn't take you seriously if you thought you were. Let them see you on the days you struggle, and let them see why you choose to believe in Christ rather than in Be Good, Feel Good, Live Your Life (God Is Watching).

Grandparents, take note: Vern Bengtson discovered the "unexpected importance of grandparents and great-grandparents" in passing on the faith.[15] Studies of grandparents are comparably recent, so the team was surprised to find that four out of ten young people had relatively the same commitment to their faith as their grandparents, and it's been that way for thirty-five years.[16] And for many whose parents split or are emotionally distant, the grandparents fill that gap.[17] They model their faith for successive generations. Remember what we said in chapter 3: Millennials want to learn from Traditionalists as long as they don't preach and harrumph. So if you don't learn to text for any other reason, do it to communicate about faith with your grandkids.

As mentioned earlier, when married evangelical parents, especially fathers, practice their faith and are involved in church, 74 percent of their kids remain evangelical.[18] If your kids see from your life that you believe righteousness is attractive and sin is ugly, then they will have to acknowledge that belief is true for you, even if they don't know whether it's true for them. That can start a dialogue. They say actions speak louder than words, but I'd suggest it's better than that: actions lead to speaking about important things.

Dialogue with Them

If we possess generational intelligence, we can dialogue with someone who is spiritual but not religious. We can even become the kind of person our emerging adults can think out loud with as we negotiate a different kind of relationship—adult to adult rather than parent to child. Too often when it comes to our children walking away from or even questioning their faith, the desire to be the parent floods back over us, and we forget everything we've learned in the earlier chapters.

You have to talk less and listen more if you want to create the supportive, open setting that helps people keep their faith. If you had an open relationship with your teenager, you did a lot of listening. But even then the relationship was at best 50 percent hearing what they thought and then 50 percent telling them what they needed to think. Now the conversations need to dial down the talking and dial up—way up—the listening.

Most Millennials want to have spiritual conversations. The massive studies of college students conducted by the Higher Education Research Institute at UCLA discovered that three out of four students have "at least some interest in spirituality" and desire to spend ample time "exploring the meaning and purpose of life."[19]

That's good news. We need to encourage seeking and dialogue rather than shut them down with condemnation of their views or impatience with their questions. Researchers from the University of Connecticut and Oregon State University found that the biggest reason people lose their faith, or "de-convert," is that the de-converters reported "sharing their burgeoning doubts with a Christian friend or family member only to receive trite, unhelpful answers."[20]

Mailing young adults books they can't relate to and trying to stamp out their doubts may be well intentioned, but they make the person with doubts feel that faith is hopeless for them or that people who have it are hopelessly naive.

When my youngest brother was born with Down syndrome and a hole in his heart, and then died in surgery a year and a half later, my sixteen-year-old brain could not understand why God did that or allowed that to happen. Thank goodness for parents and other people who let me talk. Over time, I came to the conclusion that instead of damaging faith, how Christianity deals with pain and tragedy is the most powerful reason to believe in it instead of other religions. But by then it was no longer my parents' faith; the struggles had made it mine.

So I advise parents and grandparents to be vulnerable about their own struggles in faith. You can get further in your discussions if, rather than shutting down questions, you invite them and talk openly through them. In other words, I encourage you to follow the same advice I mentioned in the last chapter: relax and be a person your children can think out loud with.

The good news is that you have more influence than you may realize. *Time* columnist Joel Stein says that Millennials don't necessarily respect authority, but

> they also don't resent it. That's why they're the first teens
> who aren't rebelling. They're not even sullen. "I grew
> up watching *Peanuts*, where you didn't even see the
> parents. They were that 'Wah, wah' voice. And MTV was
> always a parent-free zone," says MTV president Stephen
> Friedman, 43, who now includes parents in nearly all
> the channel's reality shows. "One of our research studies
> early on said that a lot of this audience outsources their
> superego to their parents. The most simple decision of
> should I do this or should I do that—our audience will
> check in with their parents.[21]

"Superego" is pyschobabble for what the Bible calls our conscience. MTV learned that Millennials rely on their parents to help them form their consciences. Your kids want to hear from you. They want to know your thoughts and why you believe the way you do. They just don't want you to push it down their throats.

So we listen to the way they see the world. And instead of saying, "We taught you better than this. You know what's right. This is what God commands. Do you want to go to hell?" we ask a lot of questions (see the list on pages 118–19 to get you started), and we share the reasons why we believe what Scripture teaches rather than simply listing off the commandments. Not because we don't believe the commandments are true but because if our children have left the faith, they probably know what the commandments are but think they don't work in real life.

If God is great and God is good, then there's a good reason behind every command he gives us, and in today's world we have to emphasize the reason instead of the command so that people are willing to see the beauty of the command before they accept it. Billy Graham's declaration "The Bible says" just doesn't work after all the generational shifts in thinking. That's not to say we can never use Scripture, but if the Bible doesn't mean that much to someone else, it's not going to win your argument and bring him or her out of darkness and into the light.

Place Them in God's Hands

If parents or grandparents can have conversations, engage with questions, and raise some of their own without freaking out, yelling, or preaching too much, then we're in a good place. But we can't do that consistently unless we place our kids in God's hands. The first way we do that is to parent as God parents. We cannot do with our children what God won't do with us.

We so desperately want them to do what is right that we manipulate and control instead of letting them choose—even if it means their own destruction. Think about it. If God took away humans' freedom to do evil, the world's greatest problems would go away. But he'll do anything—including dying—instead of that. He wants us to choose to love him over all the alternatives, even if our free will creates mass destruction. It goes back to my first faith-shaking doubt: How can there be so much suffering, so much evil, if God is good and promises to take care of us? Because God would rather have people choose horribly than not be able to choose at all. We cannot convince our kids to believe; we can't sell them on loving God. It's not our job.

Relaxing doesn't mean we don't care. It means we pray for our children, but we give up our messiah complex, thinking we can "save" our children. Instead we allow them to make their choices, and we place them in God's hands.[22]

It's the hardest thing, though, to hand our kids over to God, isn't it? Nothing in my sermons or workshops on the spiritual life of the generations grabs people more than this idea that we must hand our children over to God. I watch people struggle through the idea. Some grow still, almost frozen, while others physically shake. Many parents cry. People want to stay after and talk with me about this topic more than any other. While their stories are different, they fall into two themes: 1) "It's so hard, Haydn. I've loved this child from before he was born, and I've done everything to keep him safe and happy. How can I let go of that now, especially when this is the most important thing?" Or 2) "This was the breakthrough for me. For the last five years I've thought it was my job to preach and push when I need to listen and love."

The desperate mother at the beginning of the chapter follows the first theme. Far more than we realize, we are all control freaks with our kids, and the emerging adulthood years force us to face this and let go. So I asked the mother, "Who loves your son more, you or Jesus?" Quietly, she replied, "I know the answer is Jesus, but it doesn't feel that way. It feels like he's not doing enough or my son wouldn't be drifting away."

That's it, isn't it? That's the heart of our desperation, the reason why we struggle to control our emerging adults. It's difficult to place our kids in God's hands when he is so committed to free will that he makes us no guarantees, except one: he loves them with a big love, a God-sized love, and has since before he laid the foundations of the earth, and through that love he is always at work, 24-7, calling them—and he will never quit.

Love Them

What helps prodigals come home? First and foremost, *love* them. Keep a loving, open relationship. This is going to be difficult, because chances are both of you harbor a lot of pain. But you must love them anyway and remember that people can and do change—kids do grow up as they grow older. Have some faith that God is hard at work in the course of their lives. Frequently, a rebellious, antagonistic stance in an eighteen-year-old mellows considerably by the time that child marries and has children. Prodigals do return to the fold, and some of it is simply a consequence of aging.[23]

What do you do if your children appear to leave and will never come back? You bite your tongue until it bleeds, do you not? And you hold on to the side of the bed at night, and you pray for all you're worth. And you place them in God's hands because they never were yours, were they? The central relationship in their life is with God, not with you, even if they don't believe he exists or they ignore him. Every one of them has to look Jesus in the eye and decide. We cannot decide for them, and it breaks our hearts.

God has his own timing. Sometimes it's like those police shows where a cop is working a stakeout for six months and somebody else barges in and ruins it. God is on a stakeout, and sometimes we can be the one barging in. God says, *Relax. I've got this.* When we love as much as God loves, we give up guarantees along with trying to control someone's free will. Some prodigals don't come home, but many do. Vern Bengtson, who for almost forty years has been studying prodigals and how families pass on their faith, understands coming home:

> I was born into a highly religious family with a tradition of devotion that goes back to at least the 16th century.

My father was a pastor in the Evangelical Covenant Church. . . . Despite my strong religious heritage, I consider myself a religious prodigal. For many years, my own mother worried that she would not see me in heaven.

After being involved in the church in a minor way most of my adult life, I had a spiritual reawakening about four years ago. I woke one Sunday morning missing choir music. As I walked in the door of a massive Gothic church in downtown Santa Barbara, the choir was roaring away and the congregation was shouting praise. Light from the stained glass windows filtered down on the congregation and reflected back up into the great barrel-vaulted ceiling. I was overcome by emotion. To borrow the language of C. S. Lewis, I was "surprised by joy," and I haven't been the same since. That was a religious reawakening in which, after 65 years of searching, I found a faith community that meant something to me profoundly. Prodigals can come home.[24]

For our part, we quit shoving commandments in their faces and telling them what they're doing is wrong. Then we do what we can. We relax and we pray and we give them up to God. We listen to our emerging adults far more than we talk. And then we wait for God to provide the opportunity to say or do something that might influence them. And most of all, we love them with a big love, just as God does.

CHAPTER 10

What Do I Do When My Kid Is Putting Off Marriage but Not Sex?

CONNIE WRUNG HER hands as she confessed that her twenty-four-year-old daughter had started having sex with her boyfriend.

"My husband and I raised her in the church. Until recently she believed that sex outside of marriage is wrong," Connie told me. "But she informed me that as soon as she can get a better job, she's moving in with her boyfriend. She says they love each other and plan to get married in a few years."

"Do you like the guy?" I asked.

"We did until we heard this. So why don't they just get married? If they're already committed to each other, I don't understand what she's waiting for."

"Why are my kids putting off marriage but not sex?" is a question I hear all the time from parents, especially committed Christians. I'm not surprised. Talking about sex has never been easy, but parents and churches today are overwhelmed by the new morality and confused by the changes emerging adulthood is creating for marriage.

> We are overwhelmed by how sex-saturated our world is today. While parents used to worry about MTV's suggestive music videos, today it seems all of cable after 8 p.m. is MTV. We don't know how to shield our children now that middle schoolers face pressure to get involved sexually. We read that 20 percent of Millennials have texted sexually explicit pictures to someone.[1] Most of all, we feel overwhelmed that everywhere we turn, people think that unmarried sex is fine and it's the Christians who are messed up.

> We wonder how to explain Christian marriage. When the Traditionalists and Baby Boomers got out of high school or college, they assumed they would marry whether they were religious or not. But today we read that confidence in marriage is declining and more people are living together without being married. Parents and churches struggle to explain the beauty of Christian marriage to Gen Xers and Millennials who have seen so many marriages end in divorce.

> We wonder if there's something wrong with Millennials for not getting married earlier, even though we don't want them to. I hear this frequently from the older generations who married at twenty-three: "I don't get it; I had two kids and a mortgage by twenty-seven. What's wrong with them?" But at the same time, as we saw in chapter 8, the older generations tell their twentysomethings, "Don't be in a hurry to get married. It's so much easier when you can afford it and don't have to struggle financially."

> We don't know what to say about sex now that emerging adults marry five years later than the Boomers did. We know that Scripture is clear—all sex is for marriage. But we also know that people married at seventeen in Bible times rather than at twenty-seven, as they do today. We may not voice it, but many of us wonder if it's possible for twentysomethings to obey these teachings in today's world. My friend Annie was in a Bible study at her church with ten other married women last year when the topic of saving sex for marriage came up. She said her heart broke that she was the only one who thought it was possible.

Despite these questions and the awkwardness we feel when talking about sex, most parents and churches do attempt to talk about the facts of life. We explain that God designed sex for marriage. Often we promise that sex will be much better if emerging adults will wait. But there are two facts of life we don't talk about that hurt our young people.

We don't talk about the fact that most Christian singles are having sex. According to Princeton religion researcher Robert Wuthnow, evangelical Protestants are the most likely to say that premarital sex is always wrong (about 42 percent), yet *69 percent* of unmarried evangelicals ages twenty-one to forty-five and 78 percent of mainline Protestants had sex with at least one partner during the past year.[2]

Christian emerging adults want to believe that obeying God will be better for them, but in their hearts they agree that Homer Simpson's definition of Christianity applies to sex: "You know, the one with all the well-meaning rules that don't work in real life. Uh, Christianity."

We make things worse when we don't bring up the additional five years Millennials wait until they marry compared to the

Boomers. Most of us who are older didn't wait that long for marriage, so we don't know what to tell them. Some of us doubt that anything will work, so we say nothing and hope they aren't doing what they shouldn't be doing. But it sends mixed messages to our kids when we don't talk about sex much in a world that talks about it constantly. And when singles do ask how to handle their sexual desires for five additional years, parents and churches stammer and mumble things about trusting God and holding strong. Emerging adults (and their parents and grandparents) need practical help figuring out how to deal with the additional five years until marriage. We have to start talking about this new fact of life.

One of my colleagues, Brian, knew that sex outside of marriage was wrong. He grew up in a conservative, Baptist home and attended a Christian school. He was taught not to have sex until he was married, but he was not taught *how* not to have sex until he was married. When Brian left home, he sowed his oats, so to speak—until one day when he was twenty-eight, he woke up and found himself lying next to someone he barely knew and thought, *I'm not happy*.

"I felt hollow inside," he told me. Today, in his thirties, he's still single, but he's much more content. "I wish someone could've taught me how to be single and Christian in my twenties." Telling young people to wait until they marry without telling them how isn't working.

I know I don't have all the answers, but I do have some ideas on how to start the conversation. In many ways sex is the final exam on everything we've been talking about—especially how we communicate with emerging adults. So let's look at Connie's questions systematically and see how attitudes toward marriage and sex have shifted and then how we can help our kids and the other emerging adults in our lives sort through the challenges of finding good love and good lovin'.

They Aren't Postponing Marriage as Long as We Think

Connie is right. Millennials are waiting longer to get married. When Connie's mother got married in 1962, the average age of women marrying for the first time was 20 (23 for men). When Connie got married in 1987, that had jumped to 23.6 (25.8 for men). Her 24-year-old daughter's generation postponed it to 25.5 (27 for men), until the Great Recession bumped it to 26.1 (28 for men).[3] As a result, *half* as many Millennials are married today as their parents were at their age.[4]

When parents and grandparents ask me why their Millennials are taking so long to marry, I surprise them when I say, "Emerging adults aren't marrying that much later; you got married that much earlier." I like to ask them to guess at what age people married in 1900. Most audiences say seventeen. They aren't even close. Men married at twenty-six, and that rate didn't drop below twenty-four until World War II.[5] That's when Johnny came marching home and had to make an "honest" woman of his girl. That dropped the age for men to twenty-two, while women, who had married at twenty-two in 1900, were now marrying at twenty, and that's where the age remained for twenty-five years. The GI Bill allowed Johnny to pay his bills, so he could get married and support his family at an earlier age. Traditionalists got married, got jobs, and had babies—a boom of babies—in that order.

The Baby Boomers continued to get married younger than people did before World War II. The marrying age didn't go back to where it was before World War II until the Gen Xers postponed marriage until twenty-six for men and twenty-four for women. Later Xers pushed it to twenty-seven and twenty-five, which the Millennials maintained until the Great Recession. Millennials, even in a horrible job market, are only getting married two years later than their great-great-grandparents.

No wonder Traditionalists and Boomers think Xers and

Millennials are taking forever to marry (and bring them grand-kids). We can only compare to what we have seen. Yes, emerging adults are marrying later, but not as late as their parents and churches think.

Millennials are marrying later for the same reasons we looked at in chapter 8: pursuing more education, working entry-level jobs that don't pay enough to support a family, accumulating large debts, enjoying the freedom of the twenties, trying to decide what to do, and focusing on getting established in their careers. But the most startling reason is you, their parents and grandparents. You encouraged them to postpone marriage until their late twenties. And it has been good for their marriages. One of the reasons Millennials have the lowest divorce rate is that they marry later.[6]

How We Came to Worship Sex

Millennials want to marry eventually, but like Connie's daughter, they don't think it's realistic to go without sex until you're twenty-six and finally get married. That's a huge shift—from feeling guilty you are not able to control yourself until marriage to believing that chastity is impossible and unhealthy. This new view of sex demands allegiance and trashes on Twitter anyone who disagrees. Sex rules our thinking. You could say we worship it.

We didn't always worship sex. Agatha Christie describes how Traditionalists saw sex in *A Caribbean Mystery* (1963), written about her elderly spinster sleuth, Miss Jane Marple. In the beginning of the story, Miss Marple is thinking about how kind and fond her nephew Raymond is of her, but

in a slightly exasperated and contemptuous way! Always trying to bring her *up* to date. Sending her books to read. Modern novels. So difficult—all about such unpleasant people, doing such very odd things and not, apparently, even enjoying them. "Sex" as a word had not been much mentioned in Miss Marple's younger days, but there had been plenty of it—not talked about so much—but enjoyed far more than nowadays, or so it seemed to her. Though usually labeled Sin, she couldn't help feeling that that was preferable to what it seemed to be nowadays—a kind of Duty.

She goes on to make fun of a book her nephew Raymond had sent her, where a young man told a young woman with no sexual experience, "At *nineteen?* But you *must.* It's vital." Miss Marple pities the sex-worshiping young people: "And really! To have sex experience urged on you exactly as though it was an iron tonic! Poor young things."[7]

Christie is referring to the misunderstanding of Sigmund Freud that fed the first sexual revolution: the Roaring Twenties with the flappers and the short skirts. Freud's view that sex is a major but unconscious driver of our motivations, which causes all manner of psychological problems when repressed, became popular in the 1920s. But Freud's view had been misinterpreted to say that if you deny sexual desires, then you will have emotional problems later. This misunderstanding turned sex into something "vital."

When the Great Depression hit, skirts got longer and people became more sexually conservative. Nonetheless, the belief that sex was vital continued to spread slowly with the Traditionalists. It's easy to forget that as many as half of the women in the twenties were not virgins when they married.[8] They were no strangers to sex before marriage, yet "sex was not talked about so much" and was "usually labeled Sin." But that changed. Hyperindividualism and psychology combined so that morality shifted to be focused on the self. No one could tell someone else what was right or wrong as long as it was consensual. That helped the second sexual revolution that surged during the youth of the Baby Boomers become much more powerful and more famous than the first one.

This focus on self rather than duty went beyond sex in the second sexual revolution. Many Boomers also shifted their ideas about marriage.[9] They no longer looked for a good match, but for a soul mate who would provide incredible, satisfying sex and accept them for who they were. How many plotlines from seventies movies were about understanding and accepting? *Love Story* was a particularly popular one that gave us the sappy and impractical quotation, "Love means never having to say you're sorry." (If that's the case, obviously my wife and I have never been in love.)

Sex outside of marriage is so common for Xers and Millennials that it isn't even a question of *whether* but *when*. For decades *Seventeen* magazine has been telling teenage girls to wait until they are ready, not to wait until marriage.

Religion told people for centuries how to handle sex, but now the sexual revolution claimed these ancient rules needed to make way for psychology. Christianity said that sex was good but not vital. The sexual revolution said that sex was vital and faith optional. Western culture flipped things in the sixties, and people began to judge religion by whether it bowed to sexual freedom rather than judging sex by religious teachings. In short, we began to worship sex.

The Move to Move In
The decline in faith in marriage and the belief that sexual purity is impossible have accelerated cohabitation. Between 2006 and 2010, 48 percent of women between the ages of fifteen and forty-four moved in with a man they're not married to, according to the

Centers for Disease Control.[10] Let me repeat that in case you did a double take: *48 percent.* Cohabitation is not only acceptable for this generation but expected—and for some it will replace marriage completely. It's one of the reasons married households are at a record low. In 2010, the US Census Bureau reported that the proportion of married households dropped to 48 percent. Today, 50 percent of adults are unmarried, compared with 33 percent in 1950.[11] In addition, 58 percent of all unmarried moms are cohabiting (up from 41 percent in 2002).[12] The implications for churches are staggering, as we'll see in the next chapter.

Not only is cohabiting more accepted, but it has also become the accepted way to find the right person to ensure a successful long-term relationship. Researcher Christian Smith discovered that, except with emerging adults with religious-based objections to moving in together, the rest "maintained with complete assurance that one would be stupid to get married without first having lived together for six months to a year. The person who you thought you knew so well when living apart could prove in a 24-7 relationship to have problems or incompatibilities that would make you not want" to get married.[13]

How to Help Emerging Adults Find Good Love and Good Lovin'

This chapter began with Connie asking me, "So why don't they just get married?" We've been answering this question piece by piece, so let me pull it all together: Connie's daughter is waiting to get married because she doesn't believe she's ready yet. Like many emerging adults, she may also have lost confidence in marriage, but it's obvious she has not lost confidence in love. She believes, along with most in the Western world, that sex is vital and it's not really possible or even good to go without it. Finally, we can't forget the new moral code of Be Good, Feel

Good, Live Your Life (God Is Watching) and that the greatest sin today is to judge someone else's choices. This Millennial spiritual temptation makes even children who were raised in the church, like Connie's daughter, susceptible. If a young adult has these ideas about sex and images of marriage, then sleeping with her boyfriend and moving in with him when she gets enough money isn't surprising; it's logical. It goes without saying. It may catch parents or family members by surprise, but that's because they didn't know these ideas and images have been quietly shaping emerging adults' thinking.

So what do we do?

We've not had to face later marriage since the forties, when our grandparents last married later. But they didn't spend as much time alone and weren't immersed in a culture that worships sex. I don't have all the answers, but the following suggestions are a good place to start.

Start the Conversation

I said at the beginning of the chapter that we need to start talking about sex and the additional five years until marriage. And we need to do it now. If we stay quiet because we don't know what to say, our emerging adults will wonder whether we think it's impossible to wait that long. What's more, those lessons and discussions need to happen frequently and at a much younger age than we are comfortable with. Recent studies show that girls begin to think in terms of their sexual identities as young as six.[14] Of course we only talk about what our kids are ready for, but if we listen, we will learn what they think and what they need to know.

Listen First

Listening so we know what our children think and what they need to know applies to emerging adults even more. Connie was surprised her daughter was sleeping with her boyfriend because Connie hadn't talked to her daughter about the ideas and images in our culture that were undercutting her daughter's beliefs in God's plan. We can't help our kids unless we learn what they really think.

We can't do that when we are talking. We need to ask more questions as we transition from being the parent of a child to being the parent of an adult.

Talk Why and How

Your kids likely know what the Bible says about sex, so talk why and how. Talk about why God gives the commands and how your kids can find their sexuality in God's design.

Connie thought her daughter believed sex outside of marriage is wrong. Her daughter may have known the commandments and some of the consequences like pregnancy or disease, but she didn't understand or agree with the why. She didn't believe God would give her what she needed to be happy, because she believed she needed sex.

We don't want kids who only know the rules; we want them to agree with God. Our kids become transformed spiritually when they grasp the beauty of righteousness because they see the good that comes from obeying God. Then they no longer obey only because it's God's command but because they see how God's command creates beauty and a beautiful life. That won't make their sexual desires go away, but it will make it worthwhile to learn how to deal with them when they really believe God knows what he's talking about.

Talking about the why more than the commandments helps us talk with emerging adults who no longer believe sex is only for marriage. (Not to mention people who think Christian views about sex are a little crazy.) If your kids or your colleagues think sex is vital, telling them God commands us not to do it doesn't help.

Don't start with the commandments about sex; start with why God gave them to us. We don't sugarcoat or soften what God says. We just reverse the order.

Take a moment to practice. Try the exercise I give groups when I speak in churches: give three reasons sex before marriage isn't best for us without mentioning the Bible. If God is great and God is good, then there are good reasons for his rules. Talk about those reasons more than the commandments.

This isn't as hard as it first sounds, because most sins contain their own punishment. Sexual sins certainly do. Other people's self-inflicted wounds are some of the best ways to talk about the why behind the command. This also works at home. Our four children know many people who have already faced heartbreak or harm because of their sexual decisions, as I'm sure yours do. When those stories come up, it's a wide-open opportunity to help them figure out why sex is a wonderful creation but is not worthy of worship. Don't preach; discuss.

Teach Them the Beauty of Sacred Sexuality

God made us sexual beings even if we don't ever have sex. He wants us to find our sexuality rooted in him instead of in our bodies. There are three central reasons sacred sex is more beautiful than vital sex.

1. YOU CAN BE HAPPY WITHOUT SEX.

Jesus' life shows that we can be happy without sex. Many fans of Jesus but not Christianity forget that Jesus was a virgin. Sex is so important in their worldviews that a psychologically healthy, happy celibate makes no sense to them. They can't help but try to marry Jesus off (see *The Last Temptation of Christ* or *The Da Vinci Code*, for example).

So why wasn't Jesus as sex obsessed as people are today? Jesus knew that sex, when it's removed from its rightful place, can own us. He shows us how to take sex less seriously because it's good but not vital to a vibrant, healthy life. Because Jesus didn't make sex the epicenter of his world, sex did not own him.

2. SEX IS TOO POWERFUL TO BE "VITAL."

Each generation has increasingly seen sex as more vital than the last. It's vital for finding and keeping a mate and for figuring out if he or she is "the one." Or sex is seen as vital because it's so powerful that resistance is futile. The book of Proverbs agrees that sex is powerful—too powerful to be vital: "Can a man scoop a flame into his lap and not have his clothes catch on fire? Can he walk on hot coals and not blister his feet? So it is with the man who sleeps with another man's wife. He who embraces her will not go unpunished" (Proverbs 6:27-29). Paul extends this beyond adultery and explains that not only is sex not vital, unmarried sex harms our vitality (see 1 Corinthians 6:12-20).

Christian sex keeps this power in a safe container—marriage—where it can bind two souls together. Jesus didn't talk specifically about sex much (the Bible he read talked about it a lot, and he didn't have much to add). But one statement was so important that Jesus quotes Genesis: "A man leaves his father and mother and is joined to his wife, and the two are united into one" (Mark 10:7-8; see also Matthew 19:5). That mystical unity is too powerful to turn into a trial run, as if once a couple proves they have adequate sexual skills, they can figure the rest out later. According to Jesus, our images and ideas about sex focus too much on how it feels to our bodies and not enough on what it does to our souls.

3. SEX IS TOO FRAGILE TO BE THE FOUNDATION OF A MARRIAGE.

How many love songs use the word *heaven*? Mariah Carey sang about taking her feelings higher than the heavens. Bryan Adams found "heaven" lying in his baby's arms. Belinda Carlisle discovered that, *ooh*, "heaven is a place on earth."

Looking for heaven on earth always disappoints. How could we not be disappointed when it inevitably gets boring? Because sex, like all other physical desires, will at some point become boring. When it does, it takes more or someone else to make it spine tingling again.

Sex will disappoint Christians who wait as well. This is part of the problem with abstinence approaches that promise, "If you wait until marriage, you'll have better sex." I'm the first to admit there's a strong case in the psychological literature about the benefits of married sex, and I think we should tell people about them. If God is right about sex and he knows how it works best, then it only makes sense that it works out better for people who follow his plan. But sometimes in our desire to get people to follow the Bible's teachings, we use a sales pitch the Bible never promised. The reason to have sex only with your spouse is because marriage is a God-ordained mystical unity. Marriage teaches us to love the way God loves us, which we can't do if sex (and our marriage) is all about us. I was surprised to learn that once I got married, I didn't have sex anytime I wanted (spoiler alert, I know). If the best reason to wait is to have mind-blowing sex later, then sex is still worshiped more than God, and the minute it gets boring, we're not only disappointed, but we also feel lied to and robbed.

When a couple centers their life and marriage on God, they don't take sex as seriously. They don't have a "duty" to have mind-blowing sex; they can pull it off the throne and put it back in its proper place. Then they are free to discover its unexpected surprises and a mojo that can last throughout the years. Agatha

Christie was right when she described the era before we worshiped sex: "There had been plenty of it—not talked about so much—but enjoyed far more than nowadays."

Teach Them the Beauty of Unamazing Marriage

Along with the switch to worshiping sex, there has been a more subtle change. As faith in God and religion decline, people have replaced God with a romantic life partner and family. How many movies are about the workaholic dad who finally realizes family is what life is all about? Now the generations that feel they got burned by family throw themselves into creating the perfect family, where they can find their meaning and highest joy. It sounds great—but it's idolatry. We can't make marriage or family our god any more than we can make sex a god. When we make other people our heaven on earth, they disappoint us. It's too much pressure for them to take the place of God.

Christians can get swept up into idolizing spouse and family. We've been trying to sell sacred marriage like we have sold sex—Christians do it better. If psychology sets the rules, then we'll show people that Christian marriage is emotionally healthier and happier. We are in a contest to have more amazing marriages than non-Christians do.

As Christians and parents, we help people make their marriages beautiful, not amazing. Marriage is about uniting two people who are different, who come together and learn the sacred lessons that can only come from loving somebody who gets on our very last nerve and doesn't see any reason to change. Yet this is where grace rushes in. When Jesus shows up, we love our spouse even while we are having a small homicidal fantasy about him or her. As a result of this grace in our ordinary marriages, dedicated Christians are twice as likely to be at the highest level of happiness with their marriage compared to couples who don't say, "God is at the center of our marriage."[15] That surveys consistently show Christians are happier in marriage is encouraging, but happiness is not what we seek in marriage. We seek God.

Millennials and Xers value authenticity, so we need to share stories of unawesome marriages. If we don't, how will they ever believe normal, wonderful, unawesome marriages are worth it, especially if they didn't see grace in their parents' marriage?

Ask Them How They Are Doing

Last night Laurie stayed up past midnight talking with our daughter, who is just back from college for break. Recently our daughter has moved from "hanging out with" to dating a guy, so my wife had the "what's your plan?" conversation we've had with each of our kids when they started dating. We ask our emerging adult children awkwardly direct questions about how they are preparing for the sexual temptations in their romantic relationships. Laurie and I found it hard dating for four years; we have to talk about it if our kids are going to make it six more.

I ask my boys, "How's your car running? What's your plan to stretch your money until you start your summer job? And how are you doing keeping your hands to yourself?" They don't even flinch at the question anymore.

Not all of our kids want to talk to us about sex. When Laurie told my daughter last night that she needs someone she can talk to, my daughter said it wouldn't be one of us. So have someone they trust ask them how they're doing. Sometimes those relationships happen on their own—like with my daughter, who has two women she trusts and talks to—but more often we parents need to ask other adults to invest in them. Don't try to do this alone.

If we, or other adults, ask them, we must be ready with grace when 70 percent of them tell us they've failed. There are no sins God can't forgive, although sexual sins may be harder to forgive ourselves for. Our emerging adults can't build an identity in God if they are dragging their sexual sins around.

I've asked us to start talking about sex and marriage in a way that helps people discover the God who gave us our sexuality and knows what to do with it. That's the only thing that will help us get to twenty-eight—or eighty-eight, if we never marry.

A colleague of mine who was single at thirty-three asked me at dinner one night, "Haydn, I'm not a virgin by any stretch, but my relationship with Christ matters more to me than anything else. If I don't end up getting married, how do I live without sex for the rest of my life?" The next time I saw him, I handed him a book about how to believe God is good when things are hard or even bad. He asked, "Is this going to tell me how to deal with my sex drive?"

"Nope," I said. "It's going to tell you about the central theme Jesus came to tell us about God—that he is good and that we can trust him to take care of us."

I've always thought it an epic fail to teach single Christians the theology of sex without practical ideas for setting boundaries and "not to awaken love until the time is right" (Song of Solomon 8:4). I've not covered many of them because there's so much good stuff out there that you can locate with a couple of mouse clicks.

If my colleague remained single the rest of his life, he would need to know those things. But sex had been too strong for him in the past, and it would be again. I realized I needed to give him something even stronger. He would have to make his peace with God. He would have to believe in the God Jesus believed in, or he could not live the pure life Jesus did. There's no technique or accountability partner that can help us find our sacred sexual identity. Ultimately, there's only the worship of God that can overcome the worship of sex.

Jesus gave us the only motivation that ultimately is strong enough: "Blessed are the pure in heart, for they will see God" (Matthew 5:8, NIV).

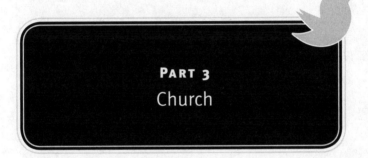

PART 3
Church

CHAPTER 11

Will Christianity Really Disappear in Three Generations?

AFTER MY BOOK *Sticking Points* was published, I hosted a webcast and included three leading writers and thinkers in the generational field. Someone recommended Monique, a virtual administrator, to handle all the details. Once the webcast was over and we wrapped up all the particulars, she asked her own questions about generational differences. When she mentioned she was a dedicated Christian, I told her I was working on this book.

She paused and then said, "I've heard the church is going to disappear in three generations."

That didn't surprise me, since it's related to the first question people ask when I mention anything regarding the spiritual life of the generations.

How bad is it?

We've heard that this will be the last Christian generation if we don't do something *now*. Ten years ago my mother-in-law, who lives with us, gave me material she had ordered on how to teach a Christian worldview to our children. She told me she had heard an interview with someone who claimed that unless we do something drastic, most of our children will leave the church, and ours will be the last generation of the Christian era. She told me she didn't know if it was marketing overstatement or really true, but she loved her grandkids and wanted to make sure we were teaching them everything they needed to know, just in case.

She's not the only one who wonders if the doomsayers are right. Over the last sixty years Christians have witnessed the shifts in thinking that we've been discussing throughout this book and watched how those shifts have affected their children and grandchildren. They've seen the Christian consensus in the United States and Canada break down. They've watched their country become more liberal on social issues. They've heard news reports that atheists and agnostics are now as numerous as Catholics and Baptists. For decades, they've heard ministers warn that the United States is going the way of Europe—plenty of large churches with lots of empty pews. And so they wonder if those rumors are true.

Before we look in the next two chapters at concerns about the future of North American churches, we need to focus on larger concerns about the future of *Christianity*. It's fair to ask: Should we worry about the end of Christianity as we know it? Is the church heading toward a massive decline? Will we lose an entire generation?

Take heart. My answer to Monique—and to all the others who are concerned over the state of Christianity—is this: no, Christianity is not going to disappear.

Why Christianity Won't Disappear

Let's look at two reasons why Christianity isn't dead or dying.

Reason #1: The Research Doesn't Bear It Out

I get why people are confused—the statistics that get thrown around are complicated. We have heard that most people in the United States believe in God: about 80 percent are Christians, and 40 percent are born-again evangelicals.[1] So when we see outspoken atheists on the bestseller list and leading talk shows, and when we read that Millennials are five times more likely to have no religious affiliation, we freak. Everything in this paragraph is true, but it's also misleading because it doesn't tell the whole story. That's why it's helpful to walk through what the surveys show is going on with religion, Christianity, and the church.

Here's the bottom line:

It is not as bad as we've heard, but it was never as good as we thought. And it's declining, especially with the Millennials.

First, the good news: it isn't as bad as we've heard. Christianity is not going away.

PEOPLE BELIEVE IN GOD, AND MOST STILL CLAIM TO BE CHRISTIAN.
In 1944 Gallup surveyed Americans and asked them if they believed in God. Ninety-six percent said they did. When Gallup asked the same question in 2011, 92 percent said they believed in God.[2] In addition, in 2014, 75 percent told Gallup their religious preference was Christian.[3]

PEOPLE STILL CLAIM TO GO TO CHURCH.
With the worry that the United States is turning into Europe, we might think that church attendance has dropped by half in

the last two generations. Instead, according to the General Social Survey, the percentage of people who say they go to church has been stable the past forty years: 40 percent in 1972, and at 30 percent for the last two decades.[4] Gallup's numbers are even higher. In 2014, 53 percent of Protestants and 45 percent of Catholics claimed to attend church at least monthly. Eight in ten claimed to attend occasionally.[5]

THE UNCHURCHED ARE LESS NEGATIVE TOWARD CHRISTIANITY THAN WE HAVE HEARD.

Many of the stereotypes Christians believe about the unchurched aren't true. Barna discovered in a recent survey that more than 25 percent of them *are* seriously interested in faith, and nearly two-thirds have generally positive perspectives on issues of faith.

Here's more of what Barna learned about unchurched adults:

> - Twenty-one percent are born-again Christians.
> - Twenty-one percent are Pentecostal or charismatic Christians.
> - Twenty-three percent say they are "absolutely committed" to Christianity.
> - Twenty-six percent say they are currently on a quest for spiritual truth.
> - Thirty-four percent describe themselves as "deeply spiritual."
> - Forty-one percent "strongly agree" that their religious faith is very important in their life today.
> - Fifty-one percent say they are actively seeking something better spiritually than they have experienced to date.
> - Sixty-two percent consider themselves to be Christian.
> - Sixty-five percent define themselves as "spiritual" people.[6]

Finally, don't lose sight of Millennials who are doing great things for God's Kingdom. Recently, *Christianity Today* ran a lead story on "33 Under 33"—Millennial leaders who are working to further the cause of Christianity. The publication found people like Trip Lee, the "hip-hop theologian"; Nabeel Qureshi, the "ex-Muslim evangelist"; and Lila Rose, the twenty-five-year-old "pro-life headline maker." The article gained such momentum that the magazine asked its readers to send in the names of other Millennials—and was inundated with names. The magazine ran two online follow-ups to the original article. As the editors waded through the hundreds of names, this is what they discovered:

> Ever since Paul began training Timothy in the faith, every generation has had to look to the next to carry the gospel to the ends of the earth. Today, as American Christianity faces declining affiliation, intense public debates over religious freedom, changes in the family structure, and technological advances, millennial Christians have already picked up the baton.[7]

We need to turn the panic meters off. When we hear those scary statistics about religion, which often seem contradictory or confusing, we need to find a more accurate picture, because it's not as bad as we have heard, and it was never as good as we thought.

Although the good news is that it's not as bad as we have heard, there is more to the story: it was never as good as we thought, and it's declining, especially with Millennials. So that we can have a better grasp of what's going on, let's go back through the three points of good news above and see what else the accompanying studies tell us.

MAY DEFINE "GOD" DIFFERENTLY.

The first point is that most Americans believe in God and claim to be Christian—*but* the rest of the story is that many define

"God" differently, and Millennials' numbers are lower than the other generations'.

Most believe in God and claim to be Christian, but that never has translated into an equal number of "believers" (75 percent) following the teachings of Christ or attending church (even at Easter or Christmas). Many of us fooled ourselves into thinking the United States was a nation of Christians because most people selected "Christian" on surveys and had a high regard for Christian morality, the Bible, and the church.

While most people believe in God and claim to be Christians, many do not believe in the God Jesus believed in. In 2008, the massive American Religious Identification Survey found that 70 percent claimed to believe in a personal God, and 12 percent believed in a higher power who isn't personal (deistic).[8] Gallup admits that when they offer alternatives to yes or no for "Do you believe in God?" belief in God is lower than 92 percent.[9]

You'll remember from chapter 8 that emerging adults, ages eighteen to twenty-eight, have been less religious than teenagers and older adults. While 94 percent of those over thirty told Gallup they believe in God, only 84 percent of eighteen- to twenty-nine-year-olds said they believe. There has been little change in the last forty years regarding how often younger adults pray, whether they believe in God or in the accuracy of the Bible, and how important they think religion is, but none of them were as strong as most of us thought.[10] For example, Ed Stetzer discovered that 34 percent of the unchurched, ages twenty to twenty-nine, do not believe Jesus died and came back to life.[11] But an even bigger change over the last three generations is that many who believe in Jesus also believe in aspects of other religions as well.[12]

THERE ARE FEWER EVANGELICALS THAN WE THOUGHT.

In the second point we learned that people still claim to attend church—*but* the rest of the story is that the number of evangelicals is much smaller than we thought, and Protestant numbers have dropped significantly.

It's shocking to many that evangelicals are at best less than half of the 40 percent figure we have heard for years. More likely, we are less than a quarter of that number. That's 22 million (7 percent) to 62 million (20 percent), rather than 124 million (40 percent). Where did the 40 percent number come from? That's how many people throughout the years have told Gallup they are "born again."

How could surveys be off by that much? Because when people who claim to be born again are asked additional questions, many of them reveal that their beliefs are different from those of orthodox Christianity. Gallup acknowledges the challenge of defining "evangelical" and "born again." Some of their surveys try to better define "evangelical" by asking whether people believe the Bible is the actual Word of God or have tried to encourage someone to believe in Jesus Christ. When they ask those who claim to be born again those same two questions, the numbers drop to 22 percent.[13] In other words, the label "born again" has misled us into thinking evangelicals are a much bigger group than they actually are.[14] So when people come across the more accurate numbers, they understandably freak out.

Not only are evangelicals a smaller group than most think, but Protestant influence in the United States has also dropped. In the 1950s, 71 percent claimed to be Protestant, whereas in 2014, only 50 percent did.[15] Moreover, young people attend church less than the previous generations did at their age because they marry and have children later.[16]

THE UNCHURCHED ARE LESS OPEN THAN BEFORE.

Finally, in the third point we saw that the unchurched are more open than we have thought—*but* the rest of the story is that they are less open than they were previously.

As we will see later in this chapter, far more people claim no religious affiliation (called "the Nones"), and there is a growing frustration that evangelicals are rigid, rule oriented, and unloving to people who think differently than they do.[17] The Nones are not spiritual "seekers." *Eighty-eight percent* answered no to the question, "Are you looking for a religion that would be right for you?" Even though for decades churches have focused their outreach on bringing spiritual seekers into a worship service, the unchurched don't see the church as positive, so they won't come in the front door.

Ed Stetzer found that "more than 70 percent of the older unchurched seemed turned off by religion compared to 60 percent of the younger set."[18] He points out that we are racing against the clock, so to speak, before the unchurched young people lose interest in organized religion.[19] Because they aren't spiritual seekers and aren't as positive about the church, we can't expect them to return to church in the same way the Baby Boomers did. That means if many of them do come, it will be through relationships, not through the front door.

Reason #2: Jesus Said It Won't

In Matthew, we see Christ's plan for his church:

> "What about you?" [Jesus] asked. "Who do you say I am?"
>
> Simon Peter answered, "You are the Messiah, the Son of the living God."
>
> Jesus replied, "Blessed are you, Simon son of Jonah, for this was not revealed to you by flesh and blood,

but by my Father in heaven. And I tell you that you
are Peter, and on this rock I will build my church, and
the gates of Hades will not overcome it." (Matthew
16:15-18, NIV)

Death itself (Hades) can't stop the church. God promises
to fulfill his mission from generation to generation. He works
through and sometimes in spite of us, but he is always working
to make his Kingdom come and his will be done on earth as it
is in heaven.

So no, we aren't even close to being one or two or three generations away from extinction. Well-meaning Christians pounce
on one statistic, yank it out of context, and shout doomsday
warnings to motivate people to do something *now*! Then, as my
mother-in-law experienced, those inaccurate statistics take on a
life of their own as they get passed from one blog or sermon to the
next until we've heard them so much we think they must be true.

But overstating the problem is essentially screaming, "Fire!"
in a theater. You get a lot of people trampled. They get asphyxi-
ated, not from the smoke but from somebody crushing their
lungs. Churches don't do well when they're panicked. Panic is
useful for escaping immediate dangers but makes us stupid in
planning for the long term. We overreact to the small things,
miss the big things, and do the wrong things. How many of us
have experienced that?

"We're losing our young people!" someone shouts. So we
change around the worship service. Younger people don't have
that much money, so when we tick off some of the big givers
with our new worship, we panic again and lurch back the other
way to try to make them happy—"Throw in more hymns; we
are losing our best donors!"

We tend to do our worst work when we're panicked. So let's

not yell, "Fire!" and instead realize that Christianity isn't going away. But the world we live in *is* significantly changing.

What *Should* We Worry About?

The worst thing about panicking over Christianity's potential disappearance is that it sidetracks us from three challenges that we really *do* need to worry about.

Challenge #1: We Have to Connect with Five Generations

We need to worry about five generations. We've never had to deal with five generations simultaneously, and we are lost.

The church's biggest challenge right now is generational for two reasons.

First, so many of our fights are generational, even though we call them other things—worship wars, attractional versus missional strategies, large churches versus small churches, verse-by-verse or topical teaching. Every one of them is defended with Scripture as the true approach, even though how we interpret the Bible regarding each of these issues depends on our generational lenses. We think we are arguing about other things, when they are often generational.

Second, we have to figure out how we will handle five generations. For example, how do we reach the younger generations now that people are living thirty years longer and don't appreciate that we no longer offer the worship styles they are used to? Last week I discussed the challenges of negotiating different church music styles with people from three different churches. They all struggle with how to reach and retain other generations without driving away the people who like the music the way it is. (We'll talk more about getting generations to work together and handling transitions in the next two chapters.) Dealing with five generations is now the biggest issue churches face, regardless of denomination.

Challenge #2: The Nones Are Growing

The Nones have been big news over the last few years. In recent surveys we've discovered that more and more people are identifying themselves as having no religious affiliation. In a 2014 survey the Pew Research Center found that 22.8 percent of Americans—including 35 percent of Millennials—are Nones, the highest percentages Pew has ever polled.[20]

But so much of what people hear about the Nones is sensationalistic, like yelling, "Fire!" in the theater again. So let me quickly give you a more accurate picture of the Nones than what you may get from the news.

First, the Nones are getting larger. In the 1930s and '40s, only 5 percent claimed to be Nones, and they were mostly atheists and agnostics.[21] By 1990, the number had barely risen to 7 percent. But then it almost doubled by 2008 (15 percent) and increased to 22.8 percent by 2014.[22]

Second, the dramatic jump in the Nones does not mean that the younger generations are suddenly rejecting Christianity. In the past, people who didn't ever plan to be involved in church still selected "Christian" as their category. Many people in the past were Nones but didn't answer surveys that way because not being Christian carried a social stigma. Today more people feel comfortable saying they aren't Christian. Yes, more people are not connected with a church now, but it's not as sudden or scary as it looks, because there never were as many Christians as surveys indicated.

The rise of the Nones is also not as significant as the headlines make it seem, because 3.5 million people called themselves Nones but attend church weekly. They just don't want to be labeled. Twenty-seven percent of the Nones attend church between monthly and a couple of times a year.[23]

Third, most Nones are not atheists, although I've seen blogs misrepresent them that way. As I said earlier, the number of atheists and agnostics has barely risen in forty years, even though they receive more attention today. In 2012, the Pew Research Center found that two-thirds of Nones say they believe in God (68 percent). Twenty-one percent admit that they pray every day. "In addition, most religiously unaffiliated Americans think that churches and other religious institutions benefit society by strengthening community bonds and aiding the poor."[24]

But some things do worry me about the Nones. If we want to reach this group, we will have to change how we do outreach. As I mentioned earlier, 88 percent of Nones are not looking for a church to join. Although they think churches do good things in society, they think churches are too messed up to hold much value for them personally. Pew Research Center's report describes, "Overwhelmingly, they think that religious organizations are too concerned with money and power, too focused on rules and too involved in politics."[25] As we said, they will not come to our churches and find us. We will have to meet them and engage them in spiritual conversations where they are.

My second worry is that more Millennials are Nones. One of the biggest reasons the Nones are growing rapidly is that only 11 percent of Traditionalists are Nones, compared to 35 percent of Millennials. As Traditionalists die, Millennials increase the numbers of Nones.[26] In their twenties, people dip in their beliefs. And it's true that the Millennials are more willing to be open about not having a religious affiliation than previous generations. But the fact that they are more comfortable means that far more people think they don't need organized religion or the church. When it comes to the Nones, less hand wringing that the United States is no longer a "Christian nation" and more focus on reworking the way we reach people would show better results.

Don't get me wrong: doing things to bring people in the front door will still work, but only for an increasingly smaller audience. And it won't work for fifty-six million Nones.

Challenge #3: The Millennials Who Have Left the Church May Not Come Back

My writing collaborator and I put together most of this book while occupying a corner table at a local Smashburger restaurant (which has great onion strings, by the way). We had spent so much time there that the entire staff got to know us. One afternoon, the manager, Veronica, asked how the book was coming along. She said she reads business books, so we talked about my first book, *Sticking Points*. When I told her this book was a look at the spiritual lives of the generations, she lit up and told us that her grandmother was a devout Catholic. Her mother had been raised Catholic, but when she became an adult, she worked on weekends, got away from the church, and never raised Veronica to know or understand her faith.

"My mother knows how to pray because my grandmother taught her and practiced it herself," Veronica said. "But my mother wasn't that interested, so she didn't teach me. I was baptized, and we went to church from time to time when I was little, but I don't remember any of it."

Veronica could be the poster child for what many young people are experiencing. Their parents knew the faith but chose to step away. They may have baptized their children, as Veronica's mother did, but they didn't practice any religion at home. So when the next generation grew to adulthood, they didn't have the foundation their parents did.

"I want to believe, but I grew up without it, so I haven't really missed it," she admitted. But then she paused. "Except when bad things happen, you know? I didn't think I believed, but after my grandfather died last year, I missed it. When he died—he's the man who raised me—I wanted to pray, but I thought, *I don't know how to pray; I don't know what to say.* I don't have the right to pray—even though I really wanted to. Since I haven't had much to do with God until now, why do I think I can just call on him when I need him? I feel hypocritical about it."

The Millennials aren't opposed to religion. At this point in their lives, at least, they are apathetic toward it. One recent survey asked 1,200 emerging adults, "What Is Really Important in Your Life?" and allowed participants to fill in the blank. Only 13 percent listed any type of spirituality.[27]

Veronica illustrates this. She told me she wasn't raised to believe that faith could be a vital part of her life, so she doesn't think of it that way. Although Veronica baptized her son, who is now four, and takes him to his catechism classes, she admits that she feels uncomfortable because she doesn't understand any of what he's learning.

If we are going to help Millennials to come or come back to church, we need to understand why the Millennials, like Veronica, don't come now. Here are five reasons.

1. MILLENNIALS HAVE LESS PATIENCE WITH INSTITUTIONS.

As we've discussed, Millennials don't trust institutions—that includes the church. Many Millennials claim to love Jesus but want nothing to do with the church. They see the hypocrisy and scandals and consider the church untrustworthy and irrelevant.

The other side is that the Nones may not be comfortable in church since they didn't grow up in it. Veronica admits that she still attends church on Easter and Christmas and sometimes with her family, but she feels awkward and out of place.

"It's embarrassing and makes me feel uncomfortable," she told me. "The whole time I think, *Oh God, get me out of here. If you love me, get me out of here!*"

"That's sort of a prayer," I joked. "But why is it embarrassing?"

"I don't know what to do. I don't know the songs or when to stand, all that stuff."

For her, it's easier to think about spiritual things outside of institutional religion. She's not opposed to learning more, but church is a big barrier to overcome, even though her husband wants to go and she wants her son to learn about faith.

2. MILLENNIALS ARE LESS LIKELY TO BE MARRIED.

When the Baby Boomers were in their twenties, it was more unusual to be single. But with the Millennials, it's more unusual to be married. Only the shifts in thinking we've discussed have greater impact on our churches than this point.

The proportion of men who are married in their twenties is half of what it was three decades ago. This is because 1) a third of people in their thirties and early forties are single or divorced, which is almost double what it was in 1971; and 2) the proportion of the US population who have never married has risen. In 1960, 9 percent of adults ages twenty-five and older hadn't married. By 2012 that had more than doubled to 20 percent. It's not going back down any time soon.[28]

Single people are less likely to attend church than they were in the seventies. Robert Wuthnow suggests that *nearly all* of the drop in attendance by Xers and Millennials, compared to when the Boomers were emerging adults, is explained by the fact that while married Millennials come as much as the Boomers did in their twenties, Xer and Millennial singles no longer come as much as Boomers did.[29] Churches know what to do with married people but have struggled to understand and relate with those who have never married or are divorced.

"Never married" no longer means just single, as we covered in the last chapter. About 24 percent of never-married Americans ages twenty-five to thirty-four cohabited in 2013.[30]

Millennials and Gen Xers believe their sex lives are their decision and not the church's—or anyone else's—business. And because the church overall isn't good at welcoming those who cohabit without approving of their behavior, young adults who live together often don't feel comfortable in church. Ed Stetzer discovered that two out of three divorced people and those living together feel their lifestyle would not be accepted at most Christian churches.[31] While most of those who are unchurched believe that the church is generally helpful to society, less than half of those who cohabit agree.[32]

We conservative Christians are making welcoming someone without approving of their behavior harder than it needs to be. We follow Jesus—who loved and welcomed *all* people without ever compromising his beliefs. We must first love those who are living together and then later teach them about why God is such a fan of marriage. If we don't love those who cohabit, we won't be able to communicate with potentially half of the young people out there.

3. MILLENNIALS ARE WAITING LONGER TO HAVE KIDS.

People are having fewer children and having them later. According to the US Census Bureau, the Traditionalists had 3.7 children, but by the mid-1970s, the Boomers were having 2, where the average has stayed ever since.[33]

I can't overstate how much these two trends—fewer and later marriages and fewer and later children—have rocked and will continue to rock the church. Marriage and children bring people to church. Rodney Stark and Byron Johnson of Baylor University wrote in the *Wall Street Journal* that recent research "confirms if people do not marry, and if they do not have children, there is a real decline in church attendance—a finding that is particularly striking among the poor and less educated."[34]

Researcher Robert Wuthnow agrees. In the past forty-five years, he suggests, the profile of nonattenders has changed. In the early seventies, both those who attended church and those who didn't were married and had children, because married people were more common than singles. Today, the typical church attender is married with kids, and the typical nonattender is single without kids.[35]

The church no longer mirrors society, but we haven't noticed. We know how to reach married people with children, but there are fewer of them and more singles, so church attendance is struggling. That also explains why fewer men come to church, especially younger ones. Almost twice as many unmarried twenty-something women attend than men, and while attendance goes up as women get older, it doesn't get any better for men.[36] That has huge implications for young women who look to church for Christian men to marry, because that gap is bigger today.

What is your church doing to help emerging adults grow spiritually, especially the males? How will your church learn from other churches that serve singles effectively?

4. MILLENNIALS THINK CHRISTIANS ARE TOO JUDGMENTAL.

This may be the biggest challenge for the future. As you may recall, the new and unsustainable way Millennials make moral decisions leads many to believe that individuals determine what is right or wrong for themselves as long as they don't hurt anyone else and that it's wrong for one person to impose morality on other people. It's arrogant for individuals to apply their moral standards to everyone, in every culture and every situation. The greatest sin, according to this thinking, is to judge someone else.

Churches that teach orthodox views of right and wrong—the

ones Christians have accepted for centuries—are turning off our own young people. Ed Stetzer reported that a significant number of early emerging adults who dropped out of church for at least a year did so because they thought church members seemed judgmental or hypocritical. The research shows people no longer view Jesus as a strict judge but as someone who simply forgives and represents love.

We must say what the Bible says. If we believe God knows what is best for us, then his instructions are precious gifts. If we believe God is smart enough to be in charge of the universe, then we can be confident his commandments tell us how to live our lives in the real world because they tell us what kinds of moral choices he will bless and empower. That's why the first thing we must do is explain why the commandment makes sense before we say everyone should obey it.

5. MILLENNIALS ARE TURNED OFF BY CHRISTIANS IN POLITICS.

Republican, Democrat, and Independent: it doesn't matter what political party or generation we belong to, we're all less conservative than we were twenty years ago. But Millennials and Nones in particular vote overwhelmingly Democratic. Our culture has become politically charged, and that polarization has seeped into our churches so that everything becomes Republicans versus Democrats. Two out of three Nones think religious institutions are too involved in politics, but so do 40 percent of those who claim a religious affiliation—and remember, both groups think churches are too into power.[37]

I respect your freedom of speech. I think Christians ought to be salt and light in every area, including politics. But we need to adjust how we communicate, because the growing divide between red and blue is not the focus of the gospel, and it is pushing people away from Christianity. Because so many of the Nones are Democrats, many researchers believe they are less rejecting religion than rejecting equating Christianity and conservative politics. They would rather not be labeled by denomination or even as Christian, because they think religious institutions have missed the point. We need to start listening to where they think we've got our priorities out of whack.

Conservative Christians are predominantly Republican.[38] That's why they need to be careful what they say (and how they say it) on Facebook or blogs. Who would have thought that our belief in Jesus isn't turning people off as much as belief in the Republican platform? (Sadly, I know a lot of dedicated Christians who can't tell the difference between the two and seem to put more energy into "restoring a Christian America" than into growing the Kingdom of God.)

In 2008, the Obama campaign surprised the nation by unleashing the power of social media to raise money and elect candidates through true grassroots mobilization. But by 2012 people on both sides of the political divide were worn out by how politicized and nasty social media became in each election cycle. During the 2012 presidential campaign, one out of five social media users unfriended people on Facebook and other social networking sites because they were tired of the political rants.[39] My son Max found an add-on for Facebook that turned any political comment into pictures of puppies and kittens.

Throughout the book I've stressed listening first, starting with the "why" rather than the commandments, and showing kindness and understanding to people who misunderstand Christianity. But in the last presidential election, most of the comments from Christians I read online didn't do those things. I know the technology is new, but the intensity (and meanness) with which many conservative Christians defend their political beliefs online puts up a big billboard that says to Democrats,

Don't come to my church. We communicate that we have nothing in common.

I get it; it's impossible for anyone, religious liberals or conservatives, to keep faith out of politics. But that creates a danger when the megaphone that is social media amplifies the desire for a Christian nation more than the desire for Christ himself. We cannot afford to misunderstand how big a turnoff mixing politics with religion is to those we are trying to reach with the Good News.

Be Good, Feel Good, Live Your Life (God Is Watching) Is the Real Worry

Throughout this book, at the base of one challenge after another, we find the same hacked Christianity we examined in chapter 7. The increase in the Nones; the changing attitudes toward marriage, sex, and moral judgment; and the feelings that churches are too judgmental, rules based, and caught up in politics lead back to Be Good, Feel Good, Live Your Life (God Is Watching).

We're going to have to deal with it. This may be the most important message of this book. Christian Smith, whose research introduced us to this hacked form of Christianity, wonders if the church can handle it if the Millennials come back:

> Returning to church as full-fledged young adults
> with children in tow—yet having spent a decade
> or two forming their assumptions, priorities, and
> perspectives largely outside of church—they may very
> well bring to the churches of their choice motives,
> beliefs, and orientations difficult to make work from
> the perspective of faithful, orthodox Christianity. The
> phrase "consumer-oriented" comes to mind. The burden
> then placed on the tasks of serious Christian formation,

education, and discipleship can be weighty. One has
to wonder whether such church returnees may not be
shaping the church more than the church shapes them.[40]

I don't think there's any question that they will shape the
church more unless we get ready. And the only way to do that is to
understand. We're poised to lose a good chunk of the Millennials,
not because they don't want God, but because they don't want Be
Good, Feel Good, Live Your Life (God Is Watching).

I never worry that Christianity will disappear, but I am terrified that the Millennials who grew up in the church aren't significantly more orthodox in their theology than those who didn't.
The commandments of Jesus make sense only if the God of Jesus
makes sense. If we don't believe in the God Jesus believed in, we
can't live the kind of life Jesus lived.

The God Jesus believed in is amazing and beautiful, and this
little, wimpy, shrunk-down god of Be Good, Feel Good, Live
Your Life (God Is Watching) that has taken over is boring. I
don't blame Veronica and all the others for saying, "I don't get it."
Because Be Good, Feel Good, Live Your Life (God Is Watching)
isn't God. If we don't do anything else, we've got to show people
the difference between the wimpy god of hacked Christianity
and the God of glory revealed in the Bible.

So I'm not scared that the church is going to go out of exis-
tence in three generations. But I am terrified that if we don't
show people the difference, the churches that will be left won't
be worth having.

CHAPTER 12

Why Won't Younger People Come to My Church?

I wrote in chapter 2 that I first learned about generational differences at church. But I didn't mention that's where I learned firsthand how brutal they can be.

I was a part-time youth pastor while attending college. During my first year at the church, I led a summer youth camp, and we experimented with some newer approaches like integrating music, preaching, video clips, stage props, and decorations to create powerful chapel services. Many of the youth responded by deciding to become Christians, and everyone returned home with new excitement.

Once a quarter, I preached on Sunday mornings, and the week after we had returned from camp, it was my turn to speak. So I preached part of the sermon that I'd given at camp about moving from religion (focusing on believing the "right" doctrines and obeying the "right" commands) to pursuing a relationship with God. I also described five reasons why the younger generation faced greater pressures in their spiritual lives than the previous generations had. Finally, I explained why a number of our young people had made commitments at that camp to follow Christ—because we were using different methods, even though it was the same message.

To my surprise, not only did the five who had been baptized at camp come forward at the end of the sermon, as we had planned, but another four adults from the congregation did as well.

That service thrilled me because it seemed these new communication approaches and a greater focus on a personal relationship with Christ could impact not only young people but also the other generations. It felt like a confirmation that we were on the right track: we could communicate differently without altering the message.

My excitement ended abruptly that evening.

I was well aware of the senior minister's growing frustration with both my style and my approach. He had come out of the corporate world and wore a suit and tie to the office while I wore blue jeans and tennis shoes. He was especially concerned that I was not teaching enough doctrine because I wasn't following the six-year Sunday school cycle the church had used for decades. He thought I brought in too much psychology rather than just teaching the Bible.

Our church still held Sunday evening services, so that night, when the senior pastor got up to preach, he announced that instead of continuing his sermon series, he was changing the topic to address my misguided psychology from the morning's message.

He went through my sermon point by point. Each time he would say, "Boys and girls, it is misguided and unbiblical when Haydn says that . . . ," and then he'd explain why I was wrong.

Where I explained that increasing television consumption and decreasing attention spans called for greater variety to hold people's attention, he explained that the old methods worked just as well, and we weren't called to entertain.

Where I explained that because people were marrying later but experiencing puberty earlier, he said that sexual urges had not changed and that this kind of psychological theory only gave young people an excuse to mess around.

Where I explained that if we wanted to keep the newest generation in the church, we could not expect them simply to accommodate our traditional ways, he said there were no such things as generational differences.

By today's standards my "cutting edge" points were as edgy and radical as the *Dukes of Hazzard* or *Starsky and Hutch*. But the senior minister felt they were heretical.

When he finished, he shut his Bible and put his notes in his pocket. Then he walked down the center aisle, out of the sanctuary, through the lobby, and into the driver's seat of the car his wife had parked by the door. They drove off, leaving seventy stunned people in the sanctuary.

One of the elders offered a closing prayer and ended the service. Shocked, my wife and I stayed in our pew while people encircled us, telling us how sorry they were, that they didn't agree with him, and that they thought he was just jealous because so many people had responded to the sermon that morning.

But one godly and committed woman, Lola, who was also my landlord, said, "He's right, you know. The most important thing we can do is teach the Bible and preach salvation so people don't go to hell. Psychology won't save people."

As I sat there, I wondered how what had started as such a marvelous day of confirmation had turned into a scary movie.

A week later, after the elders sorted everything out, the senior minister apologized to me in front of the congregation. I knew, though, that I should start looking for another job, because it was only a matter of time before our views on how to relate to the different generations would lead us into conflict again.

Why Won't Young People Come to My Church?

People care about their churches, and most of us realize that the question is not *whether* we will need to reach the younger generations but *when*. So unless your church has already addressed the shifts we saw in the last chapter and started reaching younger generations, you have likely been involved in conversations about why younger people don't come to your church or why the children who grew up in it don't stay.

If your church is slowly dying as it gets older, the conversations become more desperate: "If we don't start finding younger families, I don't see how our church can make it." These conversations take place in church hallways, around kitchen tables, and especially in board meetings, often month after month for years.

The senior minister at my church may have done all the wrong things to reach the younger generations, but he talked with me and the elders about it constantly. Sadly, the more he asked why younger people wouldn't come to the church, the less the board explored other options for responding to the new generation. Because the minister and some of the congregation thought generational differences were nonsense, they didn't see any reason to change.

Thirty More Years

Thirty years later, generational differences are still hard to navigate. How do you keep five generations happy? And since we're living longer, churches change more slowly because those in leadership positions remain in those roles longer than they ever have before. That people live thirty years longer than they used to is one of God's most amazing blessings. But it could also send millions of people to hell.

When people didn't live as long, churches would naturally adjust to each generation. But now that people attend churches for years longer, they usually prefer to keep things as they like them rather than adjusting to the preferences of the younger generations. (And because they tend to be the largest financial givers, they don't get as much pushback.) So the younger generations leave. When people died younger, churches changed sooner. That sounds crass, but it's the reality. God blessed us with longer lives, but until we start having better conversations, that blessing may unintentionally cause churches to miss millions of people by the time they finally do change.

The Most Important Thing Your Church Can Do

"Why won't younger people come to my church?" is the question I get asked 70 percent of the time.

"Because you are asking the wrong question," I respond. "That question traps you in a dead end that keeps the younger generations away."

Why is this a dead-end question? Because the question is about you and not about them. My youth ministry was with good people who wanted to save their church, but they wanted to save *their* church—the church they liked, the church they had grown up in, the church they were used to. So they asked questions that pushed the younger generation away. They spent countless hours trying to figure out what to do to reach more young people, but they asked the wrong question. They aren't unique. I see how stuck it makes congregations all the time.

If the dead-end question doesn't work, why is it so popular? Here are the reasons I see most often:

> People don't know the best question yet.
> Blame is easier. If the people we are trying to reach are the problem, God can't hold us accountable if we don't reach them.
> People are scared that if the next generation starts coming, they will want to change things until it won't feel like the same church anymore.
> They wonder if they will be pushed into a corner for the next twenty years. (Now that we're living so much longer, this is a real fear for so many people that I've dedicated the next chapter to it.)
> They usually have hurt feelings. They wonder what is so wrong with their church that the younger generations don't like it.
> They ask it when they feel guilty that they should reach the next generation, but they don't want to. We'll see that churches have three options for dealing with five generations, but they only see one. So they end up resenting the younger generations for making them feel pressured to give up the church they love.

In contrast, imagine how much more creative the conversations could be if you asked the best question: "What will we need to do differently to reach the younger generations?"

This question is the secret to better conversations because it gets the focus off you and onto the people you are called to reach. It pushes you to quit going in circles and complaining about what is wrong with them and to start talking about your options. It is the best question I know to help you determine what God has called your church to do. The most important thing you or your church can do to reach the younger generations is to stop asking the dead-end question and start asking the best question.

Three Options for Dealing with Five Generations

My first church had three options, but because some thought that generational differences didn't exist, they asked the dead-end question for years. It trapped them into talking about the only option that doesn't work. Over time, their own kids left, and they couldn't reach other young people. They missed out on a generation, and today that church is barely surviving.

It doesn't matter whether you're a paid minister, a lay leader, or someone who holds no leadership position—*everyone* who loves their church can help their church figure out what to do if they ask the best question and start conversations about these three options.

So let's look at the three options. When I consult with churches, I usually recommend the first, and sometimes the second, but never the third because it's the one that doesn't work.

OPTION #1: CHANGE THE CHURCH NOW.

This is the best option for most churches.

It's important to hear what people who never grew up in the church have to say, so research is invaluable (this book is one resource, but there are many other helpful generational resources). Since 30 percent of the unchurched used to go to church, don't forget the valuable resource that is (or was) sitting next to you in the services. Ask people of the younger generations who still attend if they've thought about leaving or why their neighbors or the people at work don't come. Or ask the younger people who stopped coming why they quit. You will also want to understand what churches that are reaching the younger generations in your community are doing. You can't always do exactly what they are doing, but you can uncover the principles that are working. Finally, when you are done with those, you might want to get some help sorting through everything you've learned, from a denominational resource or a consultant. They can often save you months of meetings as you try to determine your next steps.

When you understand what your congregation will need to do differently to reach the younger generations, you will be excited or scared (or likely both). It's easy to get carried away when we are dreaming about new ideas and possibilities. That's why we have to pause and ask, *Will we be able to do it?* It's funny that while I get hired by churches to help them figure out how to reach the younger generations, I spend more of our time helping them figure out if they are able to do it. It's a simple question that will start important conversations to move your church forward. Let's look at the possible answers.

Sometimes the answer is yes. The church is ready, they have the right staff and leaders and the right skills and structure, and it's just a matter of moving forward.

Sometimes the answer is no. I know what you're thinking: *Some consultant you are if you let churches see the need around them and then let them say no.* But some congregations don't want to change the way they do church; the people would just leave and find another church more like theirs used to be.

Sometimes the answer is no because the church doesn't have the skills. Their church staff may be skilled at leading a more traditional congregation but not know how to relate to the younger generations. I consulted with a church in the South whose godly senior minister desperately wanted to reach young families, but after watching him interact with people of different generations, it was obvious he was completely at ease with Boomers and Traditionalists but awkward with Xers and Millennials. He was a good man, used by God, but communicating with the younger generations would never be his strength, no matter how many conferences he attended. I've learned in business, as well as in churches, that there's nothing worse than taking a person out of a job they're really good at and putting them in a spot where they are only mediocre.

Most often the answer is not yet. The congregation isn't ready, they haven't talked about the right questions from this and the next chapter, or they don't have the right staff or structure. But they could in the future.

A couple of years ago I worked with a Methodist church whose average age was fifty-five and had only ten children attending. They were worried their church would eventually die unless they reached younger families. When a church three miles from theirs, which had been their size for years, doubled in size by reaching young families, some people in the congregation pushed for a gymnasium, which was promptly voted down by half the church.

They hired me to help them decide whether they should build a gymnasium. So for a day and a half, I interviewed the fine people on both sides of the issue and discovered that they understood how to get the money for the gymnasium more than they understood what it would take to fill it with children and young families. That's why I recommended they target Boomers and Traditionalists and grow old together.

The chairman of their board told me two years later that they went ahead and built the gymnasium because my questions pushed them to decide what kind of church they wanted to be and whether they were willing to make the changes to do it. They weren't ready then, but they were later.

OPTION #2: GROW OLD TOGETHER, AND . . .

It shocks a lot of people when I suggest to churches that they grow old together.

They can still serve the younger generations while focusing on the older ones. We need some churches to grow old together because as more churches target the younger generations, some of the older members will leave because they won't want to be in a younger church.

I'm not opposed to churches talking about their options and realizing they will not be able to make the transition toward a younger congregation. I *am* opposed to churches that think they're not growing old together when they are. All churches target generations; it's just that most churches do it unconsciously. The church I served as a youth minister clearly targeted Traditionalists, all the while insisting they wanted to reach younger people.

I'm also strongly opposed to churches that grow old together but don't care about or do anything for the other generations. Selfishness has no age limitations, and churches don't retire. That's why option two is "grow old together and . . ." The "and" is what the church determines God is calling them to do beyond flipping months on the calendar.

Churches that grow older together can make major contributions to the Kingdom if they start talking about how they will do it. Fortunately, there are a number of healthy ways they can:

> Target Baby Boomers and Traditionalists as I recommended to the church with the gymnasium blueprints.
> Start new churches or satellites with very different worship services and structures to reach the younger generations.
> Raise money from their Traditionalists and Boomers, the generations blessed financially beyond any in history, to fund reaching the next generation here and around the world.
> Send their people around the world to serve and lead.
> Then, before the church shrinks out of existence, hand

the keys to the building over to another church that is reaching younger people who don't have the money to buy it.

OPTION #3: PRETEND YOU CAN REACH ALL FIVE GENERATIONS.
This is the one approach that doesn't work, but it's the option I see most often. I never recommend it, because as we've seen, a church can't reach all the generations equally well. In my experience, churches that get stuck in this option use it to protect themselves. As long as they think they can reach all the generations, they don't have to talk about their fears that another generation will come in and change things. Hoping your church can reach everyone puts the focus on your church, not on the people you're trying to reach, and in no time you'll be asking the dead-end question again. Go young or grow old together—both benefit the Kingdom of God. Just don't fool yourself into thinking you can do both if you keep doing what you've been doing.[1]

What Do We Need to Do Differently to Reach the Younger Generations?
Here are some tips for reaching Xers and Millennials in your church.

What Do We Need to Do to Reach Gen Xers?
Generation X is the least understood and appreciated generation, squished between the much larger Baby Boomers and Millennials. Churches have paid far more attention to reaching Boomers and Millennials than they have to Xers. Generation X grew up in a difficult transitional time as the divorce rate jumped and "true for you but not for me" flipped them around. They responded to the flattening world economy by focusing on their own survival and success.

1. HELP XERS FIND FAMILY IN THE CHURCH.

Many Xers build a functional family from friends. While community is important to Millennials as well, it is an even higher priority for Xers. You may remember that cynicism is one of their spiritual temptations, which can cause them to withdraw. Recognize that many Xers see playing with their kids and talking with the neighbors as just as sacred as going to a Bible class, so don't evaluate their commitment based on how many programs they attend. Get to know what else they're doing outside the church. And avoid overprogramming that pulls them away from those key relationships. You may want to reevaluate your small group reproduction plans if you expect groups to divide or change membership every two years. Churches desperately need more groups—I get that. But many Xers want stability. So figure out how to balance the two needs.

2. DISCOVER WHETHER YOU NEED MORE INTERACTIVE WORSHIP.

Gen Xers have many subgroups, and they don't all respond to the same kinds of worship services. Many of them love the polished contemporary worship services that attracted the Baby Boomers. Because they grew up with the interactivity and engagement of the Internet, others prefer less polish and more spontaneity and interaction than the Boomers (who grew up on the televised variety show).[2] Some prefer smaller settings. Most expect greater transparency and more dialogue from their leaders—if not in the service, then definitely outside it. And except for those who seek liturgical styles, they engage when you have media.

3. SHOW HOW JESUS TAUGHT A BETTER WORLDVIEW THAN "TRUE FOR YOU BUT NOT FOR ME."

It's impossible to overestimate the generational impact of going into school with one worldview and coming out with another.

Whether they grew up in the church or know little about religion, all Gen Xers have to figure out how they will handle the demands to create their own identity and develop their own morality that resulted from this shift. As I said before, I don't think everyone in the church has to be an expert in the philosophical shift from confidence in science to "true for you but not for me." But if churches are still focused on proving science is wrong and constructing proofs for Christianity, they'll miss the questions the Xers are asking.

The good news is that Jesus came to bring us real knowledge about God. Help Generation Xers understand that knowing God is possible, and teach them how to have conversations with people of their own generation who don't buy it.

4. GET COMFORTABLE WITH TECHNOLOGY.

My wife and I argued for a year and a half over whether I should be allowed to bring my tablet computer to church. She maintained it was a bad example to people who might think I was messing around on the Internet rather than paying attention in the service. I told her that because it's a full computer, I have an immense library of commentaries and theological books loaded on it, which allows me to read along with the passages the minister reads in the sermon. Not until I asked five different Gen X ministers on our church staff to show her that they also used tablets during the services did she finally relent. (But she still rolls her eyes.)

Almost five to one, people of all generations still strongly prefer to read their print Bibles.[3] I'm in the minority. But in 2014, the third highest reason people gave for their increased Bible reading was "downloaded the Bible onto my smartphone or tablet."[4] It's a new world. I don't care on what platform someone reads their Bible—I just want them to read it. So get comfortable with technology.

5. GET OUT OF THE BUILDING.

Being the first generation to access backstories through the Internet and other news outlets, Generation X doesn't trust institutions, and that includes churches. I can't blame them either. They have seen too many religious leaders who have asked people to give sacrificially and then purchased extravagantly. They've heard Christians promise a relationship with God but then put all the emphasis on the church's programs. They know that Jesus taught us to love people, but they see churches stuck inside their four walls.

Some will visit church if they have a spiritual need, but far more will get involved in spiritual conversations with the people they meet in their daily lives. Xers are more likely to meet people from the church before they meet a church's programs. And they're more likely to respect a church program that goes outside of the building to serve in the community.

What We Need to Do to Reach Millennials

The most under-ministered-to part of the church is twentysomethings. We plan things for adolescents and then expect them to transition to the adult programs once they turn eighteen. And then we wonder why they drop out. While most churches would hang their heads if they had no youth ministry, few realize they need to have something for their twentysomethings. This is a critical time for emerging adults. And what they need most are others who come alongside and help them.

1. BECOME THE OLDER FRIEND.

Millennials need help navigating the scary and exciting emerging adulthood years. Of course you should put together programs at your church for twentysomethings, but that can't replace adults investing in them. When Barna Group asked unchurched Millennials what approach churches could take to draw them in, the approach religious skeptics rated highest (14 percent) was one in which the older people regularly connected with and shared life experiences with younger adults. Building relationships and learning about Jesus are two big reasons Millennials come and stay in church. In fact, Millennials who remain involved in church after their teen years are "twice as likely as those who don't to have a close personal friendship with an older adult in their faith community (59 percent versus 31 percent)."[5]

This idea of older people investing in the lives of emerging adults is a major practical point I have made throughout this book—one I cannot say enough. Because Millennials' lives are fluid and because they have to construct their own identities, they need people who have sorted it out already and can guide them along. So why does your church's youth ministry stop after high school simply because the public school system is structured that way? Why can't a couple of the youth leaders who worked with them in high school follow up on them after they scatter to college or the workforce?[6] That simple change alone would reduce the number who drop out of church in the years immediately after high school.

The only downside of assigning a few people to follow up after high schoolers graduate is that the rest of us might think, *Now we've got it covered.* But we need Traditionalists and Boomers to get involved in the lives of Millennials. The older generations have a lot to share with Millennials, even if they are not experts in theology or have messed up along the way. Millennials respond to authenticity, not perfection. They admire their parents even though they know their flaws up close. For example, I think divorced Boomers have a lot to say to Millennials about marriage. We need to tell stories of couples who waited to have sex until marriage and grew their love through faithfulness and commitment so Millennials believe it's possible in the real world.

But God can also use people who say, "If I could do it over again, I would have listened less to psychology and more to God. I could have saved myself a lot of heartache."

Whatever your story, share what you have learned about finding your identity in God with a generation whose identities come with some assembly required.

2. USE HUMOR.

In 2011, MTV conducted a study that found "humor is the new rock and roll" for the younger generations.[7] If you can be funny, you're in. Even though Tim Harlow, my minister, is now in his fifties (and has been coloring his goatee for the last ten years), he is still reaching Xers and Millennials. The church has grown from eight hundred to eight thousand over the last thirteen years. Back then he wore dress pants and a button-down shirt. Now he untucks his shirt and wears blue jeans. But he has always let loose his sarcastic sense of humor. Humor makes him seem younger than he is and connects him with the generation half his age.

It's important to remember that for Xers and Millennials, humor is edgier and more sarcastic and may not be your style. If something the younger generations say really bothers you, you should bring it up. But be slow to take offense or roll your eyes. These younger generations love humor, and they love to poke fun, so don't take everything so seriously!

3. HELP THEM UNDERSTAND THE WHYS BEHIND THE COMMANDMENTS.

Some experts call the Millennials "Generation Y," but I think it's more accurate to call them "Generation *Why?*" because Millennials want to know the why for everything. Their parents didn't say, "Because I said so!" nearly as much as the other generations did. Especially since they've grown up marinating in a morality that is contradictory, we need to share the reasons for

Scriptures' commands, the whys behind the whats. God's morality is not contradictory or random; he is great, and his goodness is brilliant, illuminating our path through life. He has good reasons for what he says. So share them.

4. TEACH DEEPER, AND DON'T SKIP THE HARD QUESTIONS.

Millennials are more secular, more liberal, more educated, and have more information available on their phones. Boomers wanted practical, pastoral, self-help application at church. "What does the passage mean to you?" became the stereotypical Bible study question. In contrast, Millennials want to know what it means as well as what it means about living in today's world. They want to go deeper. "One out of four (23 percent) chides the local church for inadequate teaching, claiming that 'the Bible is not taught clearly or often enough.'"[8]

A recent study found that 20 percent of church dropouts admit that "God seems missing from my experience of church."[9] I've mentioned a lot of statistics in this book, but I find this one to be the most shocking: *20 percent* of the twentysomethings who leave our churches think it's because God wasn't the main event. They think church skims the surface, and they want to go deeper.

They also think Christians don't talk about the hard questions. I filled in preaching at a church that was in the middle of a series on reasons to believe in Christianity. They assigned me reasons to believe the Bible is the Word of God. They also e-mailed me five sermon manuscripts from other ministers that all pretty much covered the same five classical arguments.

The sermons were fine, but they didn't take into account that people today have heard those classical arguments dissected at college or on PBS or the Internet. For example, they all gave great examples of where archaeology has proved the historical reliability of the Bible. But they didn't mention the archaeological discoveries that don't seem to corroborate details of Israel's conquest of the Promised Land, even though these are mentioned on many websites. So I went deeper and gave three of the classic arguments for believing in the reliability of Scripture and then skeptics' counterarguments. That surprised some lifelong Christians. But they relaxed when I countered the skeptics' counterarguments. I surprised folks again when I mentioned a couple of counterarguments skeptics make to the Christian counterarguments.

As you can imagine, I had some worried people come up to me after the service, concerned I would introduce doubts that people didn't have before. Plus, they feared that if Christians don't "prove" with airtight and unassailable arguments the truth of Christianity, we will lose a generation. But their fears and approach are two generations behind. Xers and Millennials ask different questions and have access to far more information. I mentioned that I saw some of the Millennials on their phones reading about the topics during the sermon. I thought at minimum I should acknowledge what they were looking at on their phones. We are naive if we think they've not been introduced to those doubts. Their friends and teachers bring them up, and they run into these challenges on the Internet all the time.

While I may have worried some Boomers, Xers and Millennials went out of their way to thank me. One guy who grew up in that church and had moved back after college said he had never heard anyone talk about what to do when skeptics had good counterarguments to the Christian counterarguments. He said he felt like college had weakened his faith with a thousand microscopic holes, and it helped him to know that other people knew both sides and still believed.

We don't protect our young people's faith by thinking they can't handle difficult intellectual challenges. We protect them by helping them *think through* the challenges. When is the last time you've heard the shifts of thinking we talked about in the first part of this book—hyperindividualism, overconfidence in psychology, "true for you but not for me," and the new morality—dealt with in a sermon? How are we supposed to protect the two new generations if they don't know what hit them? I love the way Dallas Willard says it: "When [Satan] undertook to draw Eve away from God, he did not hit her with a stick, but with an idea."[10] Be Good, Feel Good, Live Your Life (God Is Watching) is what we get when our young people don't understand Christian theology and wonder whether they can believe the teachings of Christianity are true.

Finally, since more than half of our teens will go to college, they need intellectual preparation. They need to know what philosophies and challenges to faith they will hear and how to deal with them. We have multiyear tracks in school systems called "college prep" so our kids will succeed academically, but few churches provide college prep for their intellectual and spiritual success. And don't forget their parents. They will need to know enough about what their kids will hear to be able to have helpful conversations or at least know when to call for help. What will your church put together to help both get ready for college?[11]

5. TARGET BE GOOD, FEEL GOOD, LIVE YOUR LIFE (GOD IS WATCHING). The real God startles us, draws close to us, and amazes us. The real God sweeps into our humdrum lives and sweeps us up into his multimillennial plan to restore all things to their intended order. The real God pushes us so far out of our comfort zones that we tremble, and then promises never to leave us or forsake us. He asks us to surrender our lives and then exchanges them for the eternal kind.

But most people think God is nice, supportive, and out of the way. Yawn.

We need to take on Be Good, Feel Good, Live Your Life (God Is Watching). If we found out that someone with a stolen identity worked in our preschool classroom, we would race to deal with it. There's an imposter working in the heads of our whole church, and we can't get there fast enough to deal with the hackers.

Reaching the next generation isn't easy; it never has been. Minister and novelist George MacDonald tackled this struggle to deal with the next generation 150 years ago. He encouraged his generation then with words that apply to us today:

> We have yet a work to do, my friends; but a work we shall never do aright after ceasing to understand the new generation. We are not the men, neither shall wisdom die with us. The Lord hath not forsaken his people because the young ones do not think just as the old ones choose. The Lord has something fresh to tell them, and is getting them ready to receive his message. When we are out of sympathy with the young, then I think our work in this world is over.[12]

CHAPTER 13

What Am I Supposed to Do Now That It Doesn't Feel like My Church Anymore?

IN THE LAST chapter we looked at what your church can do to reach Generation Xers and Millennials. But in this chapter I want to turn our attention to what the church can do to help Traditionalists and Baby Boomers. These privileged generations are the first to live thirty more years. But that creates struggles no other generation has had to face. It's easy to miss how hard this can be.

I had finished speaking to church leaders one Saturday morning regarding how to help people who still struggled with the transition from traditional to more contemporary services. Two couples in their late sixties hung around after everyone else had left. All four of them talked about how excited they were that their church was reaching younger people. Then they glanced at each other, and guilt spread over their faces. They began talking about how this didn't feel like their church anymore. They didn't relate to the worship music, and they weren't fans of small groups rather than Sunday school. They felt like everything was centered around the younger generations, but the younger generations didn't give much money. Their generation still paid the bills, but that seemed all the church needed them for.

One of the men said, "The previous senior minister was ten years older than me, but the new one is the age of my kids. Now I feel old every time I look at him, and I feel pushed off to the side when I had always been in the center of things." One of the women said, "We know that supporting the shift to a younger church was the right thing to do, but now that it's worked, we don't like the church. If I were looking for one, I wouldn't come here a second time." The other man said, "We're all healthy and going to be around for probably another fifteen years. That's a long time to not feel at home in your church. What are we supposed to do?" They all nodded.

Wow.

They said out loud what so many people think but won't say. I have found it to be one of the biggest reasons people ask the dead-end question and won't talk about the three options churches have in dealing with the younger generations (see pages 200–207). They're afraid that if they change to reach the younger people, the church they love will be lost. Or they're afraid it sounds selfish to say they are targeting Traditionalists and Boomers because they don't want to change their church. As a result they often find themselves in the most precarious place of all—thinking they are a church for all the generations and then watching their church decline.

We often make it harder than it needs to be by not understanding generational differences. We may dedicate forty meetings to discussing how to change our church to reach younger people. But how often do we talk about what's going to happen to Traditionalists and Boomers when we do? We need to start talking with Boomers and Traditionalists about their struggle to welcome the Xers and Millennials without feeling like they're losing their home, because our silence is making the changes much harder than they need to be. If people can't picture where they will fit in the new future, they will naturally resist change. But we're not even talking about it until people are understandably upset.

There's a second question we are not talking about that will have even greater impact on the religious lives of Baby Boomers and Traditionalists. The Boomers are such a huge generation that they've transformed every institution, and they're already transforming retirement. Financial services companies are spending millions of dollars on ads that portray them as beginning their next adventure rather than settling into traditional retirement, because these companies know that nothing turns Boomers off faster than making them feel old or irrelevant. Many of them have twenty or thirty years left in their second adulthood. What are they going to do with all that extra time? This additional thirty years is one of the greatest changes in the history of the human race. Shouldn't you and your church start talking about how you will help them figure it out?

The questions those two couples asked me are haunting. I gave them four very practical ideas for what they should do. But these ideas apply to any Baby Boomer or Traditionalist, whether they like their church or not:

1. Give your church back to Jesus.
2. Connect with Jesus if it doesn't feel like your church anymore.

3. Sign up for whatever Jesus has planned for your next thirty years.
4. Help your church figure out second adulthood.

1. Give Your Church Back to Jesus

People say, "I'm not happy with my church," all the time, so let's get this big question out of the way: *Should* we be happy at church? It's great when we are. I prefer to be. It isn't wrong or self-centered to miss the things you liked better about your church in the good old days. But it *is* impossible for a church to give every generation precisely what they want. That means it's unlikely you will ever be completely happy at your church.

And while we prefer to be happy, the reality is that it doesn't matter if we are happy with our church. Nowhere does the Bible talk about being happy at church. Frankly, Jesus really doesn't care that much if we are. He cares if we and our church are seeking first his Kingdom, and *then* he adds all the other things he wants to give us (see Matthew 6:33).

But we get that backward. We typically ask ourselves, "Do I like this church? Am I getting something out of this church? Do I feel good after going to this church?" While we're asking those questions, Jesus asks, "Is this church faithful to my message? Does it follow my example? Does it follow my great commission to go everywhere and preach the gospel?" He has a different agenda.

So give your church back to Jesus, and let him do what he wants with it. No matter which of the three options your church chooses, it's about what Jesus wants and not what you prefer. That's what aging gracefully rather than turning into "grumpy old men" is about—getting over ourselves and losing ourselves in people and purposes that matter. Church is a great place for losing ourselves, but it's a bad place for finding happiness. If you can't get that sorted correctly, church will make you grumpy.

You've probably seen grumpy older people and promised yourself you would not turn into them. Surprisingly, it's classic at church—so classic that Lyle Schaller, the grandfather of church consultants, wrote about them multiple times.[1] Maybe the grumpy group is a Sunday school class or small group. In one church I know, it's the RV club. They camp and complain all summer long together. These church complainers feed into each other's inability to let go of the past, kill many smaller congregations, and become a constant challenge to larger ones.

Then they pounce on any mistake the younger generations make and add that to their "ain't it awful" list. And the newer generations give them plenty to talk about because, let's be blunt, they will mess things up. Just as we did. So instead of criticizing and harrumphing, we can nudge the younger generations back to a better way. They will often listen if we can keep cool and bring a knowing wink and the humility of hard-won experience.

We will struggle to keep a civil tongue until we start focusing more on the future than the past. Giving our church back to Jesus means we trust he has something fresh to tell the younger generations, and we can now be excited about what's next for us even while we miss the way our church used to be.

2. Connect with Jesus If It Doesn't Feel like Your Church Anymore

The church plays a large role in our spiritual development and growth—but it doesn't play the only role. Ultimately, the church isn't responsible for your spiritual maturity: you are. You won't be able to stand in front of God at the end of your life and say, "Well, I would have grown in my faith, but I didn't connect with the worship music."

So we need to find ways to connect with God and take care of ourselves spiritually even when the church we attend no longer plays our favorite music or no longer has preaching that speaks to us the way it used to. Because I tend to be a person of many interests who can easily get involved in too many things, my wife found a bumper sticker for me that says, "Jesus is coming soon. Look busy." If the Boomers go into their second adulthoods with the same workaholic tendencies they've used throughout their careers, they will miss one of the real opportunities of greater time and financial independence: the freedom to develop their inner lives. After we leave the full-time workforce, we have time to engage more deeply in the spiritual disciplines that grow our souls and help us connect with God in more powerful ways than we've ever experienced. It would be a shame if, in the name of finding new meaning and significance, we got ourselves so busy for God that we couldn't enjoy getting to know God and his words to us in Scripture. Boomers can be so busy trying to make the world perfect that they can easily miss the one who already is.

Let's focus on connecting with Jesus when we no longer like the music, because it comes up far more than anything else when I speak or talk to church people. Music and worship services have been at the center of tensions between the generations for thirty years. If we can find practical ways to connect with Jesus even if it's not our music, we can apply those same practical ideas to anything else we don't like when our church changes.

Confession time: I haven't liked half of our church's music for the last four years. I love the band, and the vocalists have never been better. I've never been happier with how the worship leaders lead rather than perform. I know my music sentiment is a generational thing. I liked worship music ten years ago when it had less synthesizer and more guitar. But then again, I like seventies guitar rock much more than eighties synthesizer rock—even though I went to high school and college in the first half of the eighties. Worship songs have started using a lot more synthesizer, and it gets on my nerves pretty quickly.

Ironically, my twenty-five-year-old son, who is a music minister at a new church in Rhode Island, thinks my church's music is out of date. My church uses the contemporary worship songs that are most popular across the country. Recently when he was home for a visit, he told me, "I really love the sermons. But wow, I forgot how old school your style of music is." Twentysomething worship has a slower, often Americana feel, with more theologically rich lyrics. He told me that even if they do a "traditional worship song" (I think I choked when he called Matt Redman and Chris Tomlin songs traditional), they slow it down and change the arrangement. What Boomer ever thought they'd live long enough to hear contemporary worship music called "old school"?

Simply put, music isn't a right or a wrong thing; we use the tunes of the times to speak to people. This is a cultural thing. So who gets the music they like in worship services? That's easy— the people who don't attend. We need to play whatever music people who don't come to church relate to so that music doesn't get in the way of people hearing the Word of God. You are not the "target audience" for your church's music. It's not about you; it's about what speaks to the hearts of those who have not found a transforming faith. Hell's a lousy way to spend forever. And if we get all wound up about the music we prefer, we'll never get five generations into the Kingdom of God. Sometimes we need to be lined up by the Holy Spirit and poked right in the eyes like the Three Stooges. God just needs to whap us until we snap out of it and get focused on important stuff.

So what do you do if you just don't like the music? Well, my mother-in-law brings earplugs, and then if it's still too loud (as she thinks it is at my church), she holds her ears, too. If you don't like the music, you can still worship God by concentrating on the lyrics.

By the way, a lot of churches play their music too loud. I have a high-end stereo system, and it sounds better when I crank it. That's why the people who run the sound board at church keep turning up the volume. But the goal is worship, not high fidelity. So if it's too loud, let your staff know. And if they decide they're not going to do anything about it, then find a different place to sit, because often sound systems are spotty. Sound people make the music louder to cover the sanctuary's dead spots. You can ask the person running the sound system where those are. I never cease to be amazed by the people in my own church who sit right in front and then complain because the music is too loud. I want to say to them, "Well, the speakers are right above you. It's physics, not persecution."

We have to joke about music in church, because if we don't joke about it, we growl at each other. I asked church people in St. Louis who were still struggling with changes to their worship style to turn to the person next to them and say, "I hope you like the music in this church. And if you don't, buy a CD of the worship music you like." I wasn't joking. We have music players all over our homes, in our cars, on our phones. Technology makes it easy to get the music that reaches our hearts every day of the week. An hour at a worship service with music that is not to our taste won't kill us.

Finally, this doesn't have to be either/or. I've coached hundreds of worship ministers in contemporary churches to offer monthly hymn sings on Sunday nights. Nothing elaborate, just a piano and forty-five minutes of hymns. Many churches have special services for their teenagers who don't connect with the worship in the sanctuary, but we don't think to do that for their grandparents.

That's because we think of older generations as resisting the changes we need to make to reach the younger generations rather than as needing something different when the church changes.

While it is a privilege to live another thirty years, that creates bigger challenges than simply feeling like the church they loved is gone. The even bigger question is, What do the older adults do with their lives for the next thirty years? We don't even talk about it yet because we don't realize how big an impact is coming. The next two suggestions answer that bigger question.

3. Sign Up for Whatever Jesus Has Planned for Your Next Thirty Years

This is a news flash for many: emerging adulthood is the first of two new life stages now that we are living thirty years longer. The life stages used to be childhood, adolescence, early adulthood, adulthood, and old age. Their Boomer children were the first to face emerging adulthood, but the Traditionalists are the first generation to face the challenges of constructing another life after retirement. They have the health, the money, and the freedom to live another twenty or thirty active years after they finish their working years. Another twenty or thirty years means Traditionalists get almost another adult lifetime compared to earlier generations. Second adulthood has so changed the game that Traditionalists struggle to figure it out.

Ironically, the challenges of second adulthood sound a lot like the challenges of emerging adulthood. The older generations must also construct their identity, and they have the freedom and financial support to explore and experiment. They use that time to focus on their own values and interests rather than focusing primarily on earning a living and raising a family.

While the freedom sounds wonderful, both emerging adulthood and second adulthood can be confusing and overwhelming.

I argued for three chapters that we need to adjust our approach to help emerging adults figure it out. And generational intelligence tells us we must help these pioneers find their second adulthood identity in Christ. The leading experts on the Boomers reported that Boomers are becoming more spiritual in their later years.[2] The opportunity for churches is here. Research shows that people fifty and older are less stressed because they have less to prove.[3] So now they can turn their attention from success to significance. That makes them more open to shifting focus from the external to the eternal; from figuring out who they are to figuring out who God made them to be.

My friend Tim has signed up for whatever Jesus has planned for him for the next thirty years. We were supposed to talk about a class I'm teaching for one of his business clients next month, when I mentioned that I was writing this chapter. He grew excited and said, "Let me tell you my story."

Tim had worked in advertising and marketing throughout his career but then relocated to Chicago, where he opted to work part-time in the small-groups ministry at our church. But not long after, the church hired two full-time small-group ministers, so his part-time position was no longer needed. Instead of retiring, he found a part-time job doing marketing and sales outside of the church, but he wanted to serve in some significant, Kingdom way.

While attending a conference, he sat in on a session about the future of senior ministries, thinking that was something he could start at our church. As he listened to the speaker, he became more and more excited about the possibilities. The speaker summarized ideas from *Baby Boomers and Beyond: Tapping the Ministry Talents and Passions of Adults over 50* by Amy Hansen.

Tim bought the book and devoured it. He said it described exactly what he was going through.

"I didn't want to retire. I didn't want to join the seniors ministry and have only potlucks and overnight trips," he told me. "I wanted to find significant and meaningful service that would use the skills and experience I had." He ended up calling the author and volunteering to help her promote her book!

Tim shows that we can find an exciting second adulthood if we sign up for whatever Jesus has planned for our next thirty years. He canceled a purposeless retirement. He didn't assume he could figure out his new second adulthood identity, so he asked Jesus what he has planned. He looked for ways to use his skills as well as his gifts, and now he is busy helping the church figure out second adulthood.

If you are a Traditionalist or older Boomer, you can pioneer this new life stage and then help the church help this huge generation figure out second adulthood. You can start by doing what Tim did.

Cancel your purposeless retirement. Our image of retirement is too small, even though it has become the expected ending to the successful American Dream. God has a different and better dream for retirement. He has given Traditionalists and now Boomers money, health, and opportunities that he has given to no other generation in history to accomplish his purposes. He wants you to have a big retirement, not a small one.

The good news is most Boomers don't plan to retire. Merrill Lynch found that four out of five Boomers want to continue working, but most want to do something different from what they've done for most of their careers. Nor do they want to be tied down to the same pressures or demands.[4] Many who retire come back as contractors or even do cycling, where they work forty to sixty hours a week for five months on a project, and then cycle off for another six months, when their time is their own. Tim's a great example of the new trend. He's still working, but not the crazy advertising hours from the earlier stage of life. Many will continue working full-time after they retire, especially if they are in professional jobs rather than physical labor.[5] But more and more the time will be their own.

If you are facing retirement, do what Tim did and ask Jesus what he has planned for your next thirty years. He will show you the next part of his plan, and you will have to grab on for the ride.

Look for ways to use your skills as well as your gifts. The New Testament speaks often about spiritual gifts, so churches have been attuned to assessing people's spiritual gifts and then directing them to the volunteer slots the church needs to fill that best match those gifts. But the older generations have developed skills over the years that often build on or complement their spiritual gifts. Tim looked for ways to use his gifts as well as his skills developed over an entire career in marketing.

Churches aren't ready for this yet. But to keep Boomers and Traditionalists involved, churches must get beyond identifying their spiritual gifts and then trying to place them in their open volunteer slots. Instead, they must find out what the older generations can do and then turn them loose. Many Boomers are more educated than previous generations. Some are more experienced in leading and managing than the paid staff, so they can play a critical role in leading ministries.

But I've seen firsthand in my church consulting how hard it is for many pastors to allow a much more skilled leader or manager to jump in and help. And to be fair, many people who have not worked in a church underestimate the complexity of managing volunteers rather than paid employees and get frustrated when they give the pastors advice that won't work in churches the way it did in their jobs. We will need resources to help those business leaders understand the differences so their skills aren't wasted.

As it is now, churches lose the talents of the highly skilled Boomers and Traditionalists to not-for-profit organizations that are usually more adept at tapping into their experiences, resources, and networks.[6]

One woman told me, "I was the vice president of human resources for twenty-five years, and all my church offers me is working in the nursery and folding bulletins. It needs to be done, and I don't mind helping, but I have so much more to offer. Thank goodness I found a parachurch missions organization, because they were excited about what I could help them do with their staff. I haven't had so much fun putting my human resource skills to work in ten years." Her experience is typical—and it is hurting the church.

What I bluntly tell my church clients is that many highly talented people simply don't have patience for the ways churches are overled and undermanaged. And rather than fidget in frustration during two-hour planning meetings for the annual Christmas party, they volunteer to greet people at the door or lead a small group and then find their meaning and purpose in other organizations.

4. Help Your Church Figure Out Second Adulthood
What do you do if you're like this vice president and your church doesn't understand yet how the younger Traditionalists and the Boomers are changing the church? Help them figure out second adulthood.

Traditional older adult ministries have emphasized potluck dinners, guest speakers or concerts, and overnight trips. Those are fine, and people like them (my mother-in-law has twice visited Branson, Missouri). But Boomers have redefined every other aspect of the church, so we can be assured they will redefine older adult ministries as they will retirement. Boomers are entering second adulthood, and most churches aren't talking about it yet. We have paid so much attention to reaching the younger generations that we risk Baby Boomers slipping by into purposeless retirement. Now is the time the church can reinvent what they think older adult or "seniors" ministry should look like.

Ironically, we obsessed over the Boomers when they were teenagers and college students during the sixties and seventies. But now one of the two largest generations in history is moving into two decades of unparalleled opportunity to make a Boomer-sized impact, and we're missing it.

If your church isn't seeing the future yet, let me suggest six things you can do to get started now.

Help your church become the resource for figuring out second adulthood. The church can help Baby Boomers and Traditionalists figure out their identity in Christ in their second adulthood. During the Great Recession, many churches started career centers to help the unemployed find work. Why can't we be on the cutting edge of the cottage industry helping younger Traditionalists and Boomers figure out who they want to be in their second adulthood?

Help your church help you find a place of meaningful service. You will most likely get a typical answer if you ask what you can do to help at your church. But if you want to find an area to serve that utilizes all of your experience and gifts, you'll need to lay out for your church staff what those experiences and gifts are and ask what things you could do that could best utilize them.

Churches simply haven't had much experience or practice at this. Anyone who has been a minister knows the church's most unrelenting pressures are to find volunteers to fill the basic slots to keep ministries and programs going. It's only common sense that your church is going to direct you to one of those open slots unless you help them by reframing the discussion around the experiences, skills, and interests you want to utilize.

Lead with all generations; relax with your generation. You have years of experience getting things done, so you have never entertained the idea of stepping aside. And you shouldn't. But you need to know that there are younger people who are wanting to make a contribution now rather than waiting patiently until you are ready to "retire" from your ministry. It's just like work. Many in the younger generations have told me and other interviewers that they feel held back because the older generations aren't ready to leave yet. At work the younger generations complain; at church they often check out.

So don't quit leading, but lead from the side. (Leading from the side instead of the front is the hot thing in leadership development anyway.) We are so used to the "out in front" leader that we may not notice the leaders behind him or her. Being able to lead from the side typically requires experience, and that's something the older generations have had. So put yours to work. Hand off being in charge to someone younger, and then offer your help to make sure things get done. This is nothing new; you may have been helping younger managers succeed at work for fifteen years.

Helping other generations lead makes a big contribution, but it also takes more energy to adjust to another generation's language or approaches. Sometimes we need to relax with people of our own generation who know what we're talking about. It's nice to have friends who feel like home, especially if our church doesn't so much anymore.

Help your church create alternative worship services for people who miss the "good old days." The "good old days" may have been hymns, Maranatha choruses, or David Crowder songs. Don't wait for your ministers. (I know I said earlier that I tell worship ministers to offer hymn sings, but it will have a greater chance of success if you do it.) They are busy. If someone asked my worship minister son to start an alternate service, his wife would say, "No!" He's gone enough evenings already.

Start it. Run it. You've been getting things going all your life; this will not be a big deal. If there is a generation with the experience to be self-sufficient, it's yours. Get the staff's blessing and make it happen. Use a team so no one is stuck being "in charge" every time. If workplaces can cycle to tap into older talent that isn't available the entire year, so can you. Cycle in and out of being in charge with four other leaders, and then you can be gone for a month without feeling guilty.

Find emerging adults and make an impact in their lives. If the second adulthood is a new life stage, then who better to help emerging adults sort out their new life stage than the people pioneering second adulthood? Emerging adults are more interested in people who care about them than they are in programs. And they respect people who have already navigated many of the challenges they are moving into. They need someone other than their parents to help guide them through all the choices that are both exciting and incredibly overwhelming. Emerging adults need the older generations. And they need you now.

Tithe 10 percent of your time to your church to get started. Ask Jesus what he has planned for you, and then do the next thing he puts in front of you. Ten percent of your time in retirement is a great place to get started.

We'll never like the same music or run things with the same approaches as the other generations. The way I look at it, we might as well get used to adjusting to the different generations now. Heaven will be newer generations getting to know the generations that have died before us. Generation after generation from cultures we've never seen, who worshiped God with instruments we've never heard, and in languages we don't understand, all gathered around the throne of God. They will all be singing and hanging out. I cannot wait.

But most amazing, all generations will finally be happy in church, even though no one is getting the music they liked. Not one of them will be thinking, *"Ain't it awful"* how loud the cherubim get on the chorus? What would happen if we started practicing for heaven now?

PART 4

Why We Need Each Other

CHAPTER I 4

The Ultimate
Generational Intelligence

I TOLD THE story in chapter 12 of my youth ministry taking a rough turn because I focused on how the youth could apply their faith to their everyday lives. My Traditionalist senior minister thought that if our Generation X teenagers loved God, they should want to learn about doctrine without a lot of entertainment or application. Tensions grew because he thought I was pandering to our teenagers, until those tensions came out in the Sunday evening service when he "refuted" me point by point in front of the congregation. While most of the congregation was supportive, my landlord, Lola, told me bluntly, "You know, he's right." I was so caught off guard that I couldn't think of anything to say. I smiled and thanked her for caring that our young people were taught correctly.

Why do I retell that story?

Fast-forward twenty-seven years. I hadn't spoken to Lola since I left that church to plant a new one to reach Baby Boomers. I was surprised when Lola friended Laurie on Facebook, and then I was stunned when she wrote that she wanted to stop by our house and pick up a copy of *Sticking Points*.

When Lola stopped by several days later, I was working from home, so we chatted for a while.

Remembering her previous view that generational differences are bogus, I was dying to know why she wanted the book. So I asked her.

"I think it's easy to misunderstand other people if we don't try to see where they're coming from and appreciate their different perspectives. It's important that we understand people."

I smiled. "Okay, I have to know. Do you remember when you told me that my sermon about understanding generational differences was unbiblical?"

"Yes," she replied quietly.

"How did you make this shift?"

It was her turn to smile. "I watched my kids grow up and have babies. Now, having grandchildren, I've realized that they think about things in a different way—and it has really stretched me. I want to understand them. Plus, I don't know if you heard that not long after you left, the senior minister caused a big division in the church, which left us literally sitting on two different sides of the sanctuary for years. That experience taught me that even if you're right, how you handle a situation can be very wrong. And first, we need to listen to each other so we understand how people think, and then we can help them understand what may be truer to Scripture. If we don't do that, we're all lost."

I was impressed.

Several months later, I spoke with Lola again. She told me, "Your book really opened my eyes to so many new ways to think about relationships. Now, before I get frustrated about a situation, I ask myself, *Is this generational or is this scriptural?* I'm still very conservative, but I try to see if this is something Scripture specifically addresses or if it's just a different way of approaching things. Different approaches are not worth tearing up a church over. I'm so glad that God continues to show us his grace so we can grow."

So am I. I'm also glad Lola learned the generational intelligence we defined in chapter 2: when we were born affects our relationship with God and with everyone else. It's the hidden factor in our spiritual lives, our families, our relationships, and our churches. Instead of worrying in the dark like the young woman in some scary movie, Lola turned on the lights by trying to understand why the generations think differently.

"Do Whatever It Takes"

People ask me all the time, "What are the steps for dealing with generations at home or at church?"[1] The apostle Paul makes it easy to give them what they request. In Ephesians 4:1-3, he gives us a clear command on how we must relate to one another:

> I urge you to live a life worthy of the calling you have received. Be completely humble and gentle; be patient, bearing with one another in love. Make every effort to keep the unity of the Spirit through the bond of peace. (NIV)

As we've seen throughout this book, generational differences usually undermine or even blow up those bonds of peace. They complicate our spiritual lives so we become critical of another generation's spiritual temptations without recognizing the vulnerabilities that they've spotted in ours. They complicate our families, especially the new challenges with emerging adulthood. Finally, generational differences break the bonds of peace in our churches as they cause needless fights or cause generations to quit coming. But as I've already mentioned, when we don't understand the generations, we overreact to the small things, ignore the big things, and do the wrong things. Generational differences break the bonds of peace. But when Paul wrote this, he didn't care how many generations we would face or how frustrating they would be.

Paul reminds us that all generations of Christians are already unified within the Holy Spirit, even if they don't act like it: "Make every effort to *keep the unity* of the Spirit through the bond of peace" (emphasis added). How do we keep that unity? He tells us to "make every effort." But that translation doesn't fully capture how emphatically he feels about it. This is a big deal to him. He is saying "do whatever it takes" to demonstrate that unity.

Fortunately, he doesn't leave us on our own, trying to figure out what "do whatever it takes" looks like. Instead, he provides instructions in verse 2: "Be completely humble and gentle; be patient, bearing with one another in love." This verse is meant for all relationships, not only generational ones, but it gives us a practical way to deal successfully with our generational differences so they don't break those important relationships apart.

Humbly Turn On the Lights

"Be completely humble."

Humility helps us recognize the difference between biblical necessities and generational preferences. I can't say it better than Lola did: "I try to see if this is something Scripture specifically addresses or if it's just a different way of approaching things. Different approaches are not worth tearing up a church over."

Even when we're right, how we handle a situation can, indeed, be wrong. Paul spells out the best approach for handling generational differences: "Be completely humble." In other words, even if you are *right*, shouting at other generations doesn't work. It doesn't draw people to Christ, and it certainly doesn't make them more willing to listen.

Look for generational differences first before criticizing another generation for doing something wrong. Look for ways in which they may have something to offer. We can do that only when we apply humility—by realizing there may be another way to do something instead of arrogantly insisting the way our generation does it is best.

Instead of stumbling around in the dark, we have the humility to turn on the lights. Just because the new generation is always on their cell phones, for instance, doesn't make it wrong—and it doesn't make us better because we think it's wrong. It may make younger people ineffective when they try to communicate with an older generation, but that's a different conversation from "What's wrong with you? Why can't you put down the phone?"

Lola says she doesn't like talking on a cell phone, not because she doesn't like cell phones, not because she thinks people shouldn't use them, but because she has trouble hearing on them. And she admits that after years of hearing announcements in church to turn off cell phones and put them away, it has caught her off guard the last couple of years when her minister began waiting until everyone got their phones out so they could follow along with the Scripture reading.

She could have gotten upset and said, "In my day, we brought our Bibles to church." But instead she chose to humbly look at it a different way. "I'm just happy people are reading their Bibles in church again," she told me.

This is a case in which Lola humbly turned on the lights and saw generational differences as a way to "make every effort to keep the unity of the Spirit through the bond of peace."

So with that in mind, please repeat after me (preferably with your right hand in the air):

Haydn, I promise . . .

I will chill out . . .

And let another generation . . .

Do their thing . . .

If it is not immoral . . .

Or blasphemous . . .

Or really, really disgusting. . . .

So help me, God.

Paul knew that the five generations we deal with today are nothing. We will spend eternity in heaven with hundreds of generations, so thank God that he continues to pour his grace on us so we can grow in humility now to prepare us for the heavenly generational mash-up.

Gently Listen to Their Stories
"Be completely . . . gentle."

Gentleness involves courtesy and consideration and the willingness to waive one's rights and preferences.[2] The word Paul uses describes tame animals and kind rulers. Gentleness is listed as a fruit that the Holy Spirit grows in our lives. If humility makes us willing to learn, gentleness helps us listen to the stories of people in other generations.

When we approach others humbly, willing to listen and to learn their stories, then we open the door to conversation, growth, and relationship. As we listen, we can learn more by asking questions.

Instead of complaining that the younger generation has no social skills because they're always on their phones, we can be honest and say, "You know, it would bother me if I were trying to talk to someone and they were constantly looking at their phone. But I see you with your friends, and it doesn't seem to bother you when you are talking and they are on their phone. Why not?"

We all know the difference between asking questions in a way that judges and in a way that seeks to understand. Gentleness is that difference. You may still disagree with their stories, and their explanations may not make sense to you, but listen and allow them to share. Show respect to them and make sure you aren't missing something that needs to be updated in your own way of thinking.

Then, as we listen to people's stories, we engage with them to be more open to learning from us. Gentleness *makes* people want to learn from us. Look at the reason Jesus gave for why we should listen to him: "Let me teach you, because I am humble and gentle at heart" (Matthew 11:29). Listening to people tell their stories and explain why they think the way they do and why they answer the same question differently helps us get beyond our generational differences.

Today we especially need gentleness with moral issues. Gentleness helps us relate to people who are doing things we know are immoral. An actress friend told me about a tour she did with a group of people in which she was the only Christian. One of the women in her group was liberal in her sexual exploits.

Every town, a new man. Often my friend would ask her, "What is the appeal? Don't you worry about giving that part of yourself away so easily—and with men who mean nothing to you?"

The other woman would simply shrug and smile. "I enjoy it. That's what it's about, right?"

Then one day the unthinkable happened. The woman contracted HIV.

My friend told me, "The last thing I would ever think to say is 'Well, I told you.' Why should I? She will live with this, and it will affect every part of her for the rest of her life. She needed me to be there and love her and comfort her and point her lovingly toward Christ."

That's gentleness.

Gentleness helps us listen to our children when everything in us wants to scream at them to stop. In chapter 10 we talked about showing love to our children even when we disagree about their sexual choices. We can always ask them why their choices make sense to them even if we disagree. Ask with the intention of listening to gain understanding.

Once you listen to the other generations, you start to see their characteristics playing out everywhere, in every scene. Not long ago a friend told me, "Thanks a lot, Haydn. You've gotten into my brain. I can't go anywhere anymore without thinking, *That's generational.*"

"That's great," I told her. "That's exactly what I want to happen. That every time there's a potential for conflict, before you respond, you ask yourself, *Is this generational, or is this wrong?* That will help you respond with more grace and kindness."

Patiently Bear with Them

"Be patient, bearing with one another in love."

Paul is more realistic than we are. He knows that even though all Christians are one in the Holy Spirit, churches are full of imperfect people who will get annoyed and hurt, sometimes deeply hurt. (Anyone who is surprised that churches are full of hypocrites hasn't read much of the Bible. Imperfect people who mess things up are on almost every page.) So he tells us to be patient with one another—literally, he says to be "long tempered."

We all know what it means to be short tempered, but that's the opposite of patience. Paul further defines patience as "bearing with one another," which one New Testament scholar describes as "fully accepting them in their uniqueness, including their weaknesses and faults, and allowing them worth and space."[3] Different generations definitely qualify as unique. "Bearing with" makes room for them. It's what happens when we understand others and say, "Okay, they aren't going to change right now, so I guess I must bear with them through this." I love that the great fourth-century preacher John Chrysostom defined "bearing with one another in love" as having "a wide and big soul."

I've heard people through gritted teeth say, "I've just got to bear with that other person." That's not Paul's "bearing with"; that's an uneasy tolerance—and that can turn into bitterness or anger. "Bearing with" is something you do with humility and kindness. If you're gritting your teeth, you're not "bearing with" yet. "Bearing with" means patiently loving the other person even if that person never changes and the thing that person does is always annoying.

This especially applies to generational differences because often we hold our tempers, hoping that another generation will finally "get it" and change. But when we understand generations, we are the ones who finally "get it." We realize they aren't necessarily going to change. So we will have to bear with them. (The Millennials aren't going to get off their phones, and their grandparents won't stop wanting them to.) We have to meet in the middle—or sometimes just adjust the way we do things. Even if there isn't a middle ground and we show most of the patience, we still "bear with." We don't have to approve—particularly when we know another person's moral choices are wrong, as was the case with my actress friend's coworker. But we do have to humbly, gently, and patiently "bear with," just as Christ bears with us.

While we "bear with," that doesn't mean we remain silent. As we love and listen to others' stories, we can suggest alternatives. But it's important to remember what an Xer friend likes to tell me: "You have to earn the right to speak into someone's life." Only *after* you bear with them can you suggest alternatives that will be listened to and possibly heeded. Only after someone sees your concern and love will he or she be willing to make a change or at least to see another viewpoint as a valid option.

So for those who seem surgically connected to their phones, we can suggest alternatives—by asking questions: "Do you think there might be some spiritual advantages of getting away from the phone for two or three days and disconnecting?"

Or for those who think Jesus never judges: "What if a judging God can love you more than one who accepts everything you do?"

Raising questions is a great way to suggest alternatives, and so is simply sharing your opinion. This is especially true with those who believe "true for you but not for me," who think that one person can't impose his or her views on another. But since everybody has a right to an opinion, we can share what's true for us in a nonjudgmental, non-guilt-inducing way. We can say, "Here's what I think. Here's how I do it." If you do it with humility and gentleness, it won't sound as though you've made yourself the absolute standard of truth. And you just might open someone up to finding the God who *is* the absolute standard of truth.

The Ultimate Intelligence

I'm so grateful I was able to hear the rest of Lola's story. And while I celebrate that she learned generational intelligence, I'm more excited that she proves you are never too old to learn the ultimate intelligence. Two simple words wrap up Ephesians 4:2 and show us the best way: "Be completely humble and gentle; be patient, bearing with one another *in love*" (emphasis added).

You start and end with love. Think of someone from a different generation who makes you crazy. Picture their face in your mind. Assume they never change—do you still love them? I'm not saying you have to *like* them. But do you *love* them?

It isn't enough to understand the generations. We have to love them. Just because generational intelligence helps us appreciate their perspectives doesn't mean we won't want to give them a good shake every once in a while.

Our mothers may still drive us crazy. We still won't like our kids' music or the tattoos they insist on putting in places that will stretch once they've had children. We may still roll our eyes. *But we love.*

Love is the reason we put in the work to understand the generations. When we understand people from other generations, we aren't so critical of them, and that makes it easier to love them. It doesn't make it easy, but it definitely makes it easier. We don't have to work quite as hard at it.

Paul tells us at the end of Ephesians 4:2 that we do all these things "in love."

In love we can be completely humble and gentle.

In love we can be patient and bear with one another.

Love, Paul says, is the only thing that makes it possible to put aside what we prefer for someone else's benefit. So before we deal with generational differences, we must ask ourselves, *Do I want to love this person even if they never listen to me, or do I want to fix this*

person because their generational differences are driving me crazy?
Love isn't real until we decide whether we will love someone
regardless. Unlike the long lists of virtues the Greek philosophers
constantly talked about, for Paul, love isn't abstract. He's also not
telling us to have a constant feeling that we can draw on when
we need it. He is saying that love isn't real until we deal with real
people. This kind of love shows up through the power of God in
us when we accept the challenges this person in front of us brings
with them, their burdens that we must bear.[4]

If we don't understand why people from other generations are
the way they are, then we try to change them. The irony is, when
we respond with love, people are much more likely to change.
G. K. Chesterton said it well: "Things must be loved first and
improved afterwards." When we respond in love and show some
patience, people often do change, often too slowly to realize it
until five or six years later. Suddenly grandparents realize their
grandchildren have turned out all right. We flip on the lights, and
the scary movies no longer scare us, because we can see what's
in the basement hiding (those kids wearing their flip-flops to
church!). And we nod in understanding and get on with the
business of loving and creating real relationships with real people.

That's how we "keep the unity of the Spirit through the bond
of peace." We show that the God of peace has spread his peace
over all his creation. His church is the first place where that peace
becomes evident. Paul makes it clear that this is not done in our
strength or through our relational skills; we know how well we
handle generational differences when left to our own devices.
Instead, the power comes from Christ and the calling we have
received to be part of his very Spirit and his grand plan to reunite
people divided by so many differences, including the generational ones.

We want to live a life worthy of the calling we have received.

We know that the unity that is a reality in the Holy Spirit often doesn't look very real in our homes and churches. To live a life worthy of that calling, we have to learn to work with five generations. That's why I love what Paul said in his sermon in Antioch: "After David had done the will of God in his own generation, he died and was buried with his ancestors" (Acts 13:36). If I could have a life verse, it's that one. I want to fulfill God's purposes in my generation.

To fulfill God's purposes in our generations, we will need to figure out how to speak the languages of the different generations. The real God is amazing, so we need to be able to explain him to the next generations. I know five generations freaks people out. The two new life stages worry us, we wonder whether the church will survive, and we don't know what to say or the right questions to ask. This is new, and it seems like previous generations had it easier when the United States was a "Christian nation."

But I'm excited by the five generations. I think God has big plans for them. These new generations have more education, more opportunity, more communication tools (and toys) for a reason. God did not make us live longer so we could retire in comfort; we live longer so we can reach more people, because he doesn't "want anyone to be destroyed, but wants everyone to repent" (2 Peter 3:9). God did not concentrate unprecedented wealth in our hands so we can have a big-screen TV. He gives us unimagined wealth because there are people groups throughout the world who do not know Jesus loves them. He gave us the money to reach them. I don't care what generation you are—Jesus' great commission is for all generations. We have never had five generations, and we have never lived this long. We can accomplish so much more for the glory of God and his Kingdom than ever before.

Christianity isn't dying, the Millennials aren't the problem, and the future is bright. Sure, five generations is complicated, but it's one amazing ride. And I pray that with generational intelligence, you will join me on it.

Acknowledgments

I'd like to thank:

Ginger Kolbaba. You write great books of your own, so I'm fortunate you were willing to help me translate my workshops into a book. Your years at *Leadership Journal* and *Today's Christian Woman* were the perfect combination to reach everyone who needs generational intelligence. Within two hours, it felt like I was working with my sister, not someone I had just met. Oh, and thanks for polishing my *Huffington Post* columns so I sound legit.

My agents, Mike Salisbury and Sealy Yates. Both ends of the generations—a Millennial and a Traditionalist—but fun, smart, and crazy-hard workers.

Jon Farrar and Jonathan Schindler, my editors. Jon, your vision for this book carried us far beyond what I had conceived. Jonathan, I always thought *Sticking Points* would be the best book of my lifetime because I spent over a thousand hours on it. But you figured out how to make this one even better.

Laurie Anne. You make love fun. I knew you were the one, but I didn't know you would make marriage so much better than I could have imagined. You are so fun that everyone wants to get time with you, so I never take for granted that I'm the one who gets you full-time. (Even the TV people said you were the funny one in our screen test.)

Betty Irvine. The jokes say that living in the same house as your mother-in-law is supposed to be impossible. But I'm a lucky man to have two moms. You show us every day why the Traditionalists are called the Greatest Generation. I'm not sure how I would have handled losing my eyesight to macular degeneration, losing my spouse to industrial asbestos, and losing my son's health to an industrial head injury. You inspire us with your spiritual strength and have proved how powerful multigenerational households can be for passing the faith on.

Barton and Emily. We wanted you close by, but you went where God called you, and now you call Rhode Island home. Thank you for demonstrating how Millennials can impact the Kingdom of God and the church.

Josh, Max, and Katy. When people talk about you three, they say your mother and I are blessed. I couldn't agree more. I love you guys, and I will drive you crazy this summer, now that the books are done and I can come out of my office. I have to make up the time I missed with you the past three years. Plus, how will I keep up to date on Millennials and tech when you finally move out? (But I do want you to move out—sooner rather than later—so come see me about practicing your job interview skills.)

All those who are willing to set aside their own comfort and do what it takes to keep up with all the changes in our culture and our families so they can communicate the real Jesus to people who only know hacked Christianity. You are the reason Christianity isn't dying, the Millennials aren't the problem, and the future is bright.

Discussion Guide

Chapter 1: Turning On the Lights

1. What issues "keep you up at night"? In what ways (if any) are they related to generational differences?

2. Haydn writes, "If we don't have generational intelligence, we overreact to the small things, ignore the big things, and do the wrong things, making our relationships worse" (page 6). Describe a situation where you have seen this in practice. How might generational intelligence have helped you in that situation?

Chapter 2: Generational Intelligence

1. What is "generational intelligence"? Why is it necessary with five generations in our families, communities, and churches?

2. Haydn writes, "With five generations living together and interacting with each other, we have an amazing opportunity to learn from each other so that our view of God gets bigger and our faith gets stronger" (page 20). How have other generations helped you expand your view of God or strengthened your faith? How could you create more opportunities for that to happen?

Chapter 3: Traditionalists (Born before 1945)

1. What is the difference between generalizing and stereotyping? How does this distinction help you in applying generational intelligence?

2. No matter what generation you are in, how big is the traditional American dream of retirement in your dreams for your future?

3. Haydn writes, "What do I want to do in retirement? is not a Christian question" (page 41). If you were to ask God what he wants for your retirement, what would God tell you?

Chapter 4: Baby Boomers (Born 1946–1964)

1. What is the difference between being individualistic and hyperindividualistic? How does being hyperindividualistic impact a person's relationship with Christ? Which do you think you are more like?

2. Haydn writes, "Psychology, while a helpful handmaiden to faith, is a fourth-rate substitute for it" (page 58). What does that mean? How does psychology provide help to your faith and life? When do you allow psychology too much control over your thinking?

Chapter 5: Generation X (Born 1965–1980)

1. Which of the three spiritual strengths of Generation X do you think are most important for all Christians to embrace today?

2. Why do you think "true for you but not for me" has taken over as the dominant mind-set over the past twenty years? Where do you see its impact on your friends and family?

What do you need to learn so that you can better communicate with people who now hold that view?

3. What do you think this means: "What Jesus taught doesn't work unless you believe what Jesus thought" (page 75)? Do you agree? Can you think of some things Jesus commanded that you struggle to obey? What would you have to believe about God before it would be easier to follow those commands?

Chapter 6: Millennials (Born 1981–2001)

1. Haydn summarizes the new morality as "no longer [living] a life of honor to some ideal standards. It's to be yourself, to feel good about your choices, and to do what works for you—and to not judge" (page 91). What happens when we judge whether something is right or wrong by whether it works for us rather than by an ideal standard? Why is it impossible to not judge? How can you respond effectively to someone who says you are being judgmental?

2. How much importance do you place on the church? Which of the three reasons people are less interested in church (see page 95) have you observed in Millennials, as well as in other generations? Which have impacted you? Haydn writes, "You don't have to like the local church, but you do have to love it just as Christ loves it" (page 98). How can you better love the church even when you don't like it?

3. How can the strengths of your generation help other generations overcome their temptations? How can other generations' strengths help you overcome your own temptations?

Chapter 7: What Do I Say to Friends Who Claim, "I'm Spiritual but Not Religious"?

1. What is "Be Good, Feel Good, Live Your Life (God Is Watching)"? In what ways is it different from orthodox Christianity? Why is it so dangerous?

2. What is Haydn's advice for responding to friends who claim they're "spiritual but not religious"? What would you add to this advice?

Chapter 8: When Will My Twentysomething Move out of the Basement?

1. What is emerging adulthood? Why is this life stage difficult to navigate for twentysomethings?

2. What was your experience in the years described as emerging adulthood? How was your experience different from that of a twentysomething today? How was it similar? How can you encourage and support emerging adults as they discover and define their identity?

Chapter 9: How Do I Reach My Twentysomething Who Is Drifting from God?

1. Did anything on the list of findings on Millennials and faith (pages 143–44) surprise you? In what ways did this list support or contradict your ideas of faith and the Millennials?

2. What are two dos and two don'ts for passing on your faith to your children (or grandchildren)? What are two dos and two don'ts if your child (or grandchild) is walking away from the faith?

Chapter 10: What Do I Do When My Kid Is Putting Off Marriage but Not Sex?

1. How has Western culture come to view sex as "vital"? How is this shift reflected in the ideas and images of our time?

2. Haydn writes, "Don't start with the commandments about sex; start with why God gave them to us" and encourages readers to "give three reasons sex before marriage isn't best for us without mentioning the Bible" (page 166). Try this exercise for yourself. Why is it important to give the "why" behind the commandments? How difficult is it to do so?

Chapter 11: Will Christianity Really Disappear in Three Generations?

1. Haydn writes, "It is not as bad as we've heard, but it was never as good as we thought. And it's declining, especially with Millennials" (page 177). What does he mean by this? How does your experience of the church and culture fit into this claim?

2. What information presented in this chapter worries you (if any)? What information gives you hope for the future of the church?

Chapter 12: Why Won't Younger People Come to My Church?

1. Haydn says the question he gets asked most often is "Why won't younger people come to my church?" but the best question is "What will we need to do differently to reach the younger generations?" Which question are you asking? Which is your church asking? Which of the three options (on pages 203–207) is your church pursuing? Which do you think your church should be pursuing?

2. Look again at the advice given on how to reach the younger generations (pages 207–216). Which of these suggestions is your church equipped to implement? Which are you equipped for?

Chapter 13: What Am I Supposed to Do Now That It Doesn't Feel like My Church Anymore?

1. Have you ever been part of a church that changed so much trying to serve one group that it no longer felt like home? If so, what about it made it seem that way to you? What did you do about it?

2. What is "second adulthood"? Why is it important for churches to figure it out? What is your church doing to help those facing this new life stage? What more could you be doing? If you are part of the older generations, which of Haydn's four recommendations do you need to apply first?

Chapter 14: The Ultimate Generational Intelligence

1. The apostle Paul writes that we must "make every effort to keep the unity of the Spirit through the bond of peace" (Ephesians 4:3, NIV). Why is this so essential? In what ways is this an opportunity to exercise generational intelligence?

2. The apostle Paul's prescription for "keep[ing] the unity of the Spirit" is humility, gentleness, patience ("bearing with"), and love (see Ephesians 4:2). Consider your interactions with the other generations in your church or family. Have your encounters been marked by humility, gentleness, patience, and love? Why or why not? What steps can you take to live more in step with Paul's prescription?

Notes

CHAPTER 1: TURNING ON THE LIGHTS

1. Tyler Charles, "The Secret Sexual Revolution," *Relevant*, February 20, 2012, http://www.relevantmagazine.com/life/relationship/features/28337-the-secret-sexual-revolution.
2. CJ Werleman, "Atheists Have Their Number: How the Christian Right Is Hastening Religion's Decline," *Salon*, March 25, 2014, http://www.salon.com/2014/03/25/calling_the_christian_right_soon_you_will_be_outnumbered_partner/; Steve McSwain, "'NONES!' Are Now 'DONES': Is the Church Dying?", *Huff Post Religion*, November 17, 2014, http://www.huffingtonpost.com/steve-mcswain/nones-and-now-the-dones-t_b_6164112.html; Heidi Glenn, "Losing Our Religion: The Growth of the 'Nones,'" *The Two-Way* (blog), NPR, January 13, 2013, http://www.npr.org/blogs/thetwo-way/2013/01/14/169164840/losing-our-religion-the-growth-of-the-nones.
3. There is a fifth generation that will enter our workplaces soon, which I refer to as "Next Generation" or "Always On." The research is still incomplete about this generation. See pages 85–86 for more information about them.

CHAPTER 2: GENERATIONAL INTELLIGENCE

1. Gerald C. Tiffin, "Youth Culture Today: Backgrounds and Prospects," in *Ministering to Youth: A Strategy for the 80s*, ed. David Roadcup (Cincinnati: Standard Publishing, 1980), 15–16.
2. For more on how five generations make the "wait your turn" approach to power and decision making impossible, see *Sticking Points* (Carol Stream, IL: Tyndale House Publishers, 2013), 14–17.
3. "Baby Boomers: The Gloomiest Generation," Pew Research Center, June 25, 2008, http://www.pewsocialtrends.org/2008/06/25/baby-boomers-the-gloomiest-generation/; D'Vera Cohn and Paul Taylor, "Baby Boomers

Approach 65—Glumly," Pew Research Center, December 20, 2010, http://www
.pewsocialtrends.org/2010/12/20/baby-boomers-approach-65-glumly/.

4. Shaunti Feldhahn, *The Good News about Marriage: Debunking Discouraging
   Myths about Marriage and Divorce* (Colorado Springs: Multnomah, 2014),
   19, 21.

5. Ibid., 50.

6. Ibid., 73.

CHAPTER 3: TRADITIONALISTS (BORN BEFORE 1945)

1. "About This Artwork: Grant Wood, *American Gothic*," Art Institute of Chicago,
   http://www.artic.edu/aic/collections/artwork/6565.

2. "About This Artwork: Pablo Picasso, *The Red Armchair*," Art Institute of Chicago,
   http://www.artic.edu/aic/collections/artwork/5357?search_no=3&index=11.

3. For more detail on the regionalization of the United States in 1900, see
   Frederick Lewis Allen's *The Big Change: America Transforms Itself, 1900–1950*
   (New York: Harper and Row, 1952), 3–26.

4. Haydn Shaw, "Why What You Read about Millennials Seems Contradictory,"
   Huff Post Icon Next (blog), January 13, 2015, http://www.huffingtonpost.com
   /haydn-shaw/why-what-you-read-about-m_b_6459946.html.

5. Kevin Chappell, "The Washerwoman Philanthropist," *Ebony* (December 1995):
   86.

6. Lyle Schaller, *Reflections of a Contrarian* (Nashville: Abingdon, 1989), 109–22;
   Lyle Schaller, *Growing Plans* (Nashville: Abingdon, 1983), 149–52.

7. Julia Duin, "Tithing Falls by the Wayside," *Insight on the News* 18, no. 6
   (February 18, 2002).

8. Susan B. Carter and Richard Sutch, "The Myth of the Industrial Scrap Heap:
   A Revisionist View of Turn of the Century American Retirement," *The Journal
   of Economic History* 56, no. 1 (March 1996): 5, 8, http://www.jstor.org/pss
   /2124017.

9. National Center for Health Statistics, *Health, United States, 2013: With Special
   Feature on Prescription Drugs* (Hyattsville, MD, 2014), 82, table 18, http://www
   .cdc.gov/nchs/data/hus/hus13.pdf.

10. Thom S. Rainer and Jess W. Rainer, *The Millennials: Connecting to America's
    Largest Generation* (Nashville: B&H, 2011), 88; Neil Howe and William Strauss,
    Millennials Go to College (Ithaca, NY: Paramount Market Publishing, 2007), 61.

11. Jonathan Zwickel, review of *Modern Times* by Bob Dylan, Rhapsody.com,
    http://www.rhapsody.com/artist/bob-dylan/album/modern-times.

CHAPTER 4: BABY BOOMERS (BORN 1946–1964)

1. See Daniel Yankelovich, *The New Morality: A Profile of American Youth in the
   '70s* (New York: McGraw-Hill, 1974); Yankelovich, *New Rules: Searching for
   Self-Fulfillment in a World Turned Upside Down* (New York: Random House,
   1981).

2. Yuval Rosenberg, "Talking 'bout Our Generation," *Fortune*, June 21, 2006, 106, http://money.cnn.com/magazines/fortune/fortune_archive/2006/06/26/8379997/index.htm.

3. J. Walker Smith and Ann Clurman, *Generation Ageless: How Baby Boomers Are Changing the Way We Live Today . . . and They're Just Getting Started* (New York: HarperCollins, 2007), 35.

4. The article pointed to 250,000 swimming pools in the United States.

5. Landon Y. Jones, *Great Expectations: America and the Baby Boom Generation* (New York: Coward, McCann & Geoghegan, 1980). This book is often credited with coining the term *Baby Boomer.*

6. Yankelovich, *The New Morality*, 6.

7. Cheryl Russell, "A Generation of Free Agents," *The Courier-Journal*, October 24, 1993, 5.

8. Daniel Yankelovich, interview by Ben Wattenberg, *The First Measured Century*, PBS, January 12, 2007. The transcript can be found at http://www.pbs.org/fmc/interviews/yankelovich.htm. See also research from University of Michigan psychologist Joseph Adelson, "When the Young Teach and the Old Learn," *Time*, August 17, 1970, http://www.time.com/time/magazine/article/0,9171,909577,00.html.

9. Yankelovich, *The New Morality*, 83–85.

10. John White, *The Fight* (Downers Grove, IL: InterVarsity, 1976).

11. "Pass It On," which appears on *Tell It Like It Is* by Ralph Carmichael and Kurt Kaiser, Light Records, 1969.

12. "Historic Uniform Series Now Meets 21st Century Needs," National Council of Churches, USA, March 12, 2002, http://www.ncccusa.org/news/02news20.html.

13. Barna Group, *The State of the Bible: 2014* (New York: American Bible Society, 2014), 41, http://www.americanbible.org/uploads/content/state-of-the-bible-data-analysis-american-bible-society-2014.pdf.

14. See Matthew 4:1-11.

15. Lyle Schaller, *It's a Different World* (Nashville: Abingdon, 1987), 50–99; George Gallup Jr. and Timothy Jones, *The Next American Spirituality* (Colorado Springs: Victor, 2000), 51.

16. Schaller, *It's a Different World*, 21–33.

17. John of the Cross, "Excerpts from *The Dark Night of the Soul*," in *Devotional Classics: Selected Readings for Individuals and Groups*, ed. Richard J. Foster and James Brian Smith (San Francisco: HarperSanFrancisco, 1993), 34.

18. Elmer Towns, *How to Reach the Baby Boomer* (Lynchburg, VA: Church Growth Institute, 1990), Videocassette (VHS).

19. "Quick Talk: Jennifer Lopez," The Culture, *Time*, June 23, 2014, 60.

20. It's not only Christians who see how demanding psychology can be. It shows up repeatedly in comedies, like *Unbreakable Kimmy Schmidt*, the 2015 breakout Netflix hit.

CHAPTER 5: GENERATION X (BORN 1965–1980)

1. Paul Taylor and George Gao, "Generation X: America's Neglected 'Middle Child,'" *Pew Research Center: Fact Tank*, June 5, 2014, http://www.pewresearch .org/fact-tank/2014/06/05/generation-x-americas-neglected-middle-child/.

2. Piper Lowell, "Out of Desperation," *Sojourners* (November 1994), http://www .sojo.net/magazine/1994/11/out-desperation.

3. Geoffrey T. Holtz, *Welcome to the Jungle: The Why Behind "Generation X"* (New York: St. Martin's Press, 1995), 18–19.

4. Ibid., 21.

5. US Census Bureau, "Table 78. Live Births, Deaths, Marriages, and Divorces: 1960 to 2007," http://www.census.gov/compendia/statab/2011/tables/11s0078. pdf; Karen Sternheimer, "Is Marriage Under Siege?" *Everyday Sociology Blog*, July 28, 2008, http://www.everydaysociologyblog.com/2008/07/is-marriage-und .html; "Divorce Rate Drops to Lowest Since 1970," *USA Today*, May 11, 2007, http://usatoday30.usatoday.com/news/nation/2007-05-11-divorce-decline_N .htm; Pew Research Center, *Millennials: A Portrait of Generation Next* (February 24, 2010), 46–47, http://www.pewsocialtrends.org/files/2010/10/millennials -confident-connected-open-to-change.pdf.

6. The economy boomed during the childhood of the second half of Gen X—the dot-com era. So some wonder why I say the economy was negative for both halves of Gen X growing up. The boom in the economy during the second half of Generation X held a dark secret. Even though the economy grew rapidly again during the '80s and '90s, with only a mild recession in 1990, much of that growth went to the top 10 percent of wage earners. Those in the middle- and bottom-income brackets remained almost flat. They kept hearing that the economy was growing and watched the stock market break new records, but the Xers saw the air going out of the American Dream for most of the workforce. See Jim Tankersley, "Horatio Alger, RIP," *National Journal*, September 25, 2012, http://www.nationaljournal.com/next-economy/analysis-working-hard-is-no -longer-the-ticket-to-achieving-the-american-dream-20120925 and Kirstin Downey, "Sometimes There's Upward Mobility . . . But Usually, in History, There Isn't," *National Journal*, September 25, 2012, http://www.nationaljournal .com/next-economy/in-world-history-upward-mobility-has-rarely-happened -20120925.

7. Katherine S. Newman, *Declining Fortunes* (New York: Basic Books, 1994), 53.

8. Gary Steinberg, "The Class of '90," *Occupational Outlook Quarterly*, June 22, 1994, 12.

9. Jeff Gordinier, *X Saves the World: How Generation X Got the Shaft but Can Still Keep Everything from Sucking* (New York: Viking, 2008), 129.

10. Ibid., xv–xxx.

11. Only 19 percent of Xers attended a small group in the past week, compared to 29 percent of Boomers and 34 percent of Traditionalists. Barna Group,

Generational Differences, April 20, 2008, http://www.barna.org/FlexPage.aspx ?Page=Topic&TopicID=13.

12. Eddie Gibbs and Ryan K. Bolger, *Emerging Churches* (Grand Rapids: Baker, 2005), 89–134.

13. Barna Group, *Generational Differences*, April 20, 2008, http://www.barna.org /FlexPage.aspx?Page=Topic&TopicID=13.

14. Rebecca Ryan, *Live First, Work Second: Getting Inside the Head of the Next Generation* (Madison, WI: Next Generation Consulting, 2007), 85.

15. Sylvia Ann Hewlett and Lauren Leader-Chivée, with Catherine Fredman, Maggie Jackson, and Laura Sherbin, *The X Factor: Tapping into the Strengths of the 33- to 46-Year-Old Generation* (New York: Center for Work-Life Policy, 2011), 1, 21.

16. Ibid.

17. James P. Vere, "Having It All No Longer: Fertility, Female Labor Supply, and the New Life Choices of Generation X," *Demography* 44, no. 4 (November 2007): 821–28.

18. Stephanie Armour, "As Dads Push for Family Time, Tensions Rise in Workplace," *USA Today*, December 10, 2007, http://usatoday30.usatoday.com /printedition/news/20071211/1a_cover11.art.htm.

19. Sometimes called postmodernism (at least the popular version of it), "true for you but not for me" may replace the last five hundred years of rationalism, or it may be a philosophical transition period, a flash in the pan replaced by something else. Either way, the Xers stand on the hinge of the end of a five-hundred-year era.

20. This view is often called secularism, modernism, or post-Enlightenment thinking.

21. Frank Schaeffer, *Why I Am an Atheist Who Believes in God: How to Give Love, Create Beauty and Find Peace* (North Charleston, SC: CreateSpace Independent Publishing Platform, 2014), 26.

CHAPTER 6: MILLENNIALS (BORN 1981–2001)

1. Ironically, my third son spent his Christmas money on the most expensive Polaroid camera ever made, because he is into Instagram. Using your phone to take photos of the Polaroid pictures you shot is hot on Instagram right now. It all comes full circle.

2. According to the US Census Bureau, there were more than four million births in fourteen of the twenty years from 1989 to 2009. In comparison, the first Baby Boom had four million births per year for only ten years.

3. William Strauss and Neil Howe, *Millennials and the Pop Culture* (Great Falls, VA: LifeCourse Associates, 2006), 50.

4. Anna Bahney, "High School Heroes: Mom and Dad," *New York Times*, May 16, 2004, http://www.nytimes.com/2004/05/16/style/high-school-heroes-mom-and -dad.html?pagewanted=all&src=pm.

5. John Leo, "The Good-News Generation," *US News & World Report*, October 26, 2003, http://www.usnews.com/usnews/opinion/articles/031103/3john.htm.

6. Thom S. Rainer and Jess W. Rainer, *The Millennials: Connecting to America's Largest Generation* (Nashville: B&H, 2011), 57.

7. Rainer and Rainer, *The Millennials*, 16.

8. Sharon Jayson, "Are Kids Today Having a Childhood They'll Remember?" *USA Today*, April 15, 2011, http://usatoday30.usatoday.com/news/health/wellness /story/2011/04/Are-parents-overprotecting-their-kids/46135302/1.

9. Steven Reinberg, "US Kids Using Media Almost 8 Hours a Day," ABC News online, January 20, 2010, http://abcnews.go.com/Health/Healthday/us-kids -media-hours-day/story?id=9611664. The survey finds few parents set rules as to the use of smartphones and computers.

10. McCann Worldgroup, *The Truth about Youth* (May 2011): 5, http://www.scribd .com/doc/56263899/McCann-Worldgroup-Truth-About-Youth.

11. Jeffrey Jensen Arnett and Joseph Schwab, *The Clark University Poll of Emerging Adults* (December 2012), http://www.clarku.edu/clarkpoll/pdfs/Clark_Poll_Peer %20Inst.pdf; "Why We're Officially 'Adults' at Age 28," *Yahoo! Lifestyle New Zealand*, October 18, 2012, https://nz.lifestyle.yahoo.com/marie-claire /love-and-life/relationships/a/15150188/why-we-re-officially-adults-at-age-28/.

12. Wikia in association with Ipsos Media CT, "GenZ: The Limitless Generation," press release, March 18, 2013.

13. Alesandra Dubin, "Have a Social Media Account for Your Baby? 40 Percent of Millennial Moms Do," *Today Parents*, October 18, 2014, http://www.today .com/parents/have-social-media-account-your-baby-40-percent-millennial -moms-1D80224937.

14. Ed Stetzer, "Dumb and Dumber: How Biblical Illiteracy Is Killing Our Nation," *Charisma Magazine*, October 9, 2014, http://www.charismamag.com/life /culture/21076-dumb-and-dumber-how-biblical-illiteracy-is-killing-our-nation.

15. Naomi Schaefer Riley, interview by Timothy C. Morgan, "It Takes More Than a Swank Coffee Shop," *Christianity Today* (July/August 2014): 54.

16. In answer to the longstanding survey question "Generally speaking, would you say that most people can be trusted or that you can't be too careful in dealing with people?" 19 percent of Millennials answered yes, compared with 31 percent of Gen Xers, 37 percent of Traditionalists, and 40 percent of Boomers. "Millennials in Adulthood," Pew Research Center, March 7, 2014, http://www .pewsocialtrends.org/2014/03/07/millennials-in-adulthood/.

17. Alex Oliver, "Millennials and Money," *Futures Blog*, February 7, 2011, http://blog .thefuturescompany.com/uncategorized/millennials-and-money/.

18. David Kinnaman and Gabe Lyons, *unChristian: What a New Generation Really Thinks about Christianity . . . and Why It Matters* (Grand Rapids, MI: Baker, 2007), 22.

19. Read in Rainer and Rainer, *The Millennials*, 85, 96.

20. Rainer and Rainer, *The Millennials*.

21. Christian Smith, Kari Christoffersen, and Hilary Davidson, *Lost in Transition: The Dark Side of Emerging Adulthood* (New York: Oxford University Press, 2011), 20. In this section, in addition to my own observations, I rely heavily on the research Christian Smith summarized in his book. While there are many other studies and other highly respected researchers, Smith's team's research confirms the best of it, covers the topic the most thoroughly, and uses squeaky-clean research methodologies that few others have the time or money to match. That's why when people ask me what they should read to understand the faith of emerging adults, I tell them to start with Christian Smith.

22. Dr. Seuss, *Happy Birthday to You!* (New York: Random House, 1959), 44.

23. "Demi Lovato: Why I'm Not Friends with Miley Cyrus Anymore," *FOX 411*, November 25, 2014, http://www.foxnews.com/entertainment/2014/11/25 /demi-lovato-reveals-why-her-friendship-with-miley-cyrus-ended/.

24. Smith, Christoffersen, and Davidson, *Lost in Transition*, chapter 1.

25. Christian Smith and Patricia Snell, *Souls in Transition: The Religious and Spiritual Lives of Emerging Adults* (New York: Oxford University Press, 2009), 168.

26. Ibid., 152.

27. Ed Stetzer, Richie Stanley, and Jason Hayes, *Lost and Found: The Younger Unchurched and the Churches that Reach Them* (Nashville: B&H, 2009), 59.

28. Ibid., 32.

29. Ibid., 49–50.

30. Ibid., 45, 55–56.

31. Smith and Snell, *Souls in Transition*, 89.

32. Christian Smith, Jonathan Hill, Kyle Longest, and Kari Christoffersen, *Young Catholic America: Emerging Adults In, Out of, and Gone from the Church* (New York: Oxford University Press, 2014).

33. "Kingdom of God," *Theopedia*, www.theopedia.com/Kingdom_of_God.

34. Donald Miller, "How My Faith Has Changed Since 'Blue Like Jazz,'" *Storyline* (blog), January 14, 2014, http://storylineblog.com/2013/01 /14/how-my-faith-has-changed/.

35. Donald Miller defines the spiritual church as the bride of Christ. He said, "The church is a very, very good earthly organization that almost exists as a 'para church' organization alongside Jesus' bride." (Miller, "How My Faith Has Changed.") While I do understand his point that churches can quickly turn into well-run organizations and miss their larger calling in the body of Christ, I think his distinction between the earthly and the spiritual church is precisely the problem.

36. Miller, "How My Faith Has Changed." Donald Miller has caught quite a bit of flak over his current understanding of church and has explained his beliefs in more detail in his other blog posts. See Donald Miller, "I Don't Worship God by Singing," *Storyline* (blog), February 3, 2014, http://storylineblog.com/2014 /02/03/i-dont-worship-god-by-singing-i-connect-with-him-elsewhere/ and

Donald Miller, "Why I Don't Go to Church Very Often," *Storyline* (blog), February 5, 2014, http://storylineblog.com/2014/02/05/why-i-dont-go-to -church-very-often-a-follow-up-blog/.

CHAPTER 7: WHAT DO I SAY TO FRIENDS WHO CLAIM, "I'M SPIRITUAL BUT NOT RELIGIOUS"?

1. Ed Stetzer, Ritchie Stanley, and Jason Hays, *Lost and Found: The Younger Unchurched and the Churches that Reach Them* (Nashville: B&H, 2009), 24, 41.
2. Claire Hoffman, "Katy Conquers All," *Marie Claire*, December 9, 2013, http://www.marieclaire.com/celebrity/a8596/katy-perry-interview-january -cover/.
3. Melissa Steffan, "Mumford and Sons Namesake Favors 'Jesus,' Not 'Christianity,'" "Gleanings," *Christianity Today*, March 18, 2013.
4. Stetzer et al., *Lost and Found*, 21.
5. Be Good, Feel Good, Live Your Life (God Is Watching) is my way of more easily communicating what Christian Smith and his team termed "moralistic therapeutic deism." In 2005, Smith shook church leaders when he stated in his book *Soul Searching* (with Melinda Lundquist Denton, [New York: Oxford University Press]) that most of the teenagers interviewed could not articulate much Christian theology because they believed Christianity was something different, summarized as "moralistic therapeutic deism."
6. In 2008, in the follow-up interviews, Christian Smith and his team discovered that Be Good, Feel Good, Live Your Life (God Is Watching) is still the de facto viewpoint. However, because the eighteen- to twenty-four-year-olds had more experiences outside their families and communities and interacted with people of different religious beliefs, these Millennials gave more varied answers than they did as teenagers. For example, some were more negative toward religion, while others were more committed to and better able to articulate their Christian beliefs. See Christian Smith and Patricia Snell, *Souls in Transition* (New York: Oxford University Press, 2009), 155. That's hopeful news, so let me quote their report: "Confronted with real existential or material difficulties, some emerging adults appear to have backed away from the simple verities of MTD [what we are calling Be Good, Feel Good, Live Your Life (God Is Watching)] or perhaps have moved forward into somewhat more complex, grounded, or traditional versions of religious faith. In short, there seem to be certain tests in life through which some youth find that MTD proves an unrealistic account or an unhelpful way to respond." Read more in Smith and Snell, *Souls in Transition*, 154–56. We must not miss the opening for spiritual conversations those tests in life provide.
7. Smith and Denton, *Soul Searching*, 162–63.
8. Smith and Snell, *Souls in Transition*, 155.
9. Smith and Denton, *Soul Searching*, 170–71.
10. Ibid., 163.

11. Barna Group, *Churchless*, ed. George Barna and David Kinnaman (Carol Stream, IL: Tyndale, 2014), 97–102.

12. I recommend that churches provide parents of teenagers a boot camp for how to talk about these things at home. I've found a ready audience when I've offered them. If you are a parent and your church doesn't offer something like this, ask around for some recommendations of what you can read or listen to. I'm amazed at the sophistication of the arguments my dyslexic twenty-two-year-old son, Josh, has thought about because he has listened to two or three podcasts a week for three years.

CHAPTER 8: WHEN WILL MY TWENTYSOMETHING MOVE OUT OF THE BASEMENT?

1. David P. Setran and Chris A. Kiesling did a good job pulling together the research in *Spiritual Formation in Emerging Adulthood: A Practical Theology for College and Young Adult Ministry* (Grand Rapids, MI: Baker Academic, 2013), 2.

2. "Young Adults Then and Now," United States Census Bureau, http://www.census .gov/censusexplorer/censusexplorer-youngadults.html.

3. "New Census Bureau Statistics Show How Young Adults Today Compare with Previous Generations in Neighborhoods Nationwide," United States Census Bureau, December 4, 2014, http://www.census.gov/newsroom/press-releases /2014/cb14-219.html.

4. Robin Marantz Henig, "What Is It about 20-Somethings?" *New York Times*, August 18, 2010, http://www.nytimes.com/2010/08/22/magazine/22Adulthood -t.html?pagewanted=all&_r=0.

5. Ibid.

6. Jeffrey Jensen Arnett, *Emerging Adulthood: The Winding Road from the Late Teens through the Twenties* (New York: Oxford University Press, 2004), 46.

7. University of Chicago News Office, "Most Americans Think People Need to Be 26 to Be Considered Grown-up: Seven Steps toward Adulthood Take Five Years, NORC Survey at University of Chicago Finds," news release, May 9, 2003, http://www-news.uchicago.edu/releases/03/030509.adulthood.shtml; Pew Research Center, "When Does Adulthood Begin in this Economy?" March 13, 2012, http://www.pewresearch.org/daily-number/when-does-adulthood-begin -in-this-economy.

8. Jeffrey Jensen Arnett and Joseph Schwab, *The Clark University Poll of Emerging Adults* (December 2012), http://www.clarku.edu/clarkpoll/pdfs/Clark_Poll _Peer%20Inst.pdf; "Why We're Officially 'Adults' at Age 28," *Marie Claire: Yahoo Lifestyle, Australia*, October 18, 2012, https://au.lifestyle.yahoo.com /marie-claire/love-and-life/relationships/a/15150188/why-we-re-officially-adults -at-age-28/.

9. The Council of Economic Advisers, *15 Economic Facts about Millennials*, https://www.whitehouse.gov/sites/default/files/docs/millennials_report.pdf; Jordan Weissman, "Why Do So Many Americans Drop Out of College?" *The*

Atlantic, March 29, 2012, http://www.theatlantic.com/business/archive/2012
/03/why-do-so-many-americans-drop-out-of-college/255226/; "Digest of
Education Statistics," *National Center for Education Statistics*, 2013, https://nces
.ed.gov/programs/digest/d13/tables/dt13_104.20.asp.

10. "Creative Destruction," *The Economist*, June 28, 2014, http://www.economist
.com/news/leaders/21605906-cost-crisis-changing-labour-markets-and-new
-technology-will-turn-old-institution-its.

11. Phil Izzo, "Congratulations to Class of 2014, Most Indebted Ever," *Real Time
Economics* (blog), *Wall Street Journal*, May 16, 2014, http://blogs.wsj.com
/economics/2014/05/16/congatulations-to-class-of-2014-the-most-indebted-ever/.

12. See Millennial writer Jonathan Sprowl's article, "Why Young Men Aren't
Manning Up," *Today's Christian Woman*, January 24, 2012, for an excellent
summary on why Millennial men are struggling to "man up" and what
Christians can do to help them.

13. Douglas Coupland, *Generation X: Tales for an Accelerated Culture* (New York:
St. Martin's Griffin, 1991).

14. Pew Research Center, *Millennials: A Portrait of Generation Next* (February 24,
2010), 46–47, http://www.pewsocialtrends.org/files/2010/10/millennials
-confident-connected-open-to-change.pdf.

15. "Life Expectancy Calculator," *Retirement and Survivors Benefits: Social Security
Online*, http://www.socialsecurity.gov/cgi-bin/longevity.cgi.

16. For more on the difference between involved parents and helicopter parents, see
my blog posts on Huffington Post: Haydn Shaw, "Why the Millennials' Parents
Will Continue to Stay Involved in Their Kids' Lives at Work . . . and Why
That's a Good Thing," *Huff Post Parents*, January 21, 2014, http://www
.huffingtonpost.com/haydn-shaw/why-the-millennials-paren_b_4634493.html;
Haydn Shaw, "Why You Should Go to 'Take Your Parents to Work Day,'" *Huff
Post Business*, November 6, 2013, http://www.huffingtonpost.com/haydn
-shaw/why-you-should-go-to-take_b_4222683.html.

17. Robert F. Schoeni and Karen E. Ross, "Material Assistance from Families during
the Transition to Adulthood," in *On the Frontier of Adulthood*, ed. Richard
A. Settersten Jr., Frank F. Furstenberg Jr., and Ruben C. Rumbaut (Chicago:
University of Chicago Press, 2005), 404, quoted in Christian Smith, "Getting
a Life," *Books & Culture* 13 (November/December 2007): http://www.ctlibrary
.com/bc/2007/novdec/2.10.html.

CHAPTER 9: HOW DO I REACH MY TWENTYSOMETHING WHO IS DRIFTING FROM GOD?

1. Drew Dyck, "The Leavers: Young Doubters Exit the Church," *Christianity
Today*, November 19, 2010. That one in three number drops to one in four
for children whose parents are still married, attend church, and are both
evangelical. See Ed Stetzer, "Dropouts and Disciples: How Many Students Are
Really Leaving the Church," *The Exchange* (blog), May 14, 2014, http://www.

christianitytoday.com/edstetzer/2014/may/dropouts-and-disciples-how-many-students-are-really
-leaving.html.

2. Christian Smith and coauthors explain the problems that consumerism, intoxication, and sexual liberation create for emerging adults in *Lost in Transition* (New York: Oxford University Press, 2011).

3. "Baylor Researcher Refutes Reports of Religion's Decline in America," news release, September 25, 2014, http://www.baylor.edu/mediacommunications
/news.php?action=story&story=146819.

4. "Religion among the Millennials," Pew Research Center, February 17, 2010, http://www.pewforum.org/2010/02/17/religion-among-the-millennials/.

5. For an excellent summary of the various studies that explain which beliefs decline and to what degree, see David P. Setran and Chris A. Kiesling, *Spiritual Formation in Emerging Adulthood: A Practical Theology for College and Young Adult Ministry* (Grand Rapids, MI: Baker, 2013), chapter 1.

6. David Kinnaman, *You Lost Me: Why Young Christians Are Leaving Church . . . and Rethinking Faith* (Grand Rapids: Baker, 2011), 24.

7. Setran and Kiesling, *Spiritual Formation in Emerging Adulthood*, 13. For a list of other researchers who see less of a decline, see Setran and Kiesling, *Spiritual Formation in Emerging Adulthood*.

8. Ed Stetzer, "Dropouts and Disciples: How Many Students Are Really Leaving the Church?" *The Exchange* (blog), May 14, 2014, http://www.christianitytoday
.com/edstetzer/2014/may/dropouts-and-disciples-how-many-students-are-really
-leaving.html.

9. Ibid.

10. Bengtson reported his findings in *Families and Faith: How Religion Is Passed Down across Generations* (New York: Oxford University Press, 2013). He explained the dimensions they used to measure how similar one generation's faith was to another's: intensity of faith, frequency of religious service attendance, agreement with a literal interpretation of the Bible, and agreement with the importance of religion in civic life. See Vern Bengtson, interview by Amy Ziettlow, "Religion Runs in the Family," *Christianity Today*, September 20, 2013, http://www.christianitytoday.com/ct/2013/august-web-only/religion-runs
-in-family.html.

11. Stetzer, "Dropouts and Disciples."

12. Vern L. Bengtson, with Norella M. Putney and Susan Harris, *Families and Faith: How Religion Is Passed Down across Generations* (New York: Oxford University Press, 2013), 71–98.

13. Vern Bengtson, interview by Amy Ziettlow, "Religion Runs in the Family," *Christianity Today*, September 20, 2013, http://www.christianitytoday.com/ct
/2013/august-web-only/religion-runs-in-family.html.

14. Dyck, "The Leavers: Young Doubters Exit the Church."

15. Bengtson, Putney, and Harris, *Families and Faith,* 112.

16. Ibid., 112.
17. Ibid., 105.
18. Stetzer, "Dropouts and Disciples."
19. David P. Setran and Chris A. Kiesling, *Spiritual Formation in Emerging Adulthood* (Grand Rapids, MI: Baker, 2013), 14.
20. Drew Dyck, "The Leavers," *Christianity Today.*
21. Joel Stein and Josh Sanburn, "The New Greatest Generation," *Time*, May 20, 2013, 31–32.
22. Of course I'm not saying that if they are partying every night until 3 a.m., driving drunk, addicted to drugs, or involved in crime we shouldn't intervene or get them help. We should, no matter what age they are. Sometimes, if they're dangerous, we need to draw boundaries and say they can't live with us anymore. Frederick Buechner writes that the big breakthrough in dealing with his daughter's anorexia came when he quit obsessing over whether she ate, handed her life over to God, and let her decide if she was going to eventually live or die. (Frederick Buechner, *Telling Secrets* [New York: HarperCollins, 1991.])
23. Vern Bengtson, interview by Amy Ziettlow, "Religion Runs in the Family."
24. Ibid.

CHAPTER 10: WHAT DO I DO WHEN MY KID IS PUTTING OFF MARRIAGE BUT NOT SEX?

1. Amanda Lenhart and Maeve Duggan, "Couples, the Internet, and Social Media: Main Report," Pew Research Center, February 11, 2014, http://www.pewinternet.org/2014/02/11/main-report-30/.
2. Robert Wuthnow, *After the Baby Boomers: How Twenty- and Thirty-Somethings Are Changing the Future of American Religion* (Princeton, NJ: Princeton University Press, 2007), 139.
3. "Table MS-2. Estimated Median Age at First Marriage, by Sex: 1890 to the Present," US Census Bureau, September 21, 2006, http://www.census.gov/population/socdemo/hh-fam/ms2.pdf; "Median Age at First Marriage, 1890–2010," *infoplease*, Pearson Education, 2009, http://www.infoplease.com/ipa/A0005061.html.
4. By 1960, 65 percent of Traditionalists (ages eighteen to thirty-two) were married. By 1980, 48 percent of the Boomers at comparable ages were married. In 1997, 36 percent of Xers were married. Today only 26 percent of Millennials in that age range are married. See, for example, Stephen Marche, "The Reality of Marriage Is Completely at Odds with Its Portrayal in Culture," *Esquire*, October 7, 2014, http://www.esquire.com/news-politics/a30396/marriage-gets-weird-1014/.
5. Life expectancy was only forty-seven for men, so marriage would average twenty-one years in 1900. Over half didn't make it to their silver anniversary.
6. Shaunti Feldhahn, *The Good News about Marriage: Debunking Discouraging Myths about Marriage and Divorce* (Colorado Springs: Multnomah, 2014), 35.

7. Agatha Christie, *A Caribbean Mystery* (New York: Dodd, Mead and Company, 1964), 12.

8. Ira L. Reiss writes, "This century's first Sexual Revolution was in progress [in the 1920s]. . . . The percentage of women born between 1900 and 1909 who had intercourse before marriage doubled from 25 percent to 50 percent! . . . Most of the increased sexuality occurred in stable, affectionate relationships." See Ira L. Reiss, *An End to Shame: Shaping Our Next Sexual Revolution* (Buffalo, NY: Prometheus Books, 1990), 84.

9. Daniel Yankelovich, *The New Morality: A Profile of American Youth in the '70's* (New York: McGraw-Hill, 1974), 87.

10. Emanuella Grinberg, "Report: More Women Moving In before Marriage," *CNN*, April 4, 2013, http://www.cnn.com/2013/04/04/living/women-premarital-cohabitation.

11. Kate Bolick, "All the Single Ladies," *The Atlantic*, November 2011, http://www.theatlantic.com/magazine/archive/2011/11/all-the-single-ladies/8654/.

12. Sally C. Curtin, Stephanie J. Ventura, and Gladys M. Martinez, "Recent Declines in Nonmarital Childbearing in the United States," NCHS (National Center for Health Statistics) *Data Brief*, no. 162, August 2014, http://www.cdc.gov/nchs/data/databriefs/db162.htm.

13. Christian Smith and Patricia Snell, *Souls in Transition: The Religious and Spiritual Lives of Emerging Adults* (New York: Oxford University Press, 2009), 62.

14. Jennifer Abbasi, "Why 6-Year-Old Girls Want to be Sexy (STUDY)," *Huff Post Parents*, July 24, 2012, http://www.huffingtonpost.com/2012/07/17/6-year-old-girls-sexy_n_1679088.html.

15. Feldhahn, *The Good News about Marriage*, 77.

CHAPTER 11: WILL CHRISTIANITY REALLY DISAPPEAR IN THREE GENERATIONS?

1. Frank Newport and Joseph Carroll, "Another Look at Evangelicals in America Today," *Gallup*, December 2, 2005, http://www.gallup.com/poll/20242/another-look-evangelicals-america-today.aspx.

2. Frank Newport, "More than 9 in 10 Americans Continue to Believe in God," *Gallup*, June 3, 2011, http://www.gallup.com/poll/147887/americans-continue-believe-god.aspx.

3. Frank Newport, "Three-Quarters of Americans Identify as Christian," *Gallup*, December 24, 2014, http://www.gallup.com/poll/180347/three-quarters-americans-identify-christian.aspx.

4. Byron R. Johnson, "Dispelling Rumors of Religion's Demise," *The 2014 Index of Culture and Opportunity*, The Heritage Foundation, n.d., http://index.heritage.org/culture/religious-attendance/#fn1-360.

5. Newport, "Three-Quarters Identify."

6. Barna Group, *Churchless*, ed. George Barna and David Kinnaman (Carol Stream, IL: Tyndale, 2014), 40–41.

7. Kate Shellnutt, "33 Under 33," *Christianity Today*, July 1, 2014, 34–50, http://www.christianitytoday.com/ct/2014/july-august/33-under-33.html.

8. Barry A. Kosmin and Ariela Keysar, *American Religious Identification Survey (ARIS) 2008: Summary Report* (Hartford, CT: Trinity College, 2009), http://b27.cc.trincoll.edu/weblogs/AmericanReligionSurvey-ARIS/reports/ARIS_Report_2008.pdf.

9. Newport, "Americans Continue to Believe."

10. "Religion Among the Millennials," Pew Research Center, February 17, 2010, http://www.pewforum.org/2010/02/17/religion-among-the-millennials/.

11. Ed Stetzer, Richie Stanley, and Jason Hayes, *Lost and Found* (Nashville: B&H, 2009), 28.

12. Ibid.

13. Newport and Carroll, "Another Look at Evangelicals."

14. As a result of the various interpretations people give to *born again*, different researchers get different results. Lower than Gallup, American Religious Identification Survey (ARIS) found 34 percent of American adults considered themselves "Born Again or Evangelical Christians" in 2008. Barna's recent numbers are much lower than either at 21 percent.

15. Newport, "Three-Quarters of Americans."

16. Robert Wuthnow, *After the Baby Boomers: How Twenty- and Thirty-Somethings Are Shaping the Future of American Religion* (Princeton, NJ: Princeton University Press, 2010), 62–65.

17. *"Nones" on the Rise: One-in-Five Adults Have No Religious Affiliation*, Pew Forum on Religion and Public Life, October 9, 2012, http://www.pewforum.org/files/2012/10/NonesOnTheRise-full.pdf; David Kinnaman and Gabe Lyons, *unChristian: What a New Generation Really Thinks about Christianity . . . and Why It Matters* (Grand Rapids, MI: Baker, 2007).

18. Stetzer, Stanley, and Hayes, *Lost and Found*, 50.

19. Ibid.

20. *America's Changing Religious Landscape: Christians Decline Sharply as Share of Population; Unaffiliated and Other Faiths Continue to Grow*, Pew Research Center, May 12, 2015, http://www.pewforum.org/files/2015/05/RLS-05-08-full-report.pdf.

21. Katherine Bindley, "Religion among Americans Hits Low Point, as More People Say They Have No Religious Affiliation: Report," *Huff Post Religion*, March 13, 2013, http://www.huffingtonpost.com/2013/03/13/religion-america-decline-low-no-affiliation-report_n_2867626.html.

22. *America's Changing Religious Landscape*; "Event Transcript: Religion Trends in the US," Pew Research Center, August 19, 2013, http://www.pewforum.org/2013/08/19/event-transcript-religion-trends-in-the-u-s/.

23. "Religion Trends in the US," Pew Research Center.

24. *"Nones" on the Rise*.

25. Ibid., 23.

26. *America's Changing Religious Landscape.*

27. Thom S. Rainer and Jess W. Rainer, *The Millennials: Connecting to America's Largest Generation* (Nashville: B&H, 2011), 229. Note: other surveys I've cited have shown a higher interest in spirituality for Millennials. Instead of being a contradiction in the data, this study shows the large difference between taking an interest in spirituality and making it a priority when compared to the full list of what they thought was really important in their lives: 1) Family (61 percent); 2) friends (25 percent); 3) education (17 percent); 4) career/job (16 percent); 5) spouse/partner (13 percent); 6) spiritual matters (13 percent); 7) finances (12 percent); 8) happiness (12 percent); 9) raising kids (11 percent); 10) health (10 percent).

28. Pew Research Center predicts that 25 percent of people who in 2014 are ages twenty-nine through thirty-eight will not be married in 2030. Wendy Wang and Kim Parker, "Record Share of Americans Have Never Married," Pew Research Center Social and Demographic Trends, September 24, 2014, http://www .pewsocialtrends.org/2014/09/24/record-share-of-americans-have-never-married/.

29. Wuthnow, *After the Baby Boomers*, 55.

30. Wang and Parker, "Record Share of Americans Have Never Married."

31. Stetzer, Stanley, and Hayes, *Lost and Found*, 33.

32. Ibid., 32.

33. Wuthnow, *After the Baby Boomers*, 24.

34. Rodney Stark and Byron Johnson, "Religion and the Bad News Bearers," *Wall Street Journal*, August 26, 2011, http://online.wsj.com/news/articles/SB100014 24053111903480904576510692691734916.

35. Wuthnow, *After the Baby Boomers*, 69.

36. Ibid., 55, 63.

37. *"Nones" on the Rise.*

38. "How the Faithful Voted: 2014 Preliminary Analysis," Pew Research Center, November 5, 2014, http://www.pewforum.org/2014/11/05/how-the-faithful -voted-2014-preliminary-analysis/.

39. Lee Rainie and Aaron Smith, "Main Findings: Social Networking Sites and Politics," Pew Research Center, March 12, 2012, http://www.pewinternet .org/2012/03/12/main-findings-10/.

40. Christian Smith, "Getting a Life," *Books & Culture* 13 (November/December 2007): 6, http://www.ctlibrary.com/bc/2007/novdec/2.10.html.

CHAPTER 12: WHY WON'T YOUNGER PEOPLE COME TO MY CHURCH?

1. Some congregations want to be multigenerational. If that's what God calls you to be, then do it. Just know that every approach has limitations. Multigenerational churches usually stay smaller for at least three reasons: 1) no one minister or congregation will be equally good at communicating to all five generations; 2) it takes much more energy and time to deal with the generational differences, so a multigenerational church will have less energy

for outreach; and 3) you will reach those people who value multigenerational experiences. Those who don't will look elsewhere, so your reach will not be as broad as it first appears.

2. See Rex Miller, *The Millennium Matrix: Reclaiming the Past, Reframing the Future of the Church* (San Francisco, CA: Jossey-Bass, 2004).

3. Barna Group, "The State of the Bible, 2014," American Bible Society, 2014, 50, http://www.americanbible.org/uploads/content/state-of-the-bible-data-analysis -american-bible-society-2014.pdf.

4. Ibid., 41.

5. Marian V. Liautaud, "Make Room for Me," *Christianity Today*, October 13, 2014, http://www.christianitytoday.com/le/2014/october-online-only/make -room-for-me.html?paging=off.

6. Churches donate money for ministries at universities, but there's not much for young people who don't go to college. For ideas on what some are starting to do, see Catherine Newhouse, "The Forgotten Millennials," *Christianity Today* (June 2013), http://www.christianitytoday.com/ct/2013/june/forgotten-millennials .html?share=eredwoykaAAWtw2193vt7KNCJ7lpzZ1q.

7. Thomas Pardee, "Media-Savvy Gen Y Finds Smart and Funny Is 'New Rock 'n' Roll,'" *Advertising Age*, October 11, 2010, http://adage.com/article /news/marketing-media-savvy-gen-y-transparency-authenticity/146388/.

8. Barna Group, *Churchless* (Carol Stream, IL: Tyndale, 2014), 98–99.

9. Ibid., 99.

10. Dallas Willard, *Renovation of the Heart: Putting On the Character of Christ* (Colorado Springs: NavPress, 2002), 100.

11. Great resources are out there. See Fuller Youth Project research and Sticky Faith resources (http://fulleryouthinstitute.org/sticky-faith/what-is-sticky-faith) and resources developed by Mark Mittelberg and Lincoln Christian University (http://www.roomfordoubt.com/).

12. George MacDonald, *The Seaboard Parish* (London: Tinsley Brothers, 1868), 1:7.

CHAPTER 13: WHAT AM I SUPPOSED TO DO NOW THAT IT DOESN'T FEEL LIKE MY CHURCH ANYMORE?

1. See, for example, Lyle Schaller, *The Pastor and the People*, rev. ed. (Nashville, TN: Abingdon Press, 1986), 161–68.

2. J. Walker Smith and Ann Clurman, *Generation Ageless: How Baby Boomers Are Changing the Way We Live Today . . . and They're Just Getting Started* (New York: HarperCollins, 2007), 80–83.

3. Frank Newport and Brett Pelham, "Don't Worry, Be 80: Worry and Stress Decline with Age," *Gallup*, December 14, 2009, http://www.gallup.com /poll/124655/dont-worry-be-80-worry-stress-decline-age.aspx.

4. Susan Donaldson James, "Second Adulthood: Experts Say If It's Not Scary, You're Not Growing," *ABC News*, June 14, 2007, http://abcnews.go.com /Business/LifeStages/story?id=3274901.

5. "A Billion Shades of Grey," *The Economist*, April 26, 2014, http://www
   .economist.com/news/leaders/21601253-ageing-economy-will-be-slower
   -and-more-unequal-oneunless-policy-starts-changing-now; "Age Invaders," *The
   Economist*, April 26, 2014, http://www.economist.com/news/briefing/21601248
   -generation-old-people-about-change-global-economy-they-will-not-all-do-so.
6. See this helpful interview with a sociologist who studied evangelical leaders
   at the highest levels and provides examples of why they find it hard to serve
   in local churches: Tim Stafford, "The Evangelical Elite," *Chrisitanity Today*,
   November 16, 2007, http://www.christianitytoday.com/ct/2007/november
   /33.35.html?share=eredwoykaABBZRRp5NUwCjBvzksGo2vc.

CHAPTER 14: THE ULTIMATE GENERATIONAL INTELLIGENCE

1. Chapter 3 of *Sticking Points* provides a five-step process for leading through
   generational differences in organizations. See *Sticking Points* (Carol Stream, IL:
   Tyndale, 2013), 29–39.
2. I found one of the examples Markus Barth gives of the opposite of Paul's point
   in this passage especially appropriate to our discussion about the different
   generations in church: "to subject one's neighbor to arbitrarily selected elements
   of one's own religious tradition or preference." Markus Barth, *Ephesians 4–6:
   A New Translation with Introduction and Commentary*, vol. 34A of *The Anchor
   Bible*, ed. William Foxwell Albright and David Noel Freedman (New York:
   Doubleday, 1974), 462.
3. Andrew T. Lincoln, *Ephesians*, vol. 42 of *Word Biblical Commentary*, ed. Bruce
   M. Metzger (Dallas: Word, 1990), 236–37.
4. See Barth, *Ephesians 4–6*, 460.

CHAPTER 1

Sticking Together or Coming Apart

CINDY SNEAKED OUT before the conference wrapped up. Seeing me by the registration table, she looked at her watch and asked, "Can you answer a question about your presentation? I've got a big problem on my team."

"Sure," I said. "We have a few minutes before people start coming out."

She glanced at her watch again and started in. "For six months I've been working with Human Resources, trying to figure out what to do with Cara. I'm leaving the conference early to finalize the paperwork to fire her. But after listening to you, I'm wondering if maybe there's something generational about this. I lead an information technology department, and Cara surfs the Internet three hours a day."

"Sounds like a lot," I said. "If she's surfing that much, her work must not be getting done. Who on your team is picking up the slack?"

"No work falls to other people," Cindy said. "She actually carries the heaviest workload in my department. She supports more software programs and more users than anyone else."

"Oh," I said with surprise. "Seems strange to fire your highest producer. Do her customers complain about her work?"

She hesitated. "No . . . she has the best customer satisfaction scores of anyone in our department. The vice presidents often tell me to do whatever it takes to keep her because she is the best in my department. That's why Human Resources and I have been trying so hard to figure out how to make it work with her. But we are stuck."

"If she does more work and has better results than anyone on your team, why are you firing her?" I asked.

"Because she sets a bad example for the rest of the department. I have other techs asking me why they can't surf the web if Cara can. Plus, we pay her for a full day, and she's not working three hours of it. What if everyone did that? At first I offered to promote her since she is so good; I knew that would fill her plate. But she says she likes the job she has. I've coached her for a year now that she needs to stay busy. I've offered her extra projects, but she says it wouldn't be fair."

I finished her thought. "She says that being able to surf the Internet is her reward for getting her work done faster. She shouldn't be punished by having to do 30 percent more work than everyone else without 30 percent more pay."

Cindy almost shouted, "That's exactly what she said!"

Cindy was in the middle of a sticking point.

• • •

"My wife and I have two kids in their twenties, but they are certainly not like we were," Stan, a fifty-six-year-old accountant, stated once we had found a seat. We'd met in the food line at an open house for a recent high school graduate. At first when people find out I do leadership training and consulting, they nod politely. But when I mention I've been researching the different generations for twenty years, they can't stop talking.

As I started eating, Stan continued. "By the time I was twenty-five, I already had a house, a kid, and another on the way. But my kids don't look like they're ever going to settle down."

The brisket was good, so I kept eating and listened to Stan. He went on, "Our oldest son, Brandon, is a good kid, but he's taking his time figuring out what he wants to do. He's twenty-six, and he moved back home five months ago because he says things are just too expensive on his own. Living with his parents doesn't seem to faze him or his friends. I would have died of embarrassment. And I know his mother would never have dated me if I'd lived at home, but it doesn't seem to bother his girlfriend, either. She's a really nice girl with a good job, but after dating for four years, they never talk about marriage. Most of my friends were married by twenty-six; most of Brandon's are still dating."

"That seems about right," I said. "The average age for marriage has jumped. My oldest son had thought about getting married at twenty-two, and everyone said he was crazy. *I* thought he was crazy, and I got married at twenty-two. Actually, his *grandmother* thought he was crazy, and she got married the day before she turned seventeen. It's a different world."

Stan hadn't touched his food. "I'm not saying he should get married. He has moments of maturity, but I don't think he's ready for commitment yet. He hasn't finished his college degree or found a job that he wants to stick with, and he still plays a lot of video games. It's not getting married later that I don't understand; it's that he and his girlfriend don't want to get serious. I'm a little worried about what's going to happen to him and his friends."

Stan was stuck (and his brisket was getting cold).

• • •

Hector had asked if we could talk at a seminar lunch break, and he got straight to the point: "Haydn, my team is stuck. We had an important presentation recently that started out fine but ended in disaster."

Hector Perez was a forty-three-year-old vice president of a new division formed to help his midsize manufacturing company move into green technology. Even discouraged and noticeably tired, Hector's hands never stopped moving. He waved his fork like an orchestra conductor as he talked: "Larry Broz, our CEO, is great. He asked me to fly in my team, who are mainly Generation Xers like me, to make our pitch to the management team for increasing the research and development spending on green technologies. Larry's why I left a great company to come here. He may be almost seventy, but he thinks as young as I do. And my team did great. They looked professional, they knew their stuff, and even when the executive team began to throw out strong challenges, they listened and responded like they were old pros.

"But then the meeting crashed, and our proposal went with it. One of my team members, Rachel, was texting under the table. She finished quickly, but later, when the head of operations launched into one of her pet topics, which we've all heard many times before, Rachel began texting again, in full view of the others in the meeting. The head of operations then lectured Rachel, Rachel defended herself, and I tried to make a joke about my team texting in my meetings to ease the tension, but that got the head of ops even more fired up.

"The whole meeting just imploded," Hector said. "Once the CEO got the head of operations calmed down, we met for another hour, but it was awkward, and the energy was gone. People were still thinking about Rachel using her cell phone rather than the strategy. Larry finally put the meeting out of its misery and asked the executive team to submit additional comments in writing."

Hector continued, "Rachel was just doing what our whole team does in our own meetings. She texts while I'm talking, too, but it doesn't bother me because I know she's dialed in to what we're doing. On the flight home, two of my people agreed that Rachel should have left her phone alone but complained that senior management is out of touch with how people communicate now. I'm stuck in the middle. The senior execs want me to keep my team in line, but my young team members wonder if they're just spinning their wheels here, if this is the place for them long term. If senior management can't adjust to smartphones, will they ever be able to embrace these new green technologies they want us to implement? I came here to make a difference, not keep the peace."

Hector was stuck between dueling generations.

• • •

Cindy's and Hector's companies didn't know it, but they had run into seven of the twelve most common generational sticking points I've identified from interviewing and working with thousands of people. And Stan's family was tangled in four different sticking points as well. Each generation in these situations thought the others were the problem. The groups tried in vain to ignore or avoid their generational differences. Typically, as at Hector's company, the generation in charge tells a younger generation to get it together, hoping that will solve the problem. But it never does.

These groups' approaches predictably didn't work, and they weren't sure why or what to do about it the next time. Generational friction is inevitable today, and "the next time" will come more and more often and create more and more tension. If only the companies and family I described had known the following:

- For the first time in history, we have four different generations in the workplace (and five in families). These generations might as well be from different countries, so different are their cultural styles and preferences.

- Of the four approaches organizations can take to blending the generations, only one of them works today.
- Focusing on the "what" escalates tensions, while focusing on the "why" pulls teams together.
- Knowing the twelve sticking points can allow teams to label tension points and work through them—even anticipate and preempt them.
- Implementing the five steps to cross-generational leadership can lead to empowering, not losing, key people.

But they didn't know these things. And neither do most organizations or families. Sticking points are inevitable, and they often get teams and families stuck. But they don't have to. *The same generational conflicts that get teams stuck can cause teams to stick together.*

Stuck in the past or sticking together going forward: it's a matter of turning a potential liability into an asset. And it's not that hard to do, as you will soon discover. (In later chapters, I'll pick up the stories of Cindy, Stan, and Hector and share the advice I gave them about working through their generational sticking points.)

"THEY DON'T GET IT"

The most common complaint I hear from frustrated people in all four generations is "They don't get it."

"They," of course, means a boss, coworker, or family member from a different generation who the speaker believes is the cause of a problem. And in my experience, "it" usually refers to one of the following twelve sticking points—places where teams get stuck:

1. communication
2. decision making
3. dress code
4. feedback
5. fun at work
6. knowledge transfer
7. loyalty
8. meetings
9. policies

10. respect
11. training
12. work ethic

Anyone in today's workforce can identify with most, if not all, of the twelve sticking points.

"They don't get it" is usually a sign that a sticking point is pulling the team apart. Team members of the same generation begin tossing around stereotypes, making jokes to each other about the "offending" generation. Each generation attempts to maneuver the others into seeing the sticking point their own way.

And that's the first mistake—viewing a sticking point as a problem to be solved rather than as an opportunity to be leveraged. The goal becomes to "fix" the offending generation rather than to look for ways to work with them. The irony is that when we say another generation doesn't get it, we don't get it either.

Once we get it, we realize that these sticking points are more than intergenerational differences. They are catalysts for deeper understanding and appreciation that can make teams stronger and better balanced. Sticking points can be negative if you see them as problems or positive if you see them as opportunities for greater understanding and flexibility. Sticking points can make things worse or better depending on whether the four generations can work together in the twelve places they naturally tend to come apart.

We'll spend the next two chapters looking at why generational sticking points usually get teams stuck, and we'll see how we can change them into the emotional glue that sticks teams together to achieve exciting results.

FOUR GENERATIONS: THE NEW REALITY

Generational friction is inevitable today because we've never before had four generations in the workplace.

Different researchers label the generations—or more technically, "age cohort groups"—using different terms. For simplicity's sake, I've summarized the most common names along with each generation's birth years so you can see where you and others fit.

I'm using the term *Generation X* (or *Gen X* for short), even though the members of that generation don't like the label. Who can blame them? It came from the title of a book about a lost and rootless generation—and *X* is

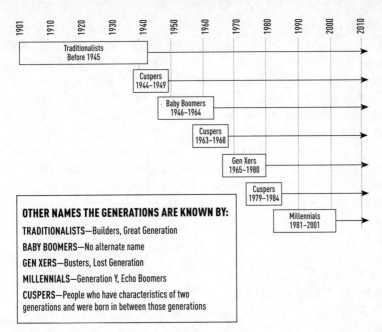

often a symbol for something that's missing or an unknown factor. But unfortunately, that's the name that has stuck.

Not everyone would agree with the dates I assign the generations. Some of us disagree by a couple of years, especially about the length of Generation X. Age cohort groups are determined by the way a generation buys, votes, and answers surveys, so of course there is no easily identified date when the Boomers ended and the Gen Xers began.

To deal with the transitional years when it is impossible to separate generations because people have characteristics of both, marketers developed the term *Cuspers*. For example, I am a Cusper, born in 1963—just when the Baby Boomer generation was ending and Generation X was beginning. Cuspers are a blend of both. I identify in some ways with Boomers and in other ways with Xers. (My wife jokes, "You overwork like a Boomer, and you are cynical like an Xer. I've married the worst of both worlds.")

While Cuspers can create problems for marketers who can't tell which generational pitch to aim at them, Cuspers are often able to bridge generations. They have one foot in both camps and can sometimes serve as translators and negotiators between generations.

I mentioned earlier that there are five generations in the home. The fifth generation (children of the second half of Gen Xers and the first half of Millennials) doesn't yet have an established name or even a start date. We assume that the Millennial generation will be about the same length as the Boomers and Xers, but that may not be the case. Assuming the fifth generation starts somewhere from 2002 to 2004, those children are already consumers and influencers of massive amounts of government and parental (and grandparental) spending. They may not be in the workplace, but they certainly are consumers.

For the first time in history, there are four generations in the workplace and five in the marketplace. This new phenomenon complicates our work and our relationships because while people of all generations have the same basic needs, they meet those needs in different ways. The rest of this book will detail the commonalities and differences among the four generations we find in the workplace.

SEVEN WAYS THE GENERATIONS WILL INCREASINGLY IMPACT YOUR ORGANIZATION

If you've never paid much attention to generational differences, here are seven organizational realities you need to be aware of. I'll divide them into internal and external impacts.

Internal Impacts:

1. *Conflicts around generational sticking points.* How do you get four generations of employees to play nice together in the sandbox? Increasingly, organizations are recognizing that younger employees don't see things the same way their elders do and that it's impossible to create policies that don't annoy someone. How do you get through the differences and get back to work? Generational friction is inevitable; generational problems are avoidable—that is, if you and your team have a working knowledge of why the generations are different and of how to lead them rather than simply manage them.

2. *Managing and motivating different generations.* Whether it's older supervisors trying to motivate younger employees or younger supervisors trying to direct people their parents' age, generational differences complicate things. While people are motivated by similar needs, how they seek to fulfill those needs differs. And that causes challenges in engaging and motivating different generations.

3. *Replacing the Baby Boomers in the war for talent.* Who will you hire following the coming exodus of Baby Boomers? Even in economic downturns, organizations compete for the best employees, what's commonly called the "war for talent." Traditionalists have already largely left the workplace. Over the next decade, many of the Baby Boomers will follow—and the ones who return will do so on their own terms. Who will replace them in your organization, and how will you adjust to the younger generation's different approach to work? How will you transfer the Boomers' experience, job knowledge, and customer relationships? Further complicating the shift, lower birthrates in the industrialized world and longer life spans could create a labor shortage over the next two decades.

4. *Succession planning.* Do you trust Generation X to run the place? The president of one of the United States' thirty largest banks confided to me, "Anywhere we have a Boomer in the succession plan for the top spots, we're pretty confident. But if it's a Gen Xer, we don't know. We just aren't sure they get the business." It's a common sentiment. Organizations made their peace with Gen Xers ten years ago, after a decade of fretting and calling them "slackers." But handing over the keys to the company causes differences in work ethic and loyalty to resurface. In the late 1990s, succession planning was a hot topic as organizations began to do the math on Boomer retirements. But it faded with the global downturn of 2002. If your organization is typical, well over half your leaders will retire in the next decade. You can't put it off any longer. Ready or not, you must have a succession plan.

5. *Leadership development.* Where will you get your leaders? Generation X is a much smaller generation, and Xers do not tend to stay in one company throughout their careers. As we'll see, the leadership development processes that served the Boomers are not working for the next generation.

External Impacts:

6. *Shifting markets.* What do the different generations want? You thought your website was great, so why isn't it working? We all know generations buy differently. That's the basis of generational market research. If your organization must market to multiple generations, you need to understand what appeals to each generation and learn to speak their language.

7. *Connecting with five generations of customers.* Most people relate well to two of the generations but not four or five. Will your salespeople miss half your customers? How will you prepare your employees to satisfy five generations of customers?

THE PEOPLE ISSUE OF THE NEXT DECADE

This generational math adds up to the people issue of the decade for your business—or hospital or government agency or political campaign or military unit or church or school or nonprofit or foundation or symphony or association or family.

In many ways, the impact on nonprofit organizations will be more intense sooner. Successful businesses can buy a little time with higher pay. Most nonprofits don't have that luxury, especially after the Great Recession that began in 2008 restructured the economy. They need to know about sticking points now. Here are some organization-specific generational challenges that will need to be dealt with in the immediate future:

- *Hospitals and medicine.* Gen Xers and Millennials did not have Sputnik and the space race to drive national passion in science. The average age of nurses in many places is increasing as medicine struggles to attract and retain Gen X and Millennial nurses. Some hospitals are already forced to hire temporary surgeons due to the shortage. (Think of the implications as the Baby Boomers hit their high-medical-need years.) Whereas businesses like Hard Rock Cafe can pick a demographic target, hospitals must serve all five generations. Without generational understanding, a highly skilled Millennial nurse can bring down customer satisfaction scores with a Traditionalist patient just by being more informal in language and approach. What to a Millennial is friendly can seem disrespectful to a Traditionalist.
- *Government.* Millennials went into government studies in much higher numbers than Gen Xers but have not been staying in government jobs. I tell my governmental clients that they have an "empty middle." With well over half their staff and most of their managers eligible to retire in the next seven years, and relatively few Gen X managers to take over, they have a generational gap that will be a challenge to fill.
- *Political campaigns.* Capturing the vote of the two younger generations was key to Barack Obama's coming from obscurity to

the presidency and then to his reelection. In the 2008 election, the first BlackBerry-carrying president lured away one of the three founders of Facebook, who at twenty-four led the customization of social-networking technology and changed the rules of politics. One example: Obama's Vote for Change site registered over one million voters with only a few part-time staff. In the past that would have required two thousand full-time staff. Campaigns at every level learned from his victory and raced to adopt technology-driven, grassroots-based campaigns. In Obama's reelection, his campaign put even more focus on social media but added precision data mining that will set the playbook for the future. Campaigns that don't take seriously all generations and their communication technologies will struggle.

- *Military.* A United States Army commander told me in 2004 that the boot camp staff's most hated recruiting slogan was "An Army of One." Recruits came in expecting the army to accommodate their goals and preferences. He and his peers begged the recruiting office to go back to "Be All You Can Be" (used 1981–2001), but that slogan has ceased to resonate with the younger generations. The Army switched slogans to "Army Strong" in the fall of 2006 because they missed recruiting goals due to the Iraq Conflict. When recruits knew they would most likely be shipped off early in their career, the self-fulfillment promises of "Be All You Can Be" couldn't be met.

- *Religious organizations.* People often turn to religion for comfort and guidance in a changing and sometimes confusing world but find that with five generations, it is impossible to keep everyone on the same page. Younger generations are not willing to wait for styles and approaches to change—they simply go somewhere else or stay home. Because religious organizations survive only if they are able to attract the next generation, this may be the most important issue they face.

- *Schools.* Similar to hospitals, K–12 schools struggle to attract and retain Gen X and Millennial teachers. In many areas, the dropout rate for new teachers is 50 percent. Internally, faculty struggle just as businesses do to understand the different generations. One med school professor told me she asked her dean if she could record herself teaching so she could work on research rather than offering ongoing classes. The school no longer required class attendance, so half her students didn't show up. (He said no.)

- *Nonprofits/foundations.* Without business-level salaries, nonprofits and foundations have to motivate and inspire each generation if they hope to win in the war for talent. Moreover, the generations have different ideas of what volunteer involvement looks like and how organizations should be run. Add to that the changing expectations of donors, and the same changes that have impacted political campaigns will continue to change fund-raising.
- *Associations.* When I ask my association clients to name their key challenges, these themes emerge: How do we get younger members to join? How do we get them to attend and, better yet, volunteer? And how do we deal with the tensions between generations when younger members try to jump in but don't want to do things the way they've always been done?
- *Families.* Raising children is definitely different today. Teens spend hours online with fifty friends and have to be forced to go outside. You know it's a different world when your child asks for the "Totally Stylin' Tattoos Barbie" for her (or his) birthday.

All organizations have to understand sticking points to ensure that their teams stick together instead of being stuck in generational conflicts. Sticking points are unavoidable; staying stuck in them is a waste. With the right tools and understanding, they can instead be huge opportunities to make our organizations more effective.

Learn how to work and communicate more effectively with other **generations**.

CP0988